Religion and Political Behavior in the United States

Religion and Political Behavior in the United States

Edited by TED G. JELEN

PRAEGER

New York
Westport, Connecticut
London

Library of Congress Cataloging-in-Publication Data

Religion and political behavior in the United States.
　　Bibliography: p.
　　Includes index.
　　1. Religion and politics—United States.　I. Jelen,
Ted G.
BL65.P7R427　1989　　322'.1'0973　　　　　88-32186
ISBN 0-275-93089-0 (alk. paper)

Library of Congress Catalog Card Number: 88-32186
ISBN: 0-275-93089-0

First published in 1989

Praeger Publishers, One Madison Avenue, New York, NY 10010
A division of Greenwood Press, Inc.

Printed in the United States of America

The paper used in this book complies with the
Permanent Paper Standard issued by the National
Information Standards Organization (Z39.48-1984).

10　9　8　7　6　5　4　3　2　1

Contents

Tables and Figures

FIGURES

Preface

This collection reflects the growing scholarly interest in religion and politics in recent U.S. history. It is by now apparent that religion, once thought to exist in an oil-and-water compact with politics, is an important force on the U.S. political landscape. Religious elites have taken extremely visible roles in contemporary public life. Such activity has raised normative questions about the boundaries between the sacred and the secular. In a more empirical vein, this political activity has generated questions about the size and importance of various politico/religious constituencies, and about the effectiveness of religiously based elite-mass communications.

The most obvious manifestation of U.S. political religion is the recent rise of the New Christian Right (NCR). Groups like Moral Majority (recently subsumed into the "Liberty Federation"), Religious Roundtable, and Christian Voice have been quite explicit in calling for a return to a "Judeo-Christian" tradition, which is sometimes thought to animate U.S. politics. Accused of violating the tradition of the separation of church and state (a phrase that appears nowhere in the U.S. Constitution), spokespersons of the NCR have replied that their reaction is merely a defensive response to a progressive secularizing of public life in the United States. Philosophically, members of the NCR have raised the question of whether or not authentic religious neutrality is possible without a consensus on fundamental values. Politically, the NCR has presented both political parties (but perhaps especially the Republican) with a potential new constituency to be taken into account when presenting candidates for public office.

A second recent interaction between the religious and the political has come about as the result of activity by the American Catholic bishops. The bishops have shifted away from concerns of sacramentalism and personal morality, and have issued statements on a number of issues of public policy.

Aside from the church's traditional opposition to abortion, the American bishops have taken positions on the nuclear arms race, U.S. policy in Central America, and the domestic economy. Moreover, certain Catholic elites, such as Chicago's Cardinal Bernardin, have attempted to weave these disparate issue positions into a "seamless garment," embracing a "consistent ethic of life." The American bishops have faced criticism from two sources: Not only have some observers felt that Catholic political activity is inappropriately partisan, but many within the Catholic tradition have argued that the American bishops have weakened the church's moral authority, by behaving in a manner more characteristic of secular political actors.

Third, the activities of recent presidential candidates have stimulated interest in religion and politics. In two recent elections, the religious affiliation of the Democratic presidential candidate has become an issue. Both John Kennedy's Catholicism and Jimmy Carter's "born-again" style of evangelical Southern Baptism received much comment during their respective (successful) campaigns for the presidency. Moreover, 1988 has been a unique year, in that two ordained ministers have sought the presidential nomination in their respective political parties. In the short run, of course, the candidacies of Marion "Pat" Robertson and Jesse Jackson were unsuccessful, since neither candidate received the nomination of his party. The long-term effects of each candidacy are more difficult to assess. Each candidate has asserted that he has mobilized large numbers of previously inactive citizens into the political process, and each has claimed to have altered his party's issue agenda. Political scientists will undoubtedly be kept quite busy investigating these claims.

In response to developments such as these, political scientists have devoted increasing attention to the interaction of religion and politics. This volume includes 15 chapters about U.S. political religion, written from what might be loosely termed a "behavioral" perspective. That is, each piece in this collection is a description or analysis of the interplay between religion and politics illustrated with some form of empirical evidence. Beyond this surface similarity, both subject areas and methods of the articles are diverse and eclectic. This diversity, in my view, reflects the current state of research into U.S. political religion.

Followers of Thomas Kuhn may comment that the study of religion and politics is "preparadigmatic." By this I mean that there is little consensus about the appropriate concepts, vocabulary, or measurement strategies to be used in this type of research. As observers of political religion, we lack generally accepted intellectual exemplars to inform our scholarly agenda. In part, this intellectual confusion is the result of the relative recency of research into religion and politics. More importantly, this lack of consensus reflects the bewildering diversity of U.S. religion. Unlike political parties, which come parsimoniously packaged as "Democratic," "Republican," or "Other," religious phenomena come in a wide variety of sizes, creeds, and experiences. The U.S. religious mosaic defies simplified description. Ultimately, "better" or "worse" classification schemes of religion seem likely to be based on their relative ability to account for political phenomena, such as election results, interest group activity, or public policy. This collection contains a number of distinctive approaches to the conceptualization and measurement of religious phenomena, and should thus inform our understanding of these issues.

The study of religion and politics also offers observers in the social sciences an unusual opportunity to observe the interplay betwen "facts" and "values." Few social scientists would subscribe to the view that a "value-free" science of human behavior is possible. However, the interaction between facts and values in much contemporary political science is often obscured, because so many of the values implicit in our research are consensual within academic institutions. At least at a general level, most social scientists would agree that tolerance is a trait to be encouraged, and that racism and sexism are inappropriate attitudes in democratic political systems. Disagreements about such topics are often concealed by a surface consensus on liberal-democratic symbols. By contrast, those of us who study religious beliefs and values are often struck by the extent to which apparent disputes about conceptualization and measurement often reflect submerged theological differences. Lacking a polite vocabulary to contain our very real religious differences, we must, of necessity, confront the fact-value issue much more directly than is typically the case in political science. The field of religion and politics has attracted people who are quite active within very specific religious traditions, people who are generally religious in a more ecumenical sense, and those who are indifferent or hostile to any beliefs in supernatural phenomena. Careful readers of this volume may find it interesting to compare the value implications of the chapters in this collection.

The book is divided into three parts. Part I contains three chapters, each dealing with the measurement of religious phenomena. While concerns with methodological issues permeate every piece in this volume, the first three chapters deal directly with problems of operationalization. Each one seeks to address the question of how the U.S. religious mosaic can be simplified and organized for analysis, while reflecting the genuine religious diversity of the U.S. population. Two of these chapters deal with the conceptualization and measurement of evangelicalism, while the chapter by Leege attempts a more general, cross-denominational scheme of classification and measurement. Part II contains eight chapters dealing with the effects of religious belief at the level of the mass public. To what extent does religion affect the political attitudes and beliefs of ordinary citizens? Part III deals with political religion at the level of religious and political elites, which include journalists, lobbyists, public officials, political contributors, and several different groups of clergy. It is our hope to make U.S. political religion more understandable to the general reader, and to provide insights to scholars and practitioners at a more advanced level.

I

Methodological Issues

1
The Meaning and Measurement of Evangelicalism: Problems and Prospects

Lyman A. Kellstedt

INTRODUCTION

Secularization theories suggest the continued decline of religion in the face of modernist tendencies. The persistence of religion in the United States and its apparent vitality is a phenomenon that does not square with the secularization hypothesis; and yet the strength of religion in the United States, in terms of growth and vitality, has not occurred across the board. So-called mainline Protestant churches have suffered serious membership losses in the past generation. Within Protestantism, most of the growth has occurred in "evangelical" denominations and churches (Kelley, 1977). Such growth should have stimulated a great deal of research in order to document and explain such vitality. Until recently, however (Hunter: 1983a, 1987a; Ammerman: 1987), little research has been done.

In political science and political sociology, evangelicalism was largely ignored until the entry into politics of groups such as the Moral Majority and such individuals as Jerry Falwell and Pat Robertson. Despite numerous studies of these groups and individuals in recent years (see the collections of Leibman and Wuthnow, 1983; Bromley and Shupe, 1984; and Johnson and Tamney, 1986), evangelicalism has been neither adequately conceptualized nor measured. To put it another way, the central features or constituent elements of evangelicalism have not been adequately specified. As a result, there is little or no agreement among scholars as to an appropriate set of operational measures of evangelicalism. In turn, this has contributed to different empirical findings from one study to the next. Thus, for example, if evangelicalism in study A is conceptualized as synonymous with a born-again experience, results from such research are likely to differ from study B where evangelicalism is conceptualized more broadly with having accepted

3

Jesus Christ as one's personal savior. All study A evangelicals should also meet study B's criterion, but the reverse is not the case. Hence study A's conceptualization would "capture" most Baptists and pentecostal groups but ignore individuals from a reformed or confessional tradition who would meet study B's criterion.

Failure to conceptualize evangelicalism adequately and to measure it in greater depth has had important substantive implications for political research. Evangelicalism is a multifaceted movement. It includes groups from across the political spectrum from left to right as Booth Fowler's research (1982) has suggested. One part of the movement, the fundamentalists, withdrew from politics after the Scopes Trial of the 1920s only to reemerge in full force in the mid-1970s under the leadership of Falwell and the Moral Majority. Unfortunately, the major data sources used by social scientists (the voting studies done by the Center of Political Studies at The University of Michigan [CPS], and the General Social Surveys [GSS], done at The University of Chicago) had no adequate conceptualization of evangelicalism and its constituent part, fundamentalism, and, as a result, no adequate measures of fundamentalism were developed. Hence we can only speculate on the impact of fundamentalism on the politics of the nation as a whole. In contrast to the fundamentalist roots of the Moral Majority, the candidacy of Pat Robertson has its roots in another wing of evangelicalism, the charismatic movement. Here again, the major surveys do not allow us to distinguish charismatics from other evangelical Christians (or from non-evangelicals for that matter). This makes studies of the possible politicization of the charismatics nearly impossible using CPS or GSS data.

The purpose of this particular research is not to resolve all the problems raised in the preceding paragraphs but to illustrate some of the difficulties in conceptualizing and measuring evangelicalism and to suggest some short-term solutions that would assist scholars to make better use of national survey data. We begin with an effort to conceptualize evangelicalism. Then we turn to the conceptualization and measurement efforts of others, examining them from the perspective of the conceptualization attempt developed in the preceding section. Next, we present a number of examples of problems encountered in the measurement of evangelicalism. Finally, we make suggestions for future research efforts in this area.

THE CONCEPTUALIZATION OF EVANGELICALISM: A BRIEF AND INITIAL FORAY

The predominant emphasis of evangelicalism is with *doctrine*. It is "right" doctrine that self-identified evangelicals look for when they "check out" a person's Christian credentials. As a result, pastors in evangelical churches tend to spend a great deal of their preaching time, and other efforts at Christian education, with doctrinal matters. So-called mainline church bodies are far less preoccupied with doctrine. Roman Catholics are far more likely to be concerned with a person's participation in the sacraments than with his or her doctrinal beliefs.

In specifying which doctrines are central, should the number chosen be kept small or should the number of criteria be large? We have developed a set of "minimalist" criteria for evangelical membership. They include four beliefs: (1) the divinity of Christ, (2) acceptance of Christ as the only way to attain eternal life or salvation, (3) an inerrant Bible, and (4) a commitment to spreading the Gospel. These criteria should be regarded as starting points subject to further conceptualization efforts and to changes that may follow from empirical research efforts. They purposely exclude a born-again experience as an essential criterion (as does Hunter, 1983a). The argument is that one can come to a belief in Christ as the means to salvation in other ways than a sudden, born-again type of experience. Individuals that are "born again" in Christ may meet evangelical criteria, but those who are not may meet the criteria as well. In addition, these criteria contain no conception of God, either in a trinitarian sense or in terms of God's essential nature. In the case of the latter, evangelicals tend to view God as very personal and ever present as opposed to abstract and less involved in the affairs of the world. Note also that the criteria do not involve religious practice, although evangelicals are likely to rank high in Bible reading, frequency of prayer, financial giving to the church, witnessing to others, and the like.

In addition to these minimalist criteria, evangelical membership depends on a series of "necessary but not sufficient" beliefs, which do not define evangelicalism but are necessary to it. Central here are beliefs in God and in life after death. Neither make a person an evangelical, but all evangelicals hold these beliefs. Third, evangelicals regard their faith as important; they receive consolation from it. Respondents that disagree do not meet evangelical membership criteria regardless of their answers to questions of doctrine discussed above. The argument here is that there is no such thing as a *nominal* evangelical; evangelicals take their faith seriously. Finally, in a survey situation some respondents answer "none" when asked their religious preference. These respondents should be excluded from evangelical membership as well, regardless of their answers on doctrinal questions.

So far we have defined evangelicalism in terms of a few doctrinal criteria and a set of necessary but not sufficient beliefs. Can denominations be said to be evangelical? We have argued elsewhere (Kellstedt and Smidt, 1988) that it may be fruitful to attempt to classify denominations into evangelical/

non-evangelical Protestant groupings, or into evangelical, fundamentalist, and pentecostal categories within evangelicalism. Certain denominations tend to emphasize the doctrinal distinctives of evangelicalism discussed above more than others. Certainly, most Baptist denominations meet the criteria without difficulty. Within the broad parameters of evangelicalism, some denominations are easy to classify into evangelical sub-groups. Thus, for example, members of Assemblies of God churches can be assumed to be pentecostal.

Briefly, let us mention two evangelical sub-groups that have had great political import in the past decade: fundamentalists and charismatic/pentecostals. Doctrinally, fundamentalists are Biblical literalists. In other words, they believe in a literal, word-for-word interpretation of Scripture. They also have had a born-again experience. In terms of life-style, fundamentalists are separatists. They are more likely to have created separate schools, radio and television ministries, and other institutional structures than other evangelicals. In addition, fundamentals are likely to self-identify as such; as Jerry Falwell has often said: "I'm a fundamentalist and proud of it" (Jelen, 1987). Finally, fundamentalists are the most politically conservative segment of evangelicalism.

The charismatic movement within evangelicalism is growing rapidly. Doctrinally the charismatic believes in a second baptism—called a Baptism of the Holy Spirit. In addition, the charismatic places special emphasis on healing, miracles, and speaking in tongues. Charismatics are born-again believers, and, like fundamentalists, often separatist in life-style and outlook. Their worship style is open, non-traditional, more emotive than other evangelicals. We feel that the charismatics are the least politicized group within modern evangelicalism, although the empirical evidence for this assertion is weak. (See Smidt, 1989, for a beginning effort to examine the political attitudes of charismatics.)

Before leaving this section, a few words should be said about blacks and Catholics and evangelicalism. James Hunter has argued that evangelicalism is a Protestant phenomenon (1983a:139–140) and that Catholics should be excluded from evangelical membership on the grounds that their sociological and religious traditions are too different to include them regardless of doctrinal beliefs.[1] We present evidence from the 1984 CPS to study in Table 1.1 to demonstrate that Catholics who meet evangelical criteria are very different politically from evangelical Protestants. First of all the data show that only a small percentage of Catholics meet evangelical criteria. This small group does behave like the Protestant evangelicals on religious variables and socio-political attitude measures (abortion and prayer). In terms of partisan identification, however, the small group of Catholic evangelicals is very Democratic. It is also far less likely to have voted for

Table 1.1
Comparison of Protestant and Catholic Evangelicals with Protestant and Catholic Non-evangelicals (1984 National Election Study—CPS)

	White Protestant Evangelicals N=232	Catholic Evangelicals N=21	White Protestant Non-Evangelicals N=786	Catholic Non-Evangelicals N=521
Attend Church Regularly	70.7%	55.0%	28.8%	43.1%
Religion Important	100.0	100.0	77.3	85.7
Religion Provides a Great Deal of Guidance	79.3	66.7	24.2	23.6
Born Again	100.0	100.0	18.3	6.3
Literal Bible	100.0	100.0	43.3	33.1
"Never" on Abortion	27.6	28.6	8.7	13.5
Pro-Choice on Abortion	11.1	14.3	36.3	36.1
Pro-School Prayer	91.0	86.7	73.7	70.1
Democratic Party Identification	40.3	66.6	39.5	53.2
Republican Party Identification	54.2	23.9	54.8	38.5
Reagan Vote	74.7	56.3	70.5	55.5
Liberal Identifier	10.7	12.5	16.9	21.0
Conservative Identifier	58.7	50.0	39.5	36.3

Reagan than Protestants. These findings argue for separating Roman Catholics from Protestants in data analysis if not for conceptual reasons.

Blacks have a Protestant religious heritage in this country. Nonetheless, their political struggles are so different from white Protestants that they should be segregated for data analysis purposes as well. Table 1.2 makes this point clearly. Black evangelicals compare favorably with whites in terms of religiosity and on attitudes toward abortion and school prayer. These black evangelicals differ significantly from black non-evangelicals in their responses to these variables. However, in terms of political ideology,

Table 1.2

Comparison of White and Black Evangelicals with White and Black Non-evangelicals (1984 National Election Study—CPS)

	White Protestant Evangelicals N=232	Black Evangelicals N= 71	White Protestant Non-Evangelicals N=786	Black Non-Evangelicals N=171
Attend Church Regularly	70.7%	65.7%	28.8%	35.2%
Religion Important	100.0	100.0	77.3	90.7
Religion Provides a Great Deal of Guidance	79.3	82.8	24.2	31.8
Born Again	100.0	100.0	18.3	22.5
Literal Bible	100.0	100.0	43.3	53.6
"Never" on Abortion	27.6	25.8	8.7	17.1
Pro-Choice on Abortion	11.1	16.7	36.3	42.4
Pro-School Prayer	91.0	97.0	73.7	81.1
Democratic Party Identification	40.3	84.2	39.5	86.2
Republican Party Identification	54.2	14.2	54.8	6.6
Reagan Vote	74.7	8.2	70.5	10.0
Liberal Identifier	10.7	31.9	16.9	29.0
Conservative Identifier	58.7	29.8	39.5	28.9

party identification, and vote choice, the two black groups do not differ. On these manifestly political variables, black evangelicals abandon their fellow evangelicals to respond with their fellow blacks. In conclusion, these first two tables demonstrate the necessity of separating Catholics and blacks from white Protestants in studies of evangelicalism where the focus of the research is on politics.

CONCEPTS AND MEASURES OF EVANGELICALISM:
GALLUP AND HUNTER REVISITED

Until recently, the measurement of evangelicalism has been left to George Gallup, Jr. and his survey organization and has been pretty much untouched by scholars. Gallup defines evangelicals in terms of the following three basic characteristics: "They describe themselves as 'born-again Christians' or say they have had a 'born again' experience; they have encouraged other people to believe in Jesus Christ; and they believe in a literal interpretation of the Bible" (Gallup, 1982, 31). Approximately 17 percent of Americans met these criteria in the early 1980s. (For a more recent use of these criteria see Wald, Owen, and Hill, 1988.) Let us turn to the specific questions that Gallup asks. "Would you say that you have been born again or have had a born again experience—that is, a turning point in your life when you committed yourself to Jesus Christ?" In 1982, 35 percent responded affirmatively to the question. Is it appropriate to exclude from the evangelical camp any person who denies having a born-again experience? What about the individual born into a Christian family who cannot remember being apart from the body of believers in Christ? Or a believer who cannot recall a specific "turning point"? Is making a commitment to Jesus Christ as Lord and Savior the same as being born again? To many orthodox Christians, the born-again language strikes of revival meetings and the "sawdust trail," as opposed to rigorous confirmation training. Not surprisingly, in an examination of data collected by Gallup for a study entitled *The Unchurched American*, we find Baptists, much more likely than Lutherans to have had a born-again experience, although the two groups differed little on other essential doctrinal beliefs. Baptists use the born-again language far more than Lutherans. Hence, on both logical and empirical grounds, we feel that the born-again experience should not be considered essential for evangelical membership.[2]

In Table 1.3 we present data from *The Unchurched American* in order to examine the born-again phenomenon more closely. Within this particular study, a total of 686 respondents, or 32.6 percent of the sample, said that they were "born again." Yet, as the data in Table 1.3 demonstrate, many of the so-called born-again respondents gave "non-evangelical" responses to other items in the survey. On conceptual grounds, it is reasonable to assume that respondents who answer that they were born again but have not committed themselves to Christ have a "low" view of Scripture, never pray, lack certainty about the resurrection, and do not associate Christ as Godly are "suspect" as evangelicals. In Table 1.4 we compare the "suspect" born-again respondents with born-again respondents that give "evangelical" answers to the questions in Table 1.3 and with declared non-born-again

Table 1.3
"Born-Again" Respondents and Other Measures (1978 Unchurched American Survey)

Item	Number	Percent of Born Again
Have not made a commitment to Christ	92	13.4%
Consider Bible a "book of legends"	38	5.7
Never pray to God	18	2.7
Not "certain" Jesus rose from dead	118	17.4
Do not believe in the resurrection	55	8.0
Believe Jesus neither God nor Son of God	64	9.6

respondents. The results are instructive: the "suspect" group differs dramatically from the other "born-again" respondents. It most closely resembles those who report not having had the experience. This analysis illustrates the problems that can develop when appropriate precautions are not followed in using the born-again question as a single operational measure for identifying evangelicals. In the 1984 CPS survey, 33 percent of white respondents who claimed to be atheists or agnostics or gave no religious preference said that they had had a born-again experience, a remarkably high and disturbing figure. Yet the analysis reveals that there are often ways to avoid such problems if other measures are available to "filter out" suspect respondents. However, if the survey being used has no other measures of evangelicalism (in contrast to *The Unchurched American* data in Tables 1.3 and 1.4), then the analyst is stuck with an inadequate measure of evangelicalism.

Second, Gallup poses the following question concerning witnessing: "Have you ever tried to encourage someone to believe in Jesus Christ or to accept Him as his or her Savior?" Forty-five percent responded affirmatively in 1982 (Gallup, 1982: 31). Is witnessing an essential criterion for evangelicalism? We prefer to consider it a desirable behavioral manifestation of evangelical beliefs rather than as a central component of the concept. In this sense, witnessing belongs in a category with an active prayer life, frequent Bible reading, and substantial financial giving. In addition, what qualifies as witnessing behavior conceptually is not as obvious as it may appear. Is the Christian neighbor whose life-style attracts people to Christ witnessing?

Table 1.4
Comparison of "Suspect" and "Non-suspect" Born-Again Respondents (1978 Unchurched American Survey)

Item	Not Born Again N=1256	Suspect Born Again N=254	Non-Suspect Born Again N=452
Attended church in last 6 months	44.0%	55.5%	75.6%
(Of attenders) Attended church at least once a week	42.7	44.5	65.3
Ever not attended church for 2 years or more	44.2	47.9	31.7
All/most of friends attend church	28.9	27.4	53.1
Prayed twice a day or more in past week	16.9	29.8	46.5
Pray at meals	22.4	24.8	47.1
Pray constantly	5.5	7.7	27.9
Watch religious TV or listen to religious radio	27.4	38.3	59.6
Church member	49.6	52.6	81.2
(Of members) active	49.2	54.4	73.9

Apart from conceptual difficulties, another problem involves the measurement of witnessing behavior and how to ascertain its frequency. In terms of the latter, the Gallup question would place in the same category the person who on one occasion encouraged a friend to accept Jesus and the person who witnesses on an every-day basis.[3] In conclusion, a more appropriate conceptual approach and operational strategy is to ascertain commitment of respondents to evangelism efforts. Such commitments are essential to evangelical membership.

In the discussion of the Gallup measures up to this point, only experiential variables are included: born-again and witness experiences. In addition, one doctrinal question is included: attitudes toward the Scriptures. "Which of these statements comes closest to describing your feeling about the Bible?" Respondents were shown a card with the following statements: "The Bible is the actual Word of God and is to be taken literally, word for word." "The Bible is the inspired Word of God but not everything in it should be taken literally, word for word." "The Bible is an ancient book of fables, legends, history, and moral precepts recorded by men" (p. 32). Only the first answer is considered "evangelical," with 37 percent holding this "literal" response in 1982. Gallup concedes that "this is a fairly strict definition, because some evangelicals do not hold to a literal interpretation of the Bible, although they accept the absolute authority of the Bible."

Most scholars would agree that evangelicals hold a "high" view of the Bible, but there is little agreement on whether a "high" view entails a "literal" view. What about those who hold that the Bible is inspired by God, believe that the original texts (if not the translations) are without error, *and* regard Scripture as authoritative today, but do not necessarily believe in a literal view of Scripture. They are inerrantists but not literalists. We ran a test with the data from Gallup's *The Unchurched American* to see if those who hold an "inspired" view of Scripture belong in the evangelical category (on the basis of that item alone). Three categories of respondents are compared: those who hold a "literal" interpretation, those who give an "inspired" response but hold other "orthodox" opinions (believe Jesus is either God or the Son of God, believe in Christ's resurrection, have made a commitment to Jesus, and believe in life after death), and those who give an "inspired" response without holding orthodox views on other "evangelical" items. We make these comparisons in Table 1.5. Note that the inspired but orthodox category is very similar to the original Gallup literal category and substantially different from the group that believes that the Bible is inspired by God but do not hold other traditional evangelical beliefs. Clearly, a person who believes that the Bible is the inspired word of God and shares other evangelical beliefs should not be excluded from evangelical membership. Again, as with the born-again question, using an item that attempts to measure some aspect of evangelical doctrine without attempting to correct for possible measurement error creates problems in assignment to evangelical membership.[4]

In summary, the Gallup measures place too great an emphasis on experience and too little on doctrine. In addition, the one doctrinal question on attitudes toward the Bible fails to include as evangelicals those who feel that the Bible is the inspired word of God and hold doctrinal positions consistent with evangelical theology. We have also argued that the born-again language is likely to turn off individuals from a reformed/confessional tradition. Finally we feel that witnessing is not an essential characteristic of evangelical membership while arguing that the Gallup item needs clarification as to frequency and type.

James Hunter based his doctoral thesis and recent book, *American Evangelicalism* (1983a), on the *Christianity Today* data collected by Gallup (1979) for the evangelical magazine. He writes: "In performing an analysis with Evangelicalism as the subject, perhaps the greatest problem is how to operationalize—that is, define—Evangelical in measureable terms. One

Table 1.5
Comparison of Gallup Category of Biblical Literalists with a Group of Biblical Inspirationalists Who Hold Other Orthodox Beliefs (1978 *Unchurched American* Survey)

	Literal N=675	Inspired but Orthodox N=314	Inspired/not Orthodox N=500
Religion Very Important in life	70.9%	70.2%	31.4%
Had Religious Training as Adult	16.5	20.3	9.4
Have Had a "Religious" Experience	46.5	45.9	16.9
Ever Gone 2 Years or More Without Church	34.0	33.3	44.4
Pray Constantly--Prayer is my Life	18.4	17.3	4.0
Born Again Plus Witness	20.1	19.8	3.0

Orthodox = Belief in Jesus as God or Son of God; belief in the resurrection; respondent has made a commitment to Jesus; and belief in life after death.

part of the problem is that there is no agreement on a conceptual definition" (p. 139). Central to evangelicalism, he argues, are the acceptance of the inerrancy of Scripture and the divinity of Christ. These core propositions of the faith were measured in the following manner in the Gallup/*Christianity Today* survey:

Which one of these statements comes closest to describing your feelings about the Bible? 1. The Bible is a collection of writings representing some of the religious philosophies of ancient man. 2. The Bible is the Word of God but is sometimes mistaken in its statements and teachings. 3. The Bible is the Word of God and is not mistaken in its statements and teachings. 4. Don't know. Which of these statements comes closest to describing your feelings about Jesus Christ? 1. Jesus Christ was a man, but was divine in the sense that God worked through Him; He was the Son of God. 2. Jesus Christ is not God or the Son of God, but a great religious teacher. 3. Jesus Christ is both fully God and fully man. 4. Don't know. (Hunter, 1983a: 140).

Note the wording difference in the question regarding Scripture and the way that Gallup usually measures attitudes in this area that we discussed above. The *Christianity Today* question does not permit a literal/inspired distinction but does allow the analyst to distinguish between inerrant responses and those that are not. Hunter considers the third option the appropriate evangelical response. On the item involving Christ, the first and third answers measure His divinity.

Hunter continues his analysis by distinguishing between confessional and conversional evangelicals. Disdaining a born-again response, the confessional chooses the fourth response to the following question:

Which one of these statements comes closest to describing your feelings about life after death? 1.   There is no life after death. 2.   There is life after death but what a person does in this life has no bearing on it. 3.   Heaven is a divine reward for those who earn it by their good life. 4.   The only hope for Heaven is through faith in Jesus Christ. 5.   Don't know. (Hunter, 1983a: 141).

The fourth option seems to capture the critical role of Christ in providing salvation.

A conversional evangelical must answer "yes" to each of the following questions:

1. Have you ever had a religious experience—that is, a particularly powerful religious insight or awakening—that changed the direction of your life or not? 2.   Is this experience still important to you in your everyday life, or not? 3.   Did this experience involve Jesus Christ, or not? 4.   Was this a conversion experience—an identifiable turning point that included asking Jesus Christ to be your personal savior, or not?[5](Hunter, 1983a: 141).

Hunter excludes Catholic and Jewish evangelicals *a priori*, arguing, as we noted above, that "Evangelicalism is, historically, a Protestant phenomenon" (p. 139). Although the number of "converted" Jews in a national sample is very small (two in this case), 75 Roman Catholics (close to 18 percent of all Catholics interviewed) met Hunter's evangelical criteria.

To summarize, Hunter defines an evangelical as a Protestant who accepts the inerrancy of the Bible and the divinity of Christ and either believes that Christ is the only hope for salvation, or has had a conversion experience, or both. Some 22 percent of Hunter's sample qualify as evangelicals using this formula. Had Catholics been included, the percentage would have been higher, much more so than the 17 percent figure Gallup reported in 1982. It illustrates the way that operational definitions determine the percentage of evangelicals that one finds in the population. Note that Hunter has no measure of witness efforts or commitments to evangelize. In sum, the conception of evangelicalism developed in the preceding section of the chapter was not adequately measured by either Gallup or Hunter. Nor were the necessary but not sufficient beliefs considered.

NECESSARY BUT NOT SUFFICIENT BELIEFS

We have argued that there are necessary but not sufficient beliefs or conditions that serve as filters or hurdles to be crossed before entry into evangelicalism can be considered. In the Gallup/*Christianity Today* survey, four of these conditions are employed: (1) Individuals were asked their religious preference. Some 125 or 8.1 percent of the sample responded "none." These respondents are excluded from evangelical membership regardless of their answers on doctrinal questions. (2) Respondents were asked: "Do you believe in God or a universal spirit?" Some 59 individuals or 3.8 percent of the sample said "no" and were excluded from further evangelical consideration. Respondents who answered these two questions in this manner were labeled "non-believers." (3) Individuals were asked to describe their feeling concerning "life after death." Fully 167 persons, or 10.8 percent of the sample, said: "There is no life after death." It makes no sense to consider a person an evangelical who does not believe in the afterlife. After all, evangelical doctrine makes faith in Christ as central to life after death. Respondents who gave this answer but considered themselves Protestants or Catholics and believed in God were placed in a category called "nominal Christians," and were excluded from consideration for evangelical membership. (4) Finally, respondents were asked: "How much consolation and help would you say you get from your beliefs about God—a lot, a fair amount, very little, or none at all?" Why has this item been employed as a filter? (a) If religious beliefs provide little or no consolation, their value is marginal (students of religion have almost always argued that one of its functions is to provide consolation). (b) What is being argued here, in addition, is that a "nominal" evangelical is a contradiction in terms. (c) The item works as expected empirically, as we shall see. Respondents who answered "little" or "none" were excluded from further consideration as evangelicals; they amounted to 97 individuals or 6.3 percent of the sample.

In Table 1.6 we look at the results of cross-tabulating an index of the four variables just discussed and a number of religious behavior and doctrine measures. As the import of religion for a person increases, the religious behavior should increase as well. Those who identify as Protestants or Catholics, profess a belief in God and life after death, and receive a lot of consolation from their religious beliefs are much more active and involved in religion than the first four groups. Table 1.6 also raises serious questions about the witness item as a measure of evangelicalism, at least without making serious efforts to clear up measurement error associated with the item. Note that over one-fifth of the non-believers claimed to have witnessed at least once per month, a very high percentage of error. In addition, only

Table 1.6
Necessary But Not Sufficient Beliefs and Religious Doctrine and Practices
(*Christianity Today* **Sample)**

	Do Not Believe in God N=152	Believe in God but Not in Life After Death N=166	Believe in God and Life After Death/ Consolation From One's Religion:		
			Little/No Consolation N= 97	Fair Consolation N=358	A Lot of Consolation N=712
Witness Regularly	21.1%	17.5%	19.6%	25.7%	44.8%
Attend Church Regularly	3.9	15.7	11.3	24.3	58.1
Read Bible Regularly	5.3	13.3	5.2	14.2	49.9
Tithe	1.3	5.4	3.1	8.1	26.7
Church Work	5.3	23.5	27.8	30.7	57.7
Church Member	11.2	54.2	59.8	65.6	85.3
Jesus God/ Son of God	38.2	65.1	78.4	92.7	96.5
Jesus Only Hope for Heaven	7.2	0.0	25.8	44.1	64.6
Bible No Mistakes	13.2	20.5	20.6	33.2	60.4
Priority of Evangelism	12.5	18.1	17.5	28.2	51.0
Salvation Important	7.9	10.2	8.2	14.2	48.7
Born Again	4.6	8.4	3.1	9.8	36.7

"Regular" witnessing is considered at least once per month; regular church attendance and Bible reading are at least once per week; regular tithing involves giving at least 10 percent of income to the church and other religious organizations.

the group receiving a lot of consolation from their religious beliefs have high percentages on the doctrinal variables across the board. On the basis of the data in Table 1.6 we feel it is reasonable to exclude the respondents who receive fair or little or no consolation from their religion from further consideration as evangelicals.[6]

What has been accomplished here? Sizable numbers of individuals have been eliminated from consideration as evangelicals on both logical and empirical grounds. When employing such a procedure, the number of evangelicals will be smaller. However, the "evangelicals" that do emerge should fit more closely with the theoretical sketch developed earlier in the chapter, or at least that part of it that emphasized the importance of the necessary but not sufficient conditions for evangelical membership.

EVANGELICALISM: THE MINIMAL DOCTRINAL ESSENTIALS

Earlier we developed a set of minimal doctrinal criteria for evangelicalism: beliefs in the divinity of Christ, salvation only through belief in Christ, an inerrant Bible, and the centrality of evangelism. The *Christianity Today* survey is the best questionnaire developed to date for the purposes of operationalizing this conception. We have already noted the questions covering the first three of our criteria. A fourth question measured the priority of evangelism: "Listed on this card are several priorities for Christians. Regardless of whether or not you consider yourself a Christian, which ONE of these actions would you say should be the TOP priority of Christians? And which could you say should be the second most important priority?" Five response options were given: (1) "Help to win the world for Jesus Christ." (2) "Concentrate on the spiritual growth of one's family and self." (3) "Join groups and support causes that will improve the entire community." (4) "Help strengthen the local church." (5) "Take part in efforts to influence local, state, and national legislation on important issues." The first option is consistent with our evangelical theory sketch—38 percent of the sample made this response their first or second priority.

Are there empirical grounds for including this priority of evangelism measure in an index of evangelicalism? The correlation of this measure with the other three criteria is relatively high. Second, the measure correlates similarly to the other evangelical items when related to a series of variables measuring religious practice (witnessing, Bible reading, attendance, and the like).[7] Hence we have a measure that appears to be reliable, is valid on grounds of content validity, and behaves as expected when correlated with theoretically related variables (in other words, has construct validity).

Despite the apparent validity of the four measures, when they are combined into an index, problems arise. What are the problems? Some 227 white Protestants and Catholics meet all four criteria. However, the survey contains a series of items that would tend to rule out respondents as "evangelical" based on their responses to these questions. Of the 227 respondents, 77 either agreed that religion provides little or no consolation in their lives, that the Devil does not exist, that God was not involved in creation, that salvation is not a personal need, or that the Ten Commandments are not valid today. Although these variables are not part of the minimal criteria for evangelicalism developed earlier, they do involve beliefs that one would expect evangelicals to disagree with. As a result, we call these 77 respondents "suspect" evangelicals.

In Table 1.7 we compare the doctrinally sound Protestant evangelicals from the *Christianity Today* survey with the "suspect" and non-evangelical groups in terms of religious practice. The suspect group is more like the non-evangelicals with regard to Bible reading, knowledge of Scriptures, church attendance, witnessing, and financial giving. As a result we conclude that the suspect group does not belong with the other evangelicals. Only studies with a large number of "religious" measures allow the scholar to make the kind of validity checks that we have instituted here. With more limited measures of evangelicalism in most other surveys, scholars will have to live with greater measurement error.

We are now at a point where we can compare the doctrinal evangelicals from the *Christianity Today* survey with those Gallup and Hunter evangelicals that do not meet the requirements we have established in this chapter. We do this in Table 1.8. Comparisons are made with the same religious practice items used in Table 1.7. Note the wide variation between Hunter evangelicals misclassified by the scheme developed for this chapter and the doctrinal evangelicals. The major reason for this is Hunter's failure to include the measure concerning evangelism priority, a measure that we have justified on both conceptual and empirical grounds. Gallup evangelicals do not differ as much from the doctrinal evangelicals in terms of religious practices. This is because of Gallup's inclusion of the witness item. The purpose of this exercise is not to argue that Hunter and Gallup measures of evangelicalism are wrong and that the one developed for this chapter is correct. Instead, it is to show that different conceptions and

Table 1.7
Comparison of Doctrinal Evangelicals with Suspect and Non-evangelicals on Religious Behavior Measures (*Christianity Today* Study—White Protestants Only)

	Protestant Evangelicals N=135	Non-Evangelicals N=575	Suspect Evangelicals N= 64
Read Bible Weekly or More	87.3%	33.3%	50.8%
Know Bible Verse	73.3	32.2	32.8
Attend Church Weekly	78.9	28.5	46.9
Witness Once a Month or More	66.7	30.9	37.8
Tithe	69.1	16.8	23.2

Table 1.8
Comparison of Doctrinal Evangelicals with Those Gallup and Hunter Evangelicals Who Do Not Meet Doctrinal Requirements: Religious Behavior Measures (*Christianity Today* Study—White Protestants Only)

	Doctrinal N=135	Gallup N= 54	Hunter N=170
Read Bible Weekly or More	87.3%	79.3%	59.1%
Know Bible Verse	73.3	61.1	44.1
Attend Church Weekly	78.9	66.7	50.3
Witness Once a Month or More	66.7	68.5	41.1
Tithe	69.1	42.0	29.3

operationalizations lead to different results. The more "pure" the measure of evangelicalism, however, the more likely that the evangelicals that emerge in the study will fit theoretical expectations.

Political analysts of evangelicalism, however, who use the data collected by others are unlikely to find such measures as were available in the *Christianity Today* survey. In addition, they will find a paucity of political measures in such "religious" surveys. Hence they will turn their attention to the surveys done at Michigan (CPS) or Chicago (GSS). There they will confront inadequate conceptualizations and operationalizations of evangelicalism. Is there anything that can be done using the measures developed by CPS since 1980? These measures include Biblical interpretation, born again, and two religious salience items. In addition, the denomination and church attendance items asked prior to 1980 remain.

In Table 1.9 we analyze 1984 data comparing groups of whites using the various available CPS measures. We assume that evangelicalism, however measured, should be related to positive feelings toward the Moral Majority and school prayer, negative attitudes toward abortion, conservative political self-identification, Republican party identification, and a Reagan vote choice. A measure of evangelicalism that best relates to each of these variables would be preferable to other measures that do not relate as well. The table compares all whites, other Protestant denominations, and three measures of evangelicalism: (1) regular church-attending members of evangelical denominations;[8] (2) doctrinal evangelicals (born-again/Biblical literalists); and (3) regular church-attending members of evangelical denominations that meet the doctrinal criteria and also regard their religion

Table 1.9
Denomination, Doctrine, and Church Attendance by Other Variables (1984 CPS Study—Whites Only)

	All Whites N=1944	Other Protestant Denominations N=537	Evangelical Denominations/ Regular Attenders N=208	Evangelical Doctrine N=325	Evangelical Denominations/ Evangelical Doctrine/ Regular Attenders N=129
Born Again	34%	25%	80%	100%	100%
Bible Inerrant	47	43	90	100	100
Religion Important	78	80	99	100	100
GT 50 Thermometer Moral Majority	25	22	48	50	65
Pro School Prayer	45	45	69	77	94
Abortion Never or Life of Mother	41	34	72	66	80
Conservative Ideology	42	48	63	56	82
Republican Party ID	44	56	56	51	59
Voted Reagan	64	71	80	74	83

as an important part of life, providing at least "quite a bit" of guidance in "day-to-day living." Obviously, the final category should be the strongest measure, the one that does the best job of minimizing measurement error with the items that we have to work with. The results in Table 1.9 bear this out. This "purist" group of evangelicals is the most positive toward the Moral Majority and school prayer, the most anti-abortion, the most conservative and Republican, and the most likely to have voted for Reagan in 1984. No doubt with somewhat improved measures the hypotheses would be even slightly better supported.

CONCLUSIONS

Future studies of evangelicalism will need more careful conceptualization and operationalization than has occurred in the past. Such research efforts need to build on the works that have preceded them. In addition, work will need to pay close attention to the major sub-groups within evangelicalism such as fundamentalists and charismatics, in both conceptual and operational senses. These groups have been and continue to be important politically, but they have not been adequately studied.

Most researchers in the field of religion and politics, however, will continue to rely on major data sources such as CPS and GSS. In these surveys we need to call for more sophisticated measures of religious doctrines and practices, religious self-identification (Guth and Green, 1986; Kellstedt and Smidt, 1988), and underlying religious world views (Benson and Williams, 1986). For evangelicalism, in particular, items concerned with the role of Christ in salvation and more adequate Bible measures are needed. Nonetheless, this study has demonstrated that more judicious use of the available items (doctrine, salience, denomination, church attendance) can lead to better measures and more adequate tests of hypotheses concerned with religion and politics.

NOTES

1. In the survey conducted by Gallup for *Christianity Today* in the winter of 1978–79, to be examined later, approximately 84 percent of Catholics would turn to the "Church" or "respected religious leaders" in testing their religious beliefs as compared with 35 percent of Protestants. The latter would turn to "what the Holy Spirit says to me personally" or to the Bible in much greater frequency than Roman Catholics.

2. Far more research is needed to settle this, however. Data presented elsewhere (Kellstedt and Smidt, 1988) suggest that born-again respondents fit the evangelical stereotype much better than non-born-again respondents who meet other evangelical criteria, after measurement errors have been corrected for.

3. Analysis of the witness item in the *Christianity Today* survey reveals that removing those who claim to witness only "less than once per month" improves the relationships of this item with external variables.

4. In the 1984 CPS survey, 16 percent of non-believers and respondents with no religious preference gave a "literal" response to the question on the Bible. Certainly, in no meaningful sense of the word is this group Biblical literalists.

5. This way of asking a born-again question is more demanding than most and produces far fewer respondents that cross over all four "hurdles." For a comparison of born-again question wordings and resulting frequencies, see Smidt and Kellstedt, 1987: 131.

6. The "fair" consolation category may give us some pause; however, the large number of respondents in the high consolation category and the wide disparity between those two groups on most of the variables examined in these tables suggests the value of the exclusion.

7. For details, see Kellstedt, 1984: 26–27.

8. For denominations that are termed "evangelical," see Kellstedt, 1986.

2
Identifying Evangelical Respondents: An Analysis of "Born-Again" and Bible Questions Used across Different Surveys

Corwin Smidt

Over the past several decades, prevailing social theories generally have suggested that the scope and influence of the religious sphere of life would increasingly diminish through the process of secularization. As a result, scholars have largely ignored religion in their political analyses. However, in recent years, various developments have occurred that seemingly run counter to such expectations; in diverse cultural settings across several different continents (e.g., Ireland, Poland, South Africa, Iran, the United States, and Latin America), religion appears to have emerged as a politically salient factor. It is not surprising, therefore, that such changes have prompted many political analysts once again to take religious variables seriously in their analyses of contemporary politics.

Unfortunately, however, several different problems confront social scientists who seek to engage in empirical analyses related to this topic. First, given that religion was largely dismissed as an explanatory variable, relatively few social scientists have devoted their scholarly endeavors to the study of the interplay of religious and political variables in American life. As a result, analysts cannot draw upon either an extensive or a firmly established body of previous research to guide their present research efforts. For example, it has not been clearly established what facet(s) of religion may be the most salient politically. Does religion primarily manifest itself politically through the effect of doctrinal beliefs upon political attitudes and behavior, through the social nature of religious groups, or through the more narrow organizational character of religious bodies? Given such uncertainty, it is not surprising that research efforts have focused upon an array of religious variables in attempting to discern which religious variables may prove to have the greatest utility in analyses of U.S. politics.

Second, this lack of a systematic body of literature might be less problematic if analysts were more familiar with and less socially separated from religious life in the United States. While being relatively distant from the phenomenon under investigation provides some analytical advantages, it also carries certain disadvantages. For example, the general lack of awareness about, familiarity with, and sensitivity to religious phenomena evident among many contemporary analysts contribute to a diminished ability (1) to detect important nuances in religious terminology and doctrinal perspectives, (2) to differentiate clearly between and among different religious phenomena, and (3) to glean important insights concerning changes within and between different religious groups. As a result, relatively crude conceptualizations of religious variables are frequently advanced and adopted by many social scientists, and this utilization of unrefined measures can prevent analysts from discerning important changes that may be taking place within and across different religious groups.

Third, given the lack of attention to religious variables and given the multi-dimensional nature of religion, there are few, if any, conventional measures of religious phenomena beyond denominational affiliation and church attendance. Many studies have remained relatively rich in the number and variety of the political and social questions posed, but relatively poor in terms of the number, variety, and quality of the religious questions asked. Some recent social surveys have incorporated new questions designed to tap various religious attitudes and activities of the respondents. However, these questions have been generally few in number and unsystematic in their focus. Even when researchers have employed relatively similar questions across their surveys, there have been important differences in question wording. However, given the general inability to discern important nuances in religious terminology, such differences in question wording frequently go undetected because of their apparent similarity.

Therefore, if one wishes to engage in an analysis of the interplay between religion and political behavior, there is at present (1) little structure to guide current research, (2) a general lack of intimate knowledge about the phenomenon under investigation, and (3) generally few, and relatively crude, measurement items with which one can work. Thus when new religious measures are employed in surveys, scholars are inclined to use the new measures without giving careful attention to the nature of the phenomenon that may be tapped by the measures. As is well known, what a measure seemingly taps and what it actually taps may be two different things. Consequently, analysts must always be sensitive to what their operational measures actually tap.

This study examines the nature of questions frequently used for identifying evangelical respondents. It seeks to demonstrate that what these questions actually tap is somewhat more complex than what initially appears. By demonstrating these subtleties, this chapter seeks to alert analysts to the differences present in what appear to be identical measures. Finally, given the variation in wording of these questions across different surveys, this study makes an initial attempt to construct from these questions relatively comparable composite measures for identifying evangelical respondents across the different surveys analyzed.

THEORETICAL FRAMEWORKS, DEFINITIONS, AND DATA

A variety of conceptual approaches can be employed in the study of evangelicals within U.S. society. One approach is to emphasize the system of religious or theological beliefs that are associated with evangelicalism. This approach seeks to assess how gradations in adhering to evangelical religious beliefs (i.e., being more or less evangelical in one's religious beliefs) may be tied to the expression of different political attitudes or behavior. A second approach is to view evangelicals simply as a particular group within society rather than as discrete individuals who may be more or less evangelical in their religious faith. Thus, according to this second approach, one either is or is not an evangelical.

Moreover, several different conceptual strategies can be employed within this latter (i.e., group) approach. One strategy, for example, is simply to view evangelicals as a categoric group that exhibits unity only through the process of abstraction. Just as one might categorize people together who have graduated from universities and label them "university graduates," so too one might categorize people together who exhibit certain stipulated characteristics and label them "evangelicals." Another strategy associated with this second approach is to view evangelicals less as an abstract category and more as a social group that possesses some form of social cohesion. Yet, even within this particular strategy, there are several different ways in which evangelicals may be viewed as exhibiting some form of social cohesion. For example, evangelicals may be viewed as members of a particular religious movement or as members of a socio-religious group[1] who interact largely within a particular subculture.

Not surprisingly, the adoption of one's approach to analyzing evangelicals significantly affects assessments of both the numerical strength and the political characteristics of American evangelicals (Smidt: 1988c). Moreover, given the fact that one is frequently working with secondary data, one's choice of analytical approach may be dictated, at least in part, by the availability of particular measures within the survey with which one is working.

Generally speaking, most analysts define evangelicals as those Protestants who emphasize that conversion is the first step in the Christian life (namely, that salvation is obtained by faith in Jesus Christ) and who regard the Bible to be the basis of religious authority. While other religious qualities may also tend to characterize evangelicals (e.g., high levels of church attendance or a belief in the divinity of Jesus Christ), such characteristics can generally be viewed either as being directly related to one of the enumerated criteria (e.g., a belief in the divinity of Jesus Christ can be directly related to an acceptance of the authoritative witness of the Bible) or as not constituting a defining quality of evangelicals when conceptualized in terms of a socio-religious group (e.g., high levels of church attendance).

Given this definition, two major measures have been conventionally employed for identifying evangelicals: (1) a question related to views of biblical authority, and (2) a question related to being "born again." Various national surveys over the past decade have incorporated related questions within their surveys. The bulk of these particular studies will serve, therefore, as the data sources upon which the analysis of this chapter will rest. The surveys utilized in this study are: (1) the Survey of the Un-churched American conducted by the Gallup Organization in April 1978; (2) the *Christianity Today* Survey of January 1979, conducted by the Gallup Organization; (3) the 1980 National Election Study conducted by the Center for Political Studies at the University of Michigan; (4) the Gallup Poll of May 13–16, 1983; (5) the Gallup Poll of September 25–October 1, 1984; (6) the 1984 National Election Study conducted by the Center for Political Studies at the University of Michigan; (7) the Gallup Poll of November 9–12, 1984; and (8) the Los Angeles Times Poll of July 8–14, 1986.

DATA ANALYSIS

"Born-Again" Variable

Despite the fact that the contemporary evangelical movement is viewed to be composed of "born-again" Christians, evangelicals have never viewed one's born-again status solely in terms of whether or not one has had a sudden Saul/Paul conversion experience. Rather, in its broadest sense, to be "born again" is simply to confess and to repent from one's sinful nature and to accept Jesus Christ as one's Savior (Poloma, 1982: 243). An acceptance of Christ as one's personal Savior and Lord can occur by means other than through an instantaneous conversion experience (e.g., one may have accepted Christ for as long as one can remember by having been raised in the faith). Hence, having an instantaneous born-again conversion experience is not the critical defining characteristic of being an evangelical; rather, it is one's personal acceptance of Christ's central role in salvation and one's personal commitment to Jesus Christ as the Lord of one's life.

However, because of its narrower connotation in referring to some relatively intense experience that marks a spiritual turning point in one's life, the born-again terminology tends to be used more frequently within some segments of orthodox Christianity than other segments. Evangelicals from more confessional traditions are less likely than evangelicals from more pietistic traditions to understand the conversion experience in terms of a specific, identifiable point in one's life. Thus, Lutherans are much less likely, for example, to claim a born-again status than are Baptists (Smidt and Kellstedt, 1987).

Actually, Gallup (1979) did differentiate between "conversionalist evangelicals" and confessional or "orthodox evangelicals" initially—with the latter group not having to respond positively to having had a born-again experience. The overlap between the two groups was large (in that many conversionalist evangelicals also met the criteria for being an orthodox evangelical), but it was by no means complete. Some significant divergences were evident between the two groups. However, as they were so closely in agreement on most items, Gallup found it practical to speak of the two as one group, and, subsequently, Gallup has generally employed a born-again question in operationally identifying evangelicals.[2] In so doing, however, Gallup narrowed both his definition of evangelicals and the resultant number of evangelicals he identified.

Subsequently, the born-again question has become one of the most commonly used measures for identifying evangelicals. However, the specific questions posed to tap this born-again phenomenon vary from survey to survey. Given different question wording, different percentages of the population admit to being born again.

This variation is evident in the data presented in Table 2.1. As can be seen from the table, the percentage of white respondents who willingly reported that they had had a born-again experience ranged from a high of approximately 40 percent in Gallup's survey of September 1984, to a low of approximately 24 percent in the Michigan study of 1980. This relatively large difference in the percentage of born-again respondents within a short interval of time suggests that this difference is due more to the manner in which the born-again questions were posed than it is reflective of any real religious change having transpired over that period of time within the American electorate. A closer inspection of Table 2.1 tends to confirm this suspicion. The data suggest that the number of born-again Christians found within the American electorate is heavily influenced by the manner in which the born-again question is posed. Note, for example, that all five Gallup surveys and the Los Angeles Times Poll (which employed the Gallup questions) indicate that approximately one-third or more of the American people claim to be born-again, while, in contrast, the two Michigan studies indicate that slightly less than one-quarter of the American people do so.

Table 2.1
Variation in Born Again Question (Whites Only)

Study	EXACT QUESTION POSED	Born Again
Unchurched American 1978	"Would you say that you have been born again, or have had a born again experience--that is, an identifiable turning point in your life?"	34.9%
Christianity Today 1979	"Have you ever had a religious experience--that is, a particularly powerful religious insight or awakening that changed the direction of your life?"	30.8%
CPS 1980	"Some people have had deep religious experiences that have transformed their lives. I'm thinking of experiences sometimes described as 'being born again in one's life.' There are deeply religious people who have not had an experience of this sort. How about you: have you had such an experience?"	23.8%

Gallup   May,   1983
              Sept., 1984
              Nov.,   1984
LA Times July,   1986
	"Would you say that you have been 'born again' or have had a 'born again' experience--that is a turning point in your life when you committed yourself to Christ?"	33.7%
		39.7%
		34.8%
		36.2%

CPS 1984	"Some people have had deep religious experiences which have transformed their lives. I'm thinking of experiences sometimes described as 'being born again in one's faith' or 'discovering Jesus Christ in one's life.' There are deeply religious people who have not had an experience of this sort. How about you: have you had such an experience?"	24.7%

What is it, then, about Gallup's questions that permit larger numbers of people to respond affirmatively to his questions than do the Michigan questions? It would appear to such systematic differences noted between the two survey organizations are because larger numbers of confessional evangelicals respond affirmatively to Gallup's born-again questions than to the Michigan questions. Confessional evangelicals may claim to be born again through having made a personal commitment to Jesus Christ—even though they might not claim to have had any particularly powerful, life-transforming experience. When one compares the Michigan questions with the Gallup questions, it is evident that the Michigan questions place a stronger emphasis upon subjective experience than do the Gallup questions. This is particularly obvious when one compares the Michigan questions with the Gallup question employed in the four later surveys (i.e., his 1983 survey, the two 1984 surveys, and the 1986 survey). In these later surveys, the born-again question is posed, at least in part, in terms of having made a commitment to Christ and not just in terms of having had some experience that marked a turning point in the respondent's life. Such terminology, namely the phrase "commitment to Christ," is much more familiar and acceptable to confessional evangelicals than either the "religious experience" or "conversion experience" terminology. Moreover, even The Unchurched American survey of 1978 appears to allow some "confessional" evangelicals to respond affirmatively to the particular born-again question included within that study. Note that in the Unchurched study, Gallup asked the respondents (1) whether they had been born again, *or* (2) whether they had had a born-again experience. Thus, even some of Gallup's 1978 respondents may claim to be born again without claiming to have had a born-again experience.

It is evident from the data presented in Table 2.2 that this does occur. In two of his studies, Gallup asked the respondents, in addition to a born-again question, whether they ever had had a "religious experience—that is, a particularly powerful religious insight or awakening." As can be seen from Table 2.2 approximately one-third of those who claim born-again status also report never having had any such powerful religious experience.

Table 2.2
Religious Experience by Whether Respondent Claims to be Born Again (Whites Only)

	Unchurched American		Gallup Survey May 1983	
	Born Again		Born Again	
	No	Yes	No	Yes
Religious Experience: Have you had "a particularly powerful religious insight or awakening?"				
No	84.5%	33.0%	82.2%	35.9%
Yes	15.5	67.0	17.8	64.1
Total	100.0%	100.0%	100.0%	100.0%
(N)	(1403)	(899)	(1591)	(729)

Thus Gallup's born-again questions are posed in such a manner that at least some respondents respond affirmatively to being born-again without claiming that they ever have had any relatively intense, born-again experience. This difference in question wording probably acccounts for the fact that Gallup's measures tend to reveal a higher percentage of born-again respondents than do the Michigan measures.

Why is it, then, that some of Gallup's respondents answer affirmatively to his born-again questions without claiming a born-again experience? Basically, it would appear that they do so simply because, at some point in time, they have made a personal commitment to Jesus Christ. Because Gallup's Unchurched American study contained the born-again and religious experience questions, as well as a question that asked respondents whether or not they had made a commitment to Jesus Christ, it is possible to ascertain whether those respondents who claim to be born again, yet deny having had any powerful religious experience, do so largely because they have made a commitment to Christ. As can be seen from Table 2.3, nearly 85 percent of those respondents who claimed to be born again among those respondents who reported *not* having experienced any particularly powerful religious insight or awakening stated that they had made a commitment to Jesus Christ. This percentage is nearly double the percentage of those who reported having committed themselves to Christ among those who claimed neither to be born again nor to have had a powerful religious experience (43.4 percent). Moreover, this percentage is nearly equivalent to the percentage of respondents who claimed to have committed themselves to Christ found among those who reported having had a powerful religious experience and who claimed to be born again (93.6 percent). Thus the data presented in Table 2.3 suggest that it is having made a commitment to Christ, rather than the religious experience per se, that tends to characterize those respondents who claim to be born again in Gallup's surveys.

On the other hand, while some respondents might claim to be born again through having made a personal commitment to Jesus Christ, not all respondents who have made such a commitment necessarily claim to be born again. This is evident from the data presented in Table 2.4. When one cross-tabulates the commitment to Jesus Christ question with the born-again question, it is evident that only slightly more than one-half (56.4 percent) of those respondents who claim to have made a commitment to Jesus Christ also claim to be born again. While some respondents may claim to be born again simply on the basis of having made a personal commitment to Jesus Christ, not all who make such a commitment necessarily claim to be born again.

However, at the same time, it must also be recognized that the use of a single born-again question as a simple means to identify evangelical Christians can

Table 2.3
Having Made a Commitment to Jesus Christ by Born Again Controlling for Having Had a Powerful Religious Experience (Whites Only)

| | | Have Not Had Powerful Experience | | Have Had Powerful Experience | |
| | | "Born Again" | | "Born Again" | |
		No	Yes	No	Yes
"Would you say that you have made a commitment to Jesus Christ or not?"					
	Yes	43.3%	84.8%	61.1%	93.6%
	No	56.7	15.2	35.9	6.4
	Total	100.0%	100.0%	100.0%	100.0%
	(N)	(1119)	(289)	(209)	(591)

Source: Unchurched American Survey.

Table 2.4
Born Again by Commitment to Jesus Christ (Whites Only)

| | | Have Made A Commitment to Jesus Christ | |
		No	Yes
"Would you say that you have been born again, or have had a born again experience--that is, an identifiable turning point in your life?"			
	No	89.6%	43.6%
	Yes	10.4	56.4
	Total	100.0%	100.0%
	(N)	(1416)	(792)

Source: Unchurched American Survey.

result in some serious measurement problems. If evangelical Christians can be characterized by anything, it is that they have made a commitment to Jesus Christ. Yet, as can be seen from Table 2.4, approximately 10 percent of those who claim never to have made a commitment to Jesus Christ still answer affirmatively that they either have been born again or have had a religious experience that constituted a turning point in their life. Obviously, religious experiences are not limited to Christians. Moreover, non-Christians, as well as Christians, can have religious experiences that can change their lives. Therefore, the born-again questions as they are now structured do not discriminate between and among Christians, Hindus, Moslems, or any other religionists who respond affirmatively to such born-again questions. As a result, analyses of born-again respondents are simply inadequate as a means of ascertaining the political attitudes and behavior of evangelicals.

Views of the Bible

It is the evangelical emphasis upon the Bible as the ultimate religious authority that helps, along with several other factors, to distinguish evangelical Christians from other Christians. However, while the Bible is accepted as the basis of religious authority, the nature of that authority may be viewed differently among evangelicals. Several different positions can be identified that, while interrelated, are analytically distinct. Moreover, different principles of biblical interpretation may be associated with different views concerning the nature of scriptural authority.

In terms of scriptural authority, evangelicals generally adhere to an infallible, an inerrant, or a literal view of the Bible.[3] While all inerrantists subscribe to biblical infallibility, not all who subscribe to the infallible nature of the Bible are biblical inerrantists. Similarly, while all biblical literalists subscribe to biblical inerrancy, not all inerrantists are biblical literalists. Consequently, while inerrantists are a subset of those who adhere to biblical infallibility, biblical literalists are a subset among biblical inerrantists.

Those who subscribe to an infallible view of Scripture believe that the Bible is the inspired Word of God and that it is true in all that it teaches. As such, it is the word of God to mankind—but it is not literally *the* words of God. The Bible contains a divine message, but that message is expressed in human terms. Thus, Scripture is seen to be the inspired Word of God that comes to the church mediated through the words of human writers. Infallabilists argue that the authors of the biblical books were inspired, by God, to be authors of His message. However, such writers were not mere stenographers of a message dictated by God; rather, there was an interplay between divine and human authorship. Thus the Bible is seen to be the medium of God's revelation, but it is not necessarily identical with the truth itself.

Nevertheless, from this perspective, Scripture is infallible in that it does not deceive humans concerning matters of salvation. It is not, however, intended to be an encyclopedia of information on every human topic; one does not go to the Bible necessarily "to answer human philosophical questions or to gain accurate information concerning history, science, geography, or astronomy" (McKim, 1985: 93). It isn't that Scripture does not offer information about such topics, but the nature of the information given is governed by the purpose of God's revelation.

Obviously, views concerning the nature of scriptural authority affect the principles by which it should be interpreted. For example, evangelicals who subscribe to biblical infallibility tend to argue that the Bible, given its particular purpose, should be viewed as a religious document. Accordingly, naturalistic accounts about creation, such as the account of creation in Genesis 1 written in poetic form, may reveal truths about creation, but such accounts are not to be understood either as a precise, literal account of the creation process itself or as a general "scientific" statement concerning the specific, sequential nature of that process. Consequently, infallibilists stress that the revelational truths contained in the story of creation in Genesis 1 are truths such as God is the creator of the universe, that people are the creatures of His creation, that men and women who have been created in the image of God have been given a mandate to rule over this created world, while, at the same time, they have a responsibility to be good stewards of that created order. Therefore, evangelicals who subscribe to biblical infallibility are likely to hold that Genesis 1 is a true account of the creation process, but they are likely to stress the poetic, rather than the "scientific," nature of that account.

The inerrancy position is more stringent than the infallibility position. The inerrancy position posits that the Bible is, at least in terms of the original documents, totally without error in all its statements whether they relate to religious faith, historical events, or natural occurrences. Biblical inerrantists are likely to stress that the account in Genesis 1 is a true account—both religiously and scientifically. Many inerrantists would recognize that the term "day" discussed in the account does not necessarily refer to a twenty-four-hour span of time (as the account is poetic and as God is eternal and exists outside of the dimension of time). However, such inerrantists might well insist that the creation sequence is true in terms of the natural history of matter and that many, if not most, scientific accounts of the origins of the universe can be harmonized with the account of Genesis 1.

Finally, biblical literalism is a specific principle of interpretation related to biblical inerrancy. The position of inerrancy does not necessarily require a literalistic interpretation. For example, a biblical literalist would, by definition, adhere to a belief in an historical, six-day creation, while a biblical inerrantist need not necessarily do so.

Unfortunately, analysts frequently use the terms "biblical inerrancy" and "biblical literalism" synonymously, and, at times, analysts have even equated the position of biblical infallibility with biblical literalism (e.g., Rothenberg and Newport, 1984: 16). Given such confusion, it is not surprising that questions attempting to tap respondents' views of the Bible can vary considerably in what the items measure. Some operational measures may tap biblical literalism, others may tap biblical inerrancy, while still others may tap biblical infallibility. Table 2.5 reveals how various surveys have used different questions to tap respondents' views of the Bible. Three different questions have been employed by these surveys, and each question tends to tap different aspects of the nature of biblical authority.

As can be seen from Table 2.5, both the question used by Gallup in his Unchurched American survey and the Gallup question used in the 1983, 1984, and 1986 surveys taps primarily whether or not the respondent could be classified as a biblical literalist. When given these three specific options concerning their biblical views, the vast majority of Americans (over 85 percent) stated that they viewed the Bible to be either the actual or the inspired Word of God—with less than 15 percent attributing no divine origin to the text. Obviously, an overwhelming majority of Americans view the Bible to be divine in its origins. Consequently, this particular question format discriminates primarily between those respondents who see the Bible to be the actual Word of God that should be interpreted literally from those respondents who view the Bible to be the inspired Word of God but that should not be interpreted literally.

The second question found in Table 2.5 was used by Gallup in his *Christianity Today* survey of 1978–79. This particular measure seemingly does not attempt to identify those respondents who are biblical literalists. Rather, it appears, at least at first glance, to attempt to identify those who espouse the position of biblical infallibility, who hold that the Bible is the Word of God and that it is "true in all its assertions." Therefore, those who espouse biblical infallibility seemingly would have to agree with the first option that "the Bible is the word of God and is *not* mistaken in its statements and teachings."

However, those who espouse infallibility generally contend that scriptural passages are addressed within a context of faith and practice. Therefore, infallibilists are certainly likely to agree that the Bible is not mistaken in terms of its teachings. But it is not altogether clear how infallibilists are likely to respond to the word "statements" within this question format. Infallibilists generally contend that when the Bible touches upon matters not directly

Table 2.5
Variation in Bible Question (Whites Only)

	Unch. Amer. 1978	CT 1978-79	CPS 1980	CPS 1984	Gallup Nov. 1984	LA Times July 1986
Question #1						
The Bible is the actual word of God and is to be taken literally, word for word	37.6%				39.5%	34.1%
The Bible is the inspired word of God but not everything in it should be taken literally, word for word	49.9				47.2	53.9
The Bible is an ancient book of fables, legends, history, and moral precepts recorded by men	12.4				13.3	12.1
	100.0% (1294)				100.0% (1230)	100.0% (1751)
Question #2						
The Bible is the word of God and is <u>not</u> mistaken in its statements and teachings		42.6%				
The Bible is the word of God but is sometimes mistaken in its statements and teachings		32.1				
The Bible is a collection of writings representing some of the religious philosophies of ancient man		25.3				
		100.0% (1338)				
Question #3						
The Bible is God's work and all it says is true			44.8%	46.9%		
The Bible was written by men inspired by God but it contains some human errors			45.6	44.7		
The Bible is a good book because it was written by wise men, but God had nothing to do with it/ The Bible was written by men so long ago that it is worth very little today.			9.6	8.4		
			100.0% (1168)	100.0% (1586)		

related to faith and practice (e.g., assertions in the field of history and science), it does so only in order to illuminate and demonstrate issues related to its central concern. Accordingly, infallibilists generally argue that the Bible does not speak directly to scientific and historical questions and that such statements may or may not be totally accurate scientifically or historically. Consequently, it may be that the option "the Bible is the word of God and is *not* mistaken in its statements and teachings" taps biblical inerrancy more than biblical infallibility—in that while an infallibilist would not claim that the Bible is mistaken in its teachings, such a person might claim the Bible may, at times, be "mistaken" in its "scientific" and historical statements.

Perhaps one final observation should be made concerning this second question found in Table 2.5. For whatever reasons, it is evident that the second question attracted more people at the lower end of the index than was true for the other two questions. With Gallup's *Christianity Today* Bible question, the percentage of people reporting the "weakest" interpretation of Biblical authority is nearly twice that evident with his previous question and nearly three times that evident with the Michigan question. While it is not immediately clear why this particular wording should attract so many more people, relatively speaking, than the other "weaker" options, the dramatic differences in percentages associated with the different "weak" options reveal that the wording of such closed-ended question options can have a major impact on the resulting distributions when tapping respondents' views of the Bible.

As literalists are a subset of biblical inerrantists, and as inerrantists are a subset of biblical infallibilists, operational measures that tap biblical literalism should identify a smaller segment of the population than a measure tapping either biblical inerrancy or biblical infallibility. On the other hand, one might question whether such nuances concerning the nature of biblical authority would necessarily be detected by the mass public. If so, one might expect little, if any, difference in the relative distributions associated with different measurement items. If respondents react more to the relative placement of the positions concerning various views of the Bible than to the actual wording of the various options, then one might expect that some who accept the authoritative nature of the Bible may respond affirmatively to the answer that most strongly emphasizes that authority (e.g., literalism) regardless of whether they truly believe the Bible to be *the* word of God or the *inspired* word of God.

The "problem" with the Gallup question is that literalism in biblical interpretation is a very narrow operational criterion in identifying evangelicals. Even some evangelicals who subscribe to biblical inerrancy would likely contend that "the Bible is the inspired word of God but not everything in it should be taken literally, word for word." At the same time, however, it is possible that many non-evangelicals might also give such a response. Is it possible, then, to find some way that would enable analysts to differentiate between evangelicals and non-evangelicals who give the "inspired" response to Gallup's Bible question?

Fortunately, it appears that it is possible. After the initial *Christianity To-day* survey of 1979, Gallup's operational definition of evangelicals has included the criterion that the respondent affirm that he or she has engaged in lay evangelism. So, for each of the last three surveys employing Gallup's operational measures, there is a question that asks the following: "Have you ever tried to encourage someone to believe in Jesus Christ or to accept Him as his or her Savior?" As Hunter (1981: 366) notes, it is true that evangelicals place a heavy emphasis upon evangelism, but such personal efforts are not considered to be essential for one's inclusion within the evangelical circle. To require an affirmative response to such a question is too restrictive a criterion for classification as an evangelical.

On the other hand, given the emphasis upon witnessing among evangelicals, such a question could perhaps be used in conjunction with Gallup's Bible question in order to differentiate between evangelicals and non-evangelicals among those who gave an "inspired" response to the Bible question. However, it would be advantageous to test whether such a procedure has any empirical basis. Fortunately, the Gallup survey of May 1983 and the Los Angeles Times poll of July 1986 contain some additional religious questions that permit a partial test for the "validity" of utilizing such a procedure. As can be seen from the May 1983 Gallup survey presented in Table 2.6, those respondents who believed the Bible to be the inspired word of God and also witnessed were very similar in their religious characteristics to those who fell in the literal category. At the same time, however, such respondents were also substantially different from those respondents who similarly believed the Bible to be the inspired word of God

Table 2.6
Comparison of Gallup Category of Biblical Literalists with a Group of Biblical Inspirationalists Who Witness: 1983 (Whites Only)

	Literal (N=614)	Inspired, but "Evangelical" (N=448)	Inspired, not "Evangelical" (N=824)
Religion very important in Life	71.0%	67.6%	35.3%
Have had a "religious experience"	40.2%	41.3%	19.4%
"Born Again"	53.5%	41.5%	8.6%

Source: Gallup Study of May 1983.

but who had not witnessed. The percentage of those "inspired, but evangelical" respondents who reported (1) that religion was very important in their life, (2) that they have had a "religious experience," and (3) that they "have been 'born again' or have had a 'born-again' experience" reflects the percentages evident among biblical literalists, but are substantially different from those evident among "inspired, but not evangelical" respondents.

The same conclusion can be drawn from the Los Angeles Times poll of July 1986. Given that several additional religious questions were asked in the 1986 survey, an additional as well as more extensive test can be made for the validity of this separation procedure. Once again, as can be seen from Table 2.7, those respondents who believed the Bible to be the inspired word of God and also witnessed were very similar in their religious characteristics to those who fell in the literal category, and, at the same time, they tended to be distinctively different from those respondents who also believed the Bible to be the inspired word of God but who had not witnessed. The percentages of those "inspired, but evangelical" respondents who reported (1) that religion was very important in their life, (2) that they "have been 'born again' or have had a 'born-again' experience," (3) that they believe in life after death, and (4) that they believe that a devil exists that tempts you and that a hell exists to which sinners are condemned almost mirror the percentages evident among biblical "literalists," while, at the same time, they are substantially different from the percentages evident among the "inspired, but not evangelical" respondents. In fact, the percentage of the "inspired, but evangelical" respondents who express a belief in the existence of life after death actually exceeds the percentage evident among the Biblical "literalists." Only on two items (i.e., whether or not the respondent believed that Jesus Christ was God and whether or not the respondent believed that all living creatures were created in their present form within the last ten thousand years[4]), did the "inspired, but evangelical" respondents fall only halfway between the "literal" respondents and the remaining "inspired, but not evangelical" respondents.

Therefore, it would appear that those respondents who report the Bible is the inspired (rather than the actual) word of God and who, at the same time, have reported having tried to encourage someone to believe in Jesus Christ should not necessarily be excluded from the ranks of evangelicals. Such respondents mirror other literalists in their religious chracteristics, while they are significantly different from other respondents who express the same views concerning the Bible but who report never having witnessed to others.

However, if such "inspired, but evangelical" respondents are combined with other Protestant, "born-again," biblical literalist respondents, will

Table 2.7
Comparison of Gallup Category of Biblical Literalists with a Group of Biblical Inspirationalists Who Witness: 1986 (Whites Only)

	Literal (N=597)	Inspired, but "Evangelical" (N=400)	Inspired, not "Evangelical" (N=541)
Religion very important in life	74.3%	65.6%	27.4%
"Born Again"	66.5%	58.5%	11.7%
Believe in life after death	84.6%	89.9%	73.9%
Believe Jesus Christ was God	95.3%	88.6%	81.4%
Believe in Devil which tempts you and a Hell to which sinners are condemned	89.0%	79.1%	55.7%
Believe all living creatures were created in their present form within last ten thousand years	57.8%	42.2%	24.0%

Source: LA Times Poll of July 1986.

such a combination markedly change the resultant composition of the evangelical category? Not all literalist respondents analyzed in Tables 2.6 and 2.7 were necessarily Protestant in religious faith or willing to classify themselves as being born again. Consequently, it is not clear how such a combination would, if at all, alter the religious character of the resultant evangelical category if only the narrower definitional approach were employed.

As can be seen from Table 2.8, the combining of those Protestant, "born-again," "inspired, but evangelical" respondents with those respondents who are Protestant, born-again, biblical literalists has minimal effects upon the religious character of the rsulting evangelical category. The resultant percentages for each of the six "test items" evident with the more inclusive definitional approach are virtually identical to the percentages derived when the narrower approach is utilized. The corresponding percentages associated with each approach do not differ by as much as 5 percent on any of the six religious faith questions. In fact, even with regard to the

Table 2.8

Comparison of Refined Measure Tapping Evangelicals with Measure Using "Literalists" Only

	Protestant Born Again, Literalists Only (N=318)	Protestant Born Again, Literalists, plus "Inspired" Evangelicals (N=506)
Believe in God or universal spirit	99.6%	99.2%
Believe Jesus Christ was God	97.4%	95.3%
Believe in Devil which tempts you and a Hell to which sinners are condemned	96.6%	93.9%
Believe in life after death	88.3%	89.3%
Religion very important in life	85.0%	80.3%
Believe all living creatures were created in their present form within last ten thousand years	63.3%	59.3%

Source: LA Times Poll of July 1986.

item dealing with whether all living creatures have been created in their present form within the last ten thousand years, hardly any change is detected; whereas 63.3 percent of the Protestant, born-again, biblical literalists stated that they believe all living creatures were created in their present form within the last ten thousand years, the percentage drops only to 59.3 percent when the "inspired, but evangelical" respondents are added to the initial category.

CONCLUSION

It is a well-established fact of survey research that question wording has a significant impact upon measurement results. Unfortunately, identical questions and responses for identifying evangelical respondents were not employed across all of the surveys analyzed. Consequently, the analysis presented in this chapter suggests that the following operational criteria be employed for identifying evangelicals:

- Unchurched American survey: Protestant, who responded affirmatively to the question "would you say that you have been 'born again' or have had a 'born-again' experience—that is, an identifiable turning point in your life?" and who stated that the Bible is the actual word of God and should be taken literally, word for word.

- *Christianity Today* survey: Protestant, who responded affirmatively to the question of whether or not they had had a religious experience that changed the direction of their life, and who expressed that "the Bible is the word of God and is *not* mistaken in its statements and teachings."

- 1980 and 1984 CPS studies: Protestant, who responded affirmatively to the question of whether or not they had had a "deep religious experience which (had) transformed their lives, and who expressed that "the Bible is God's word and all it says is true."

- Gallup polls of 1983, 1984, and the LA Times poll of 1986: Protestant, who responded affirmatively to the question "would you say that you have been 'born again' or have had a 'born-again' experience—that is, a turning point in your life when you committed yourself to Christ," and who stated either (1) that the Bible is the actual word of God and is to be taken literally, word for word, or (2) that the Bible is the inspired word of God and who have also reported having tried to encourage someone to believe in Jesus Christ.

Obviously, for comparisons across different surveys employing different questions, the operational measures must be seen as "roughly equivalent" rather than precisely the same. Fortunately, however, it is possible to assess in an indirect manner whether these differences in operational measures across different survey organizations may be significant in nature. Because the CPS 1984 survey and the Gallup survey of November 1984 occurred at roughly the same cross-section in time, comparisons of the two different operational measures for evangelicals can be made in order to assess their equivalence. Table 2.9 presents the relationship between these two different, but roughly equivalent, operational definitions of evangelicals and responses to two questions that were least likely to be affected by question wording—namely, reported voting turnout and reported presidential vote. As can be seen from Table 2.9, these two different operational measures utilized for identifying evangelicals appear to be tapping the same general segment of the electorate. While 69.8 percent of the evangelicals in the Gallup survey reported that they had voted in the 1984 presidential election, 70.1 percent of the evangelicals in the CPS study reported that they did so. Moreover, while 80.1 percent of the evangelicals in the Gallup survey reported that they had voted for Reagan in 1984, 76.3 percent of the evangelicals in the CPS study responded that they did so. On the other hand, among non-evangelicals, 62.0 percent and 61.0 percent in the Gallup and CPS studies, respectively, reported that they had voted for Reagan.

Table 2.9
Comparison of Resultant Percentages Associated with the Utilization of the Different Operational Measures for Identifying Evangelicals (Whites Only)

	Gallup November 1984		CPS 1984	
	Nonevan.	Evan.	Nonevan.	Evan.
Voted				
Yes	72.5%	69.8%	76.2%	70.1%
No	27.5	30.2	23.8	29.9
Total	100.0%	100.0%	100.0%	100.0%
(N)	(1718)*	(532)*	(1431)	(288)
Presidential Vote				
Mondale	37.1%	19.9%	39.0%	23.7%
Reagan	62.9	80.1	61.0	76.3
Total	100.0%	100.0%	100.0%	100.0%
(N)	(1192)*	(346)*	(1022)	(198)

*Weighted.

Consequently, it would appear (1) that these two different, but roughly equivalent, operational measures for identifying evangelicals across the two different survey organizations do tap the same general segment of the electorate, and (2) that both of these operational measures meaningfully differentiate evangelicals from other segments of the electorate.

At a minimum, however, identical operational measures do exist across time for both the CPS studies and for the later Gallup and Los Angeles Times polls conducted during the 1980s. Consequently, at a minimum, different baselines can be established for these CPS and the later Gallup/Los Angeles Times surveys, and the analyst can determine whether or not similar *patterns* are evident among evangelicals across time for both the CPS and the later Gallup/Los Angeles Times studies. If the resultant percentages are roughly equivalent and the patterns similar across the CPS and the later Gallup/Los Angeles Times surveys, then greater confidence can be placed in the specific percentages—in that the similar, though slightly different, operational measures would thereby appear to be tapping the same general pool of evangelical respondents.

NOTES

1. Lenski (1963: 21) coined the term "socio-religious group" to refer to both the communal and associational facets associated with different religious groups.

2. However, Gallup has recently begun to employ a new operational measure for identifying evangelicals. This new measure is a single question that moves toward tapping group identification.

3. Other perspectives could be employed in analyzing the nature of biblical authority. For example, a more "simplistic" perspective that is somewhat less sensitive to the nuances of the analysis would be to analyze whether the words of Scripture (1) are, (2) contain, or (3) become God's revelation to human beings.

4. It should be noted that less than 60 percent of the respondents who stated that "the Bible is the actual word of God and is to be taken literally, word for word" stated that they believed that "all living creatures were created in their present form within the last ten thousand years." This somewhat "surprising" result indicates one of two different things—or a combination of both. First, it may be that Gallup's Bible measure taps relative assessments of biblical authority more than it taps whether or not the Bible should be literally interpreted, and thus those being surveyed respond more to the ranking of "actual" versus "inspired" than they do to the coupled phrases regarding literalism in interpretation. Second, it may be that the question tapping the age of living creatures is seriously flawed. The problem stems from the presence of the phrases "living creatures" and "in their present form," and from the fact that the phrase "within the last ten thousand years" flows from the word "form" rather than from the word "created." Thus, even if one believed that dinosaurs lived more than ten thousand years ago, one might still be inclined to agree with the statement because (1) no dinosaurs are presently living, and (2) the form of living creatures has remained virtually unchanged over the last ten thousand years. It is true that a more careful analysis of the statement might reveal that the latter interpretation may not be a proper interpretation of the statement; however, individuals respond to such phrases rather than analytically evaluate such response items. Consequently, any possible ambiguity can result in measurement error.

3
Toward a Mental Measure of Religiosity in Research on Religion and Politics

David C. Leege

Do religious differences lead to political differences? Although that is the usual way of posing the question in the United States, it is an odd sequence, when one considers the broad sweep of Western history. For it was political differences that defined religious differences. Being a Lutheran or a Catholic, an Anglican or a Puritan, had little to do with the religious values one *chose*; it had nearly everything to do with being a Hessian or a Burgundian, or being among the titled elite or the aspiring counter-elite, respectively. To be sure, through homilies or other methods of Christian formation, the educated people and even a few ordinary folks might learn different outlooks on the world, on the nature of salvation, and on ethical obligations, but the fact that these outlooks differed depended in the first instance on the religious direction of a regime and its surrounding political community.

Sociologists of religion should not think it odd, therefore, that measures of religious beliefs, when properly controlled for social location, have explained little of the variance in political values, while measures of ethnic assimilation, communalism, and regionalism did much better (see, for example, Fee et al., 1980; Leege and Welch, 1989). Immigrants to these shores brought memories of a system where religion was first and foremost a characteristic of the regime and political community. Yet the values they found in the developing U.S. system were ones of voluntary choice regarding religion. Choice involves achievement, in Weberian terms, not ascription. They had known little of that possibility, and so religious and political tribalism were linked more closely than were religious and political beliefs.

Only a thoroughly Americanized sociology of religion would, as Lenski (1963) did, treat the religious factor as an *independent* variable. We would do well to remember that the "communities of memory" Bellah and associates (1985) describe are, in the first instance, rooted in political differences, rather than religious outlooks. Until recent times, the child born into a Western Minnesota town had no more choice about his Lutheranism than did his Scandinavian ancestors. And the child reared in the Bible Belt of Northern Louisiana had no more capacity to select values outside those taught in the Baptist Sunday School than did that Minnesota child. Was it any different in Mormon Utah or Irish Catholic South Boston? For a long time politics determined religion, not the inverse.

Perhaps that is why the sequence of studies beginning with Glock and Stark (1965, especially Stark and Glock, 1968) and culminating in Hoge and De Zuleuta's work (1985) on religious salience has looked for a measure that captures the extent to which an individual *really* identifies with his or her religious body. Given our frame of reference as social scientists, we have never been satisfied with ascriptive characteristics; they are only surrogates for a person's deeper values and we must penetrate further to determine how strongly a person holds those values.

It is in this tradition that scholars study religion and politics, rather than politics and religion. And it is within American notions that an individual has a unique outlook on the world, that we seek a mental, not a social, measure of religiosity. The notion that it is worthwhile to measure mental characteristics of religiosity assumes that society is fairly well assimilated, highly mobile both geographically and socially, moderately educated into common symbol systems, yet still amenable to contacts with varied symbol systems. All of these are assumptions behind recent works in the sociology of religion and our own efforts to develop a measure of foundational religious beliefs in the Notre Dame Study of Catholic Parish Life.

This chapter (1) explores several efforts to develop deeper, mental measures of religiosity, (2) describes the early procedures we used to shape our measures of foundational religious beliefs, and (3) assesses our measure in contrast with the results from a standard scale-building approach. Any new effort at measurement is tentative. The proof of the utility of a measure is not that it meets a set of statistical criteria applied singularly to it as a variable, but that it enters significantly into a network of predictions linking religion and politics. We have more confidence in our measure than in some alternatives, but much work needs to be done with it before we will understand what we have. Clearly, whether religious differences lead to political differences depends on what is selected as "religious" and what is taken to exemplify "political."

THE SEARCH FOR A MENTAL MEASURE

That U.S. political scientists are paying attention at all to religion and politics owes much to two developments, one intellectual and one based on current events. The intellectual concern was stimulated by the Committee on Political Sociology of the International Sociological Association (ISA). Beginning in 1959 it gained infrastructure and introduced American scholars to the intellectual concerns of Europeans through meetings, collaborative research, and finally the data confrontation seminars sponsored by the Inter-University Consortium for Political Research in the 1960s and early 1970s. Volumes such as *Party Systems and Voter Alignments* (Lipset and Rokkan, 1967) showed that one could not understand the politics of Western democracies without a grasp of religious histories and identities. Rose and Urwin (1969), using manifest social classifications, showed that "religious divisions, not class, are the main social basis of parties in the Western world today" (p. 12). American Philip Converse—who along with the European leaders of the Committee on Political Sociology of ISA served on the International Advisory Council of Rose's Survey Research Centre at Strathclyde—noted that religion should be a priority variable for comparative electoral research and suggested that it could be characterized in any of five ways: denominational affiliation, frequency of church attendance, "other indicators of the strictness of religious practice" such as Lenski's "associational involvement" and "communal involvement," and "intensifier" registers such as we-they negative feelings toward religious outgroups (Converse, 1968: 7–9).

Current events provided the impetus for research using these alternate measures of religiosity. In an exceptionally clever piece on religion and politics in the 1960 election, Converse (1966) used elaboration strategies to show the utility of all five measures of religiosity.

Somewhat independently, sociologists of religion were interpreting responses to the massive social and cultural changes in the United States in the 1960s through the use of religious variables. Glock and Stark (1965), among others, offered five dimensions of religiosity—the experiential, the ritualistic, the ideological (beliefs), the intellectual (cognitive), and the consequential. Much of the research in the Glock-Stark tradition focused on religious beliefs. Generally the research found that the more orthodox the belief, the more politically conservative, the more racially prejudicial and anti-Semitic, the less civil libertarian, and the less compassionate the person. Social scientists of the period were decidedly for compassion and social change, and perhaps Rokeach (1969–70) summarized their sentiments in asking of what value was Christian religion if its effect was to produce closed-minded bigots. Recall that this was during the heyday of the secularization hypothesis.

Although most of the measures of this genre were mental measures, some scholars put their political persuasions aside and asked searching questions about the utility of the measures. Perhaps the most influential of these was

Milton Yinger who in 1969 argued that the Glock-Stark strategy was capable of measuring religious views *not* held (and which the investigator thought important), but it could not show whether or how a person *is* religious. Batteries of agree-disagree items define religiosity by the investigator's sampling of the universe of content.

Yinger and scholars since that time have turned to anthropologist Clifford Geertz (1973) for conceptual orientation. What they seek are not universes of content based on conventional doctrinal symbols alone, but on the operating religious symbol system of the individual. The contents of that symbol system, argued Geertz, are responses to recurrent "ultimate" problems of human existence, rites, and beliefs organized to cope with such problems, and groups that instill loyalty while propagating such rites and beliefs.

Some scholars such as Greeley (1981, 1984) have argued that the imagery one associates with God prefigures an encompassing view of the world and social relations. In this approach to religion as a mental measure, one captures its content by looking for latent structure among a variety of descriptors of God. We have also used this approach (Welch and Leege, forthcoming) and find it reasonably powerful in understanding the relationship between deep religious worldviews and sociopolitical attitudes. Nevertheless, insofar as it derives structure from correlational and factorial procedures, it classifies people not according to *their own* operating symbol system but by degrees of centrality or deviation from a group norm. In short, the model of mind is not *ipsative*; its analytic procedures drive individuals away from their unique choices toward general patterns (see Stephenson, 1953 and S. Brown, 1980 for the argument in favor of "ipsative" measurement).

To be sure, the very process of doing social research is one of fitting patterns, once discovered or imposed, to disparate phenomena. Nevertheless, we wanted a mental measure of religiosity not limited to the content sample we had selected. We found conceptual orientation not only in Geertz but in the measurement ideas in Benson and Williams' (1986) recent study of *Religion on Capitol Hill*.

Our conceptual desiderata for a measure ran as follows: insofar as religion involves ordered symbol systems that give meaning to both the perceived and imagined worlds, and therefore involves mental operations, it must be measured in a way that captures *the individual's own idea elements and their ordering*. When such idea elements concern (1) fundamental problems of human existence to which religion is thought to respond, (2) ways in which these problems are overcome, and (3) outcomes that result from this process, we open the possibility that religious beliefs are both dogmatic and predogmatic. That is, while people heavily socialized by a religious body are likely to have some of their perceptions of reality channeled by dogmatic symbols, there are also deeply held feelings about physical and social realities that both antedate religious socialization and develop concurrently. Thus measures based on Christian beliefs may or may not tell much of the story, but they can never tap much more than an individual's deviation from a group norm (whether that norm is set by the investigator who selects items, or later examines correlations among latent-structure measures based on distances from group means, slopes, or whatever). Mental measures of religiosity ought to tell *how the individual* is religious, in both a predogmatic and dogmatic sense. When they do so they are likely to tap foundational religious beliefs.

The methodologically obvious approach to the problem is open-ended questions or an in-depth interview that allows the individual to offer his or her own symbols and structure. That strategy may be possible when the investigator works with a dozen or so ordinary respondents, as in Q-method, or with 80 or so articulate members of an elite, as did Benson and Williams. It is not a viable strategy for mass samples that involve no face-to-face contact with the investigator or his associates.

We found Benson and Williams especially helpful in determining the content of the stimuli. They conceptualized and found four dimensions of foundational religious beliefs: agentic-communal, restricting-releasing, vertical-horizontal, and comforting-challenging. *Agentic* religiosity focuses on me and my problems; *communal* religiosity identifies the common needs of people in their social state. *Restricting* religious values set limits, boundaries, and regulations; *releasing* religious messages offer forgiveness and the freedom from guilt that allows one to experience a fuller, newer life. *Vertical* religion is directed upward to or downward from God; *horizontal* religion is directed outward to other people. Religion as *comfort* offers solace and assurance; religion as *challenge* impels one to serve, to transform persons or society.

The first two are of greatest interest to us in our long-term work on culture, religion, and politics because they bear on Tocqueville I (that is, *Democracy in America*) and Tocqueville II (that is, the arguments of Bellah et al. [1985] in *Habits of the Heart*). If, as Tocqueville claims, the genius of the U.S. political system is in the mores of the people, and if those mores are rooted in the religious values of the people, then the struggle between individualism and communitarianism and the search for boundaries that make commitment possible must also be found in the deepest religious values of the American people (Bellah et al., 1985). That is why a "me-centered" religiosity (Benson and Williams agentic; Leege and Welch individualistic) and a "community-building" religiosity (Benson and Williams communal; Leege and Welch communitarian) should have different political consequences. That is also why an approach to religion that is constricting, bounding, and legalistic should have different political consequences than one that is releasing, liberating, and fulfilling.

While there have been other attempts to develop mental measures of religiosity, we felt that some (e.g., King and Hunt, 1972) were basically more sophisticated refinements of the Glock-Stark strategy, or others either were variants of the religious imagination approach discussed earlier (e.g., Vergote, 1969 and 1972) or were addressed to dimensions we thought were already captured by the Benson-Williams strategy (e.g., Vergote, 1970, on horizontal and vertical, or Gorsuch and Smith, 1983, on "nearness to God"). Therefore, we had a number of conceptual and operational cues that shaped our measure of foundational religious beliefs.

FOUNDATIONAL RELIGIOUS BELIEFS: AN IPSATIVE MEASURE

The measure that appears as Figure 3.1 began with the code categories Benson and Williams abstracted from their open-ended responses. In a number of pretests, some with knowledgeable individuals and others with ordinary parishioners, we back-translated several alternate wordings, instructions, and question layouts. "The basic human problem" offered a *problem*, "the path to salvation" a *process*, and "the outcome of salvation" an *outcome*. By drawing arrows from one box to another, the respondent could offer a sequence, simple or complex, but *it was the respondent's sequence*, not ours. Finally, both the presence of open boxes and the instructions encouraged respondents to offer their own wording in case our back-translations and pretests had failed to yield something close to their own feelings. The identical question was utilized on all four of our samples: parishioners (N = 2,667), lay leaders (N = 212), paid staff (N = 89), and pastors (N = 35).

How did it work as a measure? First, in terms of ease of response, the data presented in Table 3.1 indicate that a very high percentage of parishioners, 86 percent, and nearly all of the elite samples were able to diagram at least one sequence. About 15 percent of the parishioners, lay leaders, and staff were likely to depict at least two sequences, and almost that same proportion offered a third. Pastors, on the other hand, were more likely to eschew distinct multiple sequences in favor of a complex single sequence. Finally, a small proportion of ordinary parishioners—but considerably larger proportions of elites—offered their own wording for a problem, process, or outcome rather than select our wording; one's own wording was more likely to be offered for the processes than for the problems or outcomes. In short, while the question regarding foundational beliefs offered considerable structure to respondents, it did not constrain them either to single, simple sequences or to our wording of the fundamental human problem to which religion responds, the solution to the problem or the path to salvation, and the outcome of salvation.

Figure 3.1
Measurement of Foundational Religious Beliefs

Now we are going to ask you to be an artist. Religion always identifies a basic human problem, something that is wrong with humans and their world. Then religion talks about a path to salvation, that is, a way that basic human problems can be overcome. Finally, religion talks about outcomes of salvation — a change in persons' lives or the way the world is as a result of salvation. Below is part of a picture that shows several kinds of basic human problems, paths to salvation, and outcomes of salvation. Think about your religious beliefs. Now you be the artist. What do you think is the basic human problem that religion deals with? What do you think is the path to salvation? When you decide these, draw an arrow from the box that describes the basic human problem (Under "A") to the box that describes the path to salvation (Under "B"). Finally, what do you think is the outcome of salvation? Now draw an arrow from the box you have chosen under B to the box you have chosen under C — the outcome of salvation. If any of our descriptions in the boxes under A or B or C do not really describe what you think is the basic problem, or the path, or the outcome, then you can try to write in something in your own words. We have left some open boxes for you to write in something if you want. But be sure to connect whichever boxes you choose for A, B, and C with arrows.

(A) THE BASIC HUMAN PROBLEM	(B) THE PATH TO SALVATION	(C) THE OUTCOME OF SALVATION
Something lacking in my individual life	Doing good works to earn God's favor	My life on earth is changed; I feel fulfillment, meaning, joy
Separation of human beings from God; sinfulness	Trusting in God's free gift of forgiveness	I will live forever with God in heaven after I die
Lack of human community or closeness between people	Relying on the Church's sacraments to set things right	The world will be changed so that people live together in peace and harmony
	Working hard to make our society better and more just	

Table 3.1
Characteristics of Response to Foundational Beliefs Question by Type of Respondent

Characteristic	Parishioners	Lay Leaders	Paid Staff	Pastors
Proportion completing at least one sequence	86%	92%	94%	97%
Proportion using two or more sequences	15	14	15	3
Proportion using three sequences	12	13	14	3
Proportion using complex (i.e., two or more problems-processes-outcomes) patterns within the same sequence	6	12	15	26
Proportion of entries in a sequence that involve own wording:				
Problem	3.3%	7.9%	6.7%	17.1%
Process	6.3	12.4	11.2	11.4
Outcome	2.2	5.4	10.1	8.6

As a first attempt at a measurement problem, we have both a standardized instrument that can be used in a paper-pencil format, and an instrument that allows for individual definitions. The instrument is much closer to models of mind incorporated in ipsative measures such as Q-method than to normative measures incorporated in standard survey research methodology. Yet it is much simpler to administer than the cumbersome card-sorting feature of Q-method. Finally, the fact that religious elites are more likely than the rank-and-file to use their own wording or to select complex patterns agrees with our expectations that they would have more complex cognitive structures related to religious values.

Eliciting responses is easy compared to the classification of response patterns. We decided initially to work with only two of Benson and Williams' dimensions: agentic-communal and restricting-releasing. The vertical-horizontal dimension appears, both conceptually and empirically, to collapse into the first, and the comforting-challenging dimension appears to collapse into the second. For the purposes of this chapter we will discuss primarily our handling of the agentic-communal dimension.

The Appendix to this chapter shows the full range of coding decisions that we made. Our classifications addressed an entire string or path, not simply one or two or three components of it. The easiest classifications, of course, concerned exclusive paths.

An exclusively agentic path was one that selected as the problem either "something lacking in my individual life" or "separation of human beings from God, sinfulness," then drew an arrow to "doing good works to earn God's favor," or "trusting in God's free gift of forgiveness," or "relying on the Church's sacraments to set things right," and concluded with "my life on earth is changed . . ." or "I will live forever . . . ." The focus on such sequences is on me—my problem, my outcome. The sequence 10-21-31, for example, is easily classified as agentic (see Appendix).

An exclusively communal path would involve either "lack of human community . . ." or "separation of human beings from God" as the problem, any of the four suggested paths to salvation but most likely "working hard to make society better or more just," and concluding with "the world will be changed so that people will live together in peace and harmony." Here the focus is on human beings (plural) and their interactions, and the solution is a social, not personal matter. The sequence 12-23-32 for example, is clearly communal.

Other sequences are not so clear and must be inferred, either from the predominant direction of their content or the extent to which they approximate the performance of clearly agentic or clearly communal respondents on selected criterion variables that also have agentic or communal content.

Another complicating factor is that the same individual may have a complex set of foundational beliefs described by both agentic and communal sequences. Benson and Williams found some mixtures of religious themes in their congressional data and, in fact, the modal class of Catholics on Capitol Hill was classified as "integrated": that is, they manifested both agentic and communal elements in their foundational belief systems. We too found that even in sequences limited to the elements offered on the questionnaire, 15 percent of the Catholic parishioner sample used two or more sequences and most of these involved both a clearly agentic and a clearly communal sequence. Another 6 percent were using mixed elements within a 4-, 5-, or 6-part sequence. Some of the sequences involving the respondent's own wording combined both types of elements. Thus we anticipated that a classification scheme for Catholics would have to include three types: agentic, integrative, and communal.

We also made a change in terminology from Benson and Williams. Because the term "agentic" has special meanings in both philosophy and theology, we prefer to substitute for it "individualistic." Likewise, since the term "communal" has a special meaning in sociology, we prefer to substitute for it "communitarian." Both of these substituted terms are closer to the discourse used by Tocqueville and Bellah to analyze deeply held values and the civic order.

The initial classification efforts, without criterion variables, yielded 14 percent of the cases that lacked a sequence and were lost to further analysis, 38.1 percent that were unambiguously individualistic, 12.1 percent that were unambiguously integrative, 17.8 percent that were unambiguously communitarian, and 18 percent that needed further examination against criterion variables. Following iterations against two sets of two criterion variables, another .7 percent of the cases could not be classified and were lost from further analysis, but 38.2 percent were individualistic, 28.8 percent were integrative, and 18.2 percent were communitarian. Analyses of other portions of our data show that Catholics with deeper involvements in church life—for example, pastors, staff, and volunteer leaders—are more likely to integrate individualistic and communitarian elements in their foundational belief systems; because these are also more highly educated people with greater civic involvements, we suspect we have a finding similar to what Benson and Williams discovered for Catholics among the political elites. Religious individualism/communitarianism, because of its development, is treated as a continuous variable running from individualistic through integrative to communitarian orientations.

What about the measurement properties of our measure of foundational beliefs: religious individualism/communitarianism? Because it is an ipsative measure it is impossible to offer the standard statistical coefficients by which to assess it. The assumptions behind ipsative measurement are at odds with omnibus internal consistency tests, such as coefficient alpha, for reliability. Because sequences are unique, to subject their individual components to correlational and factor analyses would make no sense.

Nevertheless, since the classification of strings into the categories individualistic, integrated, and communitarian involves judgments, we have submitted the coding rules to a test of intercoder reliability. Using sociologists of religion of different denominational backgrounds, expertise, and stages in career, we have a coefficient of 76.4 percent agreement to offer as an interjudge reliability measure. At this writing we are in the process of developing some test-retest stability measures. We are also embarking on a series of known-groups validation tests.

Ultimately, however, the strongest argument regarding a measure is the nomothetic network of predictions that derive from it (Campbell and Fiske, 1959). If, as in our case, it can be shown to fit within a theoretically related network linking religious variables to sociopolitical variables and to offer greater success in prediction than comes from other measures or *types of measures*, we can have greater confidence in its properties. For that purpose, we have compared predictive results from our ipsative measure with results from the standard scale-building approach to measurement that could be drawn from our data base.

AN IPSATIVE MEASURE OR A STANDARD SCALE?

Many approaches are available for the classification of foundational beliefs. We could work strictly with the ipsative measure and preserve the unique individual structuring offered by the respondent. We could factor analyze individual elements in the measure to see whether a latent structure resides in the data across all respondents. We could, as Benson and Williams did, address many more batteries from the instrument—for example, images of God, religious behaviors, closeness to God while doing different types of activities—and utilize either conventional summated scale-building techniques or explanatory factor analysis. This section compares the results of the latter approach with the results from our ipsative measure.

The logic of standard approaches to scale-building is straightforward: incorporate as many items (or indicators) as possible into a common measure produced by factor analytic technology, or select specific items that are theorized to be related and construct an index that meets standard scale-building criteria. After consultation with Benson we also decided to use items from the religious imagination batteries, closeness to God battery, expectations of pastor battery, and religious practices battery to develop indexes and factor scales.

In this scale-building effort, we selected six items for the agentic position and nine items for the communal position; the items were similar to ones used by Benson and Williams to produce their agentic-communal measure. Interitem and item-test operations reduced the agentic indicators to three items with a corrected coefficient alpha of .80. The items were: I feel extremely close to God while being absolved or anointed; I feel extremely close to God while praying privately; and God is my constant companion. Similar operations reduced the communal indicators to four items with a corrected coefficient alpha of .77. The items were: I feel extremely close to God helping individuals in need; I feel extremely close to God working for justice and peace; God is more present in relationships with others than in an individual's life (strong agreement); and (high order of importance attached to the priest) leading the parish in projects to help the poor and minorities attain justice.

Is it possible to combine the agentic and communal items into a single, one-dimensional ordinal scale? We tried several approaches. First, once respondents were assigned scale positions on each, we combined them into a fourfold table: low agentic/low communal (17.2 percent), high agentic/low communal (21.5 percent), high agentic/high communal (38.1 percent), low agentic/high communal (14.5 percent), and unable to classify due to missing data (8.7 percent). A common scale derived from the merged scale-positions, however, is difficult to interpret. Is it an ordinal scale arranged in the sequence we have listed? Should the high agentic/high communal—which we have called "integrative"—be on the extreme end of the continuum rather than between agentic and communal? What should be done with respondents who are low on each? Can the agentic scale and the communal scale actually be combined into a common index? We have serious reservations about this conventional approach to scale-building with our data. An effort to correlate the two yielded rather low coefficients, although the large sample size was significant at $< .001$ (Cramer's $V = .14$, Pearson's $r = .21$). A second approach is to factor analyze (1) all 15 of the original items or (2) the 7 items that survived scale-building techniques. Neither of these efforts yielded a single factor nor intelligible multiple factors. Finally, we also tried to add classifications from the ipsative measure to the conventional scale. The results made little sense, because as Table 3.2 clearly shows, the two approaches to measurement classify respondents with only minimal overlap (Cramer's $V = .11$, Pearson's $r = .09$, $p = < .001$).

If we treat the seven items as a conventional fourfold ordinal scale, as we have done in procedure 1 above, what differences are apparent between its results and results from our ipsative measure of religious individualism/communitarianism? Using each measure as a dependent variable and examining

Table 3.2

Relationship between Two Procedures for Classification of Agentic-Communal Dimension

| Ipsative Measure | Multiple-Item Index: | | | | |
	Low Agentic Low Communal	High Agentic Low Communal	High Agentic High Communal	Low Agentic High Communal	Row Total
Agentic	46.6% (192)	52.9% (285)	45.1% (407)	30.5% (103)	45.0% (987)
Integrative	29.4 (121)	31.2 (168)	34.8 (314)	39.6 (134)	33.6 (737)
Communal	24.0 (99)	16.0 (86)	20.2 (102)	20.9 (101)	21.4 (468)
Column Total	18.8% (412)	24.6% (539)	41.2% (903)	15.4% (338)	100.0% (2192)

Based on 2,192 of 2,667 parishioners who could be classified by the two procedures. Data drawn from the Notre Dame Study of Catholic Parish Life.

religious demographic and social demographic characteristics, we find that frequency of Mass attendance and family income level explain more variance on the conventional scale, while region, political generation, and education explain more variance on the ipsative measure. Ethnicity, marital status, and gender differ little on either. Further, the proportion of variance explained by demographic characteristics is modest, regardless of which measure is used. Thus we do not think that either the conventional scale or the ipsative measure is masking a social locational variable.

Now let us turn to the other side of the predictive network, where either measure is used as an independent variable predicting political effects. When we examine predictive power against a wide range of issue positions and the liberalism-conservatism self-classification, we find rather large differences. Table 3.3 shows the R^2 for each.

Table 3.3
Variance Explained (R^2) by Two Procedures for Classification of the Agentic-Communal Dimension

Political or Social Value	Ipsative Measure	Multiple-Item Index
Ideology: Liberalism-Conservatism	.020	.003
Abortion Policy	.018	.000
Voting according to Religious Values	.016	.003
ERA	.020	.008
Threats: Secular Humanism	.023	.000
Threats: Communist Subversion	.010	.000
Premarital Cohabitation	.030	.001
Male Breadwinner	.025	.002
Husband is Boss	.015	.001
Parents Censor Books	.009	.000
Allow Homosexual Teachers	.010	.004
Sex Education Shared	.009	.005
Old-Fashioned Child-Rearing	.005	.001
Boycott Offensive TV	.004	.001
Tuition Tax Credits	.003	.000
Shared Parenting	.003	.002
Racial Intermarriage	.004	.003
Bilateral Nuclear Freeze	.003	.002
Busing for Integration	.008	.007
Approach to Social Change	.002	.001
Religious Organization Lobbying	.003	.002
Teaching Creationism	.001	.001
Increase Defense Spending	.005	.006
Capital Punishment	.000	.004
Registration of Firearms	.002	.009
Required Prayer in Schools	.002	.009
Unilateral Nuclear Freeze	.003	.010

On the liberalism-conservatism ideology measure, the ipsative measure of religious individualism/communitarianism clearly outperforms the conventional scale. On the issue batteries, the ipsative measure considerably outperforms the conventional scale on religiously influenced voting, abortion policy, ERA, and such social attitudes as cohabitation, the roles of the male as breadwinner and boss, censorship of books, and the threats of secular humanism and communist subversion. The measure slightly outperforms the conventional scale on allowing homosexuals to teach in public schools; the conventional scale, however, slightly outperforms the ipsative measure on registration of firearms, requiring prayer in the public schools, and a unilateral nuclear freeze. On the other items, the explained variance is virtually identical. Because party identification is treated as a polytomy, in our study, it is not included here.

What are we to make of these differences? First, a conventional scale with so few items, that fails to produce a single factor or interpretable factors, that cannot incorporate foundational beliefs items, and that offers so little predictive power is not very useful for a mass Catholic sample. Benson and Williams, using some similar measures, had remarkable success; but their sample was religiously far more heterogeneous than our sample was, generating greater variance to be explained.

Second, lacking convincing performance out of a conventional scale, we have reverted to our first instinct: let the respondent provide his or her own structure among idea elements that represent individualistic and communitarian religious themes. In a six-block theoretically grounded model designed to account for political values (with assimilation, gender, political generation, class, and region representing the other five blocks of predictors), the ipsative measure performed more adequately than four of the six blocks (Leege and Welch, forthcoming).

Third, given less than satisfying early measures, we are continuing other approaches to the problem. We have isolated several factors among religious practices, images of God, and closeness to God. These have been compared with religious individualism/communitarianism for their predictive power on sociopolitical variables. The results are mixed, depending on the outcome variable, but some of the imagery and devotional practices factors and the ipsative measure appear to be the most promising (Welch and Leege, 1989). We have been conceptualizing other approaches to Catholic religiosity beyond the dimensions found so productive in the congressional sample used by Benson and Williams. That work will continue, within the limits of our patience and Notre Dame's computing budget.

We must entertain the possibility that religious individualism/communitarianism is not a continuous variable at all. Perhaps it is a pair of nominal measures, and the integrated position should not be treated as a midpoint between them, but as another nominal category. We are about to undertake a variety of tests to deal with this issue. Certainly recent work on liberalism-conservatism has shown in what ways that concept is multidimensional (Conover and Feldman, 1981). Perhaps our explorations of the dimensionality issue will have similar consequences for the understanding of religious individualism/communitarianism.

Finally, we currently have some reservations about our ability to capture the other theoretically pregnant dimensions of Benson and Williams' research. For example, on the restricting/releasing dimension, using conventional scale-building techniques we have produced a 14-item legalism scale. It works reasonably well against many political variables. Factor analyzed, however, it produces four factors. Even more important, legalism represents only the restricting end of a presumed continuum. The releasing end needs measures that capture not only what the respondent has been freed *from* but also freed *for*. *In both Christian theology and predogmatic foundational beliefs, release is not the absence of restraint or the indifference of God, but it is an unburdening from guilt or fear. There are still standards within which one must live and short of which one falls. But the intervention of an external force makes those standards no longer a burden, and therefore we are free to achieve new purposes.* We have not yet found a way to characterize the concept in our data, nor have we gotten a good handle on it from the Benson-Williams volume.

Social research, like religiosity and citizenship, never involves terminal points, but is always a journey. The objectives are always on the horizon and companions lend a hand along the way. But we never really reach the ultimate goal in the world we can know because the horizon is not a fixed point in the universe. So it is with our work on religion and politics and the role of critical discourse on measurement within the social scientific community. The properties of any measure have the effect of humbling the scholar.

APPENDIX
I. Code Categories for Ipsative Measure

Column A
Basic Human Problem
    10. Something lacking in my individual life
    11. Separation of human beings from God; sinfulness
    12. Lack of human community or closeness between people
    13. Fear of the unknown, mortality
    14. Imperfections inherent in humanity
    15. Separation from God and each other; lack of love of God, self, neighbor
    16. Conflict among creatures
    17. Need for meaning, purpose
    18. Lack of conviction in beliefs

Column B

Path to Salvation

20. Doing good works to earn God's favor
21. Trusting in God's free gift of forgiveness; turning to God through prayer
22. Relying on the Church's sacraments to set things right
23. Working hard to make our society better and more just; more in tune with God's plan
24. Living the best life I can, trying to do right, looking for good in others, forgiving but recognizing that I will never be perfect and depending on the love and forgiveness of God and others
25. Doing all I can to enhance other people's lives through love
26. Finding meaning and purpose in God and living on that discovery, following God's will
27. Accepting Jesus in my life
28. Accepting life with its problems, as God's will, accepting God's will
29. Developing firm beliefs, convictions

Column C

Outcome of Salvation

30. My life on earth is changed; I feel fulfillment, meaning, joy
31. I will live forever with God in heaven after I die
32. The world will be changed so that people live together in peace and harmony
33. God and creatures are joined in mutual respect, love, value for each other
34. A higher level of intellectual or spiritual perfection, evolution
35. Christian victory, here and in afterlife

II. A Priori Assumptions about Direction of Individual Items

10. agentic
11. agentic or communal
12. communal
13. agentic
14. agentic or communal
15. communal
16. communal
17. agentic or communal
18. agentic

20. agentic
21. agentic
22. agentic or communal
23. communal
24. agentic or communal
25. communal
26. agentic or communal

27. agentic
28. agentic
29. agentic

30. agentic
31. agentic
32. communal
33. communal
34. agentic
35. agentic or communal

The individual item, however, never alone determines the classification of the string (path, sequence). Rather it is the combination of the three or more items that matters. When all three are in the same direction, for example 10-21-31 (agentic) or 12-23-32 (communal), the classification is simplified. When one or more items runs in directions contrary to other items, the intent of the sequence must either be inferred rationally or it must be tested empirically against criterion variables.

III. Classification of Paths

Agentic Paths

10-20-30	10-20-31	10-21-20-30
10-21-30	10-21-31	10-11-21-30
10-22-30	10-22-31	10-20-21-30
10-24-30	10-24-31	10-21-26-30
10-26-30	10-26-31	10-11-27-30
10-27-30	10-28-31	10-22-31-30
10-28-30	10-29-31	11-21-31-30
		10-11-20-31
11-20-30	11-20-31	10-22-20-31
11-21-30	11-21-31	11-21-20-31
11-22-30	11-22-31	10-11-21-31
11-24-30	11-24-31	10-22-21-31
11-27-30	11-26-31	17-13-21-31
11-29-30	11-27-31	10-21-22-31
	11-29-31	11-21-22-31
14-24-30		11-24-22-31
	13-24-31	10-27-26-31
17-20-30	13-28-31	10-22-27-31
17-29-30		11-20-29-31
	14-24-31	10-22-20-30
18-21-30	14-26-31	11-21-20-31
18-29-30	14-27-31	10-21-30-31
	14-28-31	10-22-30-31

10-21-34	17-26-31	10-24-30-31
10-27-34		10-27-30-31
	18-21-31	10-20-30-31
11-21-34	18-22-31	11-21-30-31
11-29-34	18-24-31	11-22-30-31
		11-26-30-31
18-27-35		11-29-30-31
18-29-35		18-29-30-31
		11-24-35-31
		11-21-22-35
		11-22-21-31
		10-11-21-30-31
		10-20-21-30-31
		11-21-22-30-31
		10-20-21-22-30-31

Integrated Paths	Communal Paths
12-23-32-31	11-23-32
10-20-30-32	11-24-32
11-20-30-32	11-25-32
11-28-30-32	11-26-32
12-20-30-32	12-20-32
11-21-31-32	12-21-32
12-23-31-32	12-22-32
12-23-32-30	12-23-32
11-23-30-32	12-24-32
10-21-23-32-30	12-26-32
11-12-20-23-31	12-27-32
11-12-23-30-32	12-28-32
11-21-22-23-31	14-23-32
15-21-23-30-31	14-25-32
17-24-23-32-31	15-23-32
12-21-30-32-31	15-25-32
10-21-23-31-32	17-25-32
10-26-24-31-32	18-23-32
12-23-30-31-32	18-24-32
14-23-30-31-32	11-24-33
15-26-30-31-32	11-25-33
10-21-23-25-32-31	12-21-33
10-11-21-20-22-32	12-24-33
16-15-21-20-30-32	12-25-33
11-21-22-20-31-32	13-25-33
10-20-21-30-31-32	15-22-33
11-25-21-30-31-32	15-26-33

11-14-24-30-31-32   15-27-33
11-23-30-31-32-33   16-24-33
10-12-22-23-31-32   16-25-33
12-21-24-30-31-32   11-23-34
                           14-23-34
                           15-25-34
                           15-25-35

                           12-23-33-20
                           11-12-21-32
                           11-20-33-32
                           10-12-23-32
                           11-12-23-32
                           12-22-23-32
                           12-23-32-33
                           15-23-32-33

                           11-12-23-32-33
                           10-11-12-23-32

IV. Rules for Classifying Respondents

1. If only one string is given, classify the respondent as *agentic, integrated,* or *communal* according to the lists that classify each sequence.

2. If two or three strings are given:
    (a) if string 1 is agentic, and succeeding strings are agentic, classify R as agentic.
    (b) if string 1 is agentic, and succeeding strings are either integrated or communal, classify R as integrated.
    (c) if string 1 is integrated, and succeeding strings are agentic, integrated, or communal, classify R as integrated.
    (d) if string 1 is communal, and succeeding strings are integrated or agentic, classify R as integrated.
    (e) if string 1 is communal, and succeeding strings are communal, classify R as communal.

3. If no valid* string is given for string 1, classify R as missing data.

4. If a valid string for string 1 is given but string 2 and string 3 are not valid, classify R by the content of string 1 along. If strings 1 and 2 are valid, but string 3 is invalid, classify R by the combined content of strings 1 and 2 as described in Rule 2.

*A valid string is defined as a string that includes at least one selection of value 10s, at least one selection of value 20s, and at least one selection of value 30s within the six options available for a string.

ACKNOWLEDGMENTS

This chapter is a revised version of materials presented at a roundtable discussion on Measurement Strategies in the Study of Religion and Politics at the annual meeting of the American Political Science Association, Washington, D.C., August 1986. The author is indebted to Michael Welch, Peter Benson, and Ted Jelen for helpful comments; to Thomas Trozzolo for data handling; and to the Lilly Endowment, Inc., which subsidized the data collection for the Notre Dame Study of Catholic Parish Life.

II

Religion and Politics Among the Mass Public

4
Fundamentalism and Economic Restructuring

Joseph B. Tamney, Ronald Burton, and
Stephen D. Johnson

In his classic essay *The Protestant Ethic and the Spirit of Capitalism*, Max Weber (1952) argued that capitalist development in Western Europe occurred, in part, because of the influence of Calvinism, especially as expressed in Puritanism. Other forms of Christianity, such as the Catholic Church, while not enthusiastically supporting capitalism, never seriously challenged the value of capitalism, until the twentieth century. At the present time there are signs that the relationship between Christianity and Western economies is undergoing important change. With the Catholic bishops playing a leading role, Christians are questioning the moral value of capitalism. The possibility exists that changes in Christianity will contribute to bringing about a new economic order in the West.

In this chapter we do three things. First, beginning with a brief summary of Calvinism in the United States, we discuss the changing relationship between official religion and capitalism. Second, we analyze data from three research projects in an effort to determine whether religious ideas are linked to support for economic restructuring in the populace. Third, we conclude with a brief discussion of whether dissatisfaction with the economic institution, rooted in religious beliefs, is likely to lead to actual social change.

U.S. CALVINISM AND THE CHRISTIAN RIGHT

The Calvinist tradition in the United States was an important social force right through the early part of the century. Calvinist leaders were critical of U.S. industrial society as it emerged. Leading Calvinist theologians condemned some business practices, such as taking undue advantage of the ignorance of buyers. Calvinists especially opposed the growing inclination to consider productivity and profits rather than service and benevolence the primary goals of business" (G. S. Smith, 1985: 137). However, Calvinists opposed structural changes in the economy, believing that economic evils can be eliminated only by the religious conversion of individuals (p. 142). "By and large, they believed, as did most evangelicals, that capitalism was the most biblical, practical, and just economic system, and they resisted all forms of collectivism" (p. 128). It was believed that taking savings from people was theft. The right to private property was considered God-given. Moreover, Calvinists believed that "because people were prone to selfishness and sloth, they would not work as diligently under socialism as they had under capitalism" (p. 131). The affinity Weber (1952) noted between early Calvinism and capitalism clearly existed in the United States during the industrialization period.

After the turn of the century the fundamentalist movement formed in the United States, influenced by Calvinistic social doctrine. Indeed, at the present time the strongest support for classical Calvinist economic philosophy is from Christian Right leaders—the political, conservative wing of fundamentalism (Tamney and Johnson, forthcoming). Jerry Falwell, a leading figure of the Religious Right in the United States, is an outspoken champion of the free enterprise economic system (Strege, 1986: 118).

In contrast, some contemporary Calvinist leaders are now urging structural economic reform (Smith, 1985: 156). Today it is mainly the Christian Right within fundamentalism that *publicly* defends capitalism on religious grounds. However, it remains true that they express, albeit in simplified form, what was, and what might still be, the dominant Christian viewpoint on economic matters.

MAINLINE PROTESTANTISM

At the beginning of this century mainline Protestantism, strongly influenced by Calvinist ideas, accepted and legitimated U.S. imperialism and the free enterprise system (Olmstead, 1970; Mead, 1973: 191). Then the rise to prominence of the Social Gospel movement introduced a critical voice into mainline Protestantism. Walter Rauschenbusch, for instance, condemned on religious grounds such capitalist institutions as private property and the goal of maximizing profit (Krueger, 1986: 26). However, within the mainline religious institutions, while the Social Gospel movement had some influence, radical ideas never did hold sway.

A popular book between the World Wars among Methodists was John Shackford's (1917) *The Program of Social Action*. The book was approved by the Committee on Curriculum of the General School Board of the Methodist Episcopal Church. It was used as a textbook for training Christian leaders.

We shall summarize the chapter entitled "The Christianization of Wealth and of Industry." Selfishness is condemned; it "is the law of the jungle, whether in the Congo or in Wall Street" (p. 130). Every person has a right to the resources "necessary to the complete life and development of the individual" (p. 130). Criteria are presented for evaluating an economy. "Does it provide the best possible conditions under which all the people may realize their fullest life? Does it guard the interest of the weak as well as of the strong? Does it tend to make good men and to help them to become brothers" (p. 137)? The author noted that workers were unjustly being paid the lowest possible wage and that workers suffered poverty and a sense of powerlessness (pp. 134–135). However, the aforementioned criteria are not used to evaluate the U.S. economy, and no specific economic policies are recommended. While by his own admission Shackford (1917: 17) was committed to the Social Gospel, there was no bite accompanying his bark. Shackford's book illustrates how the Social Gospel was rendered harmless by those ostensibly sympathetic to it.

This sense that workers were being unjustly treated, combined with a lack of decisive action, characterized mainline Protestantism throughout this century. Between the World Wars the neo-orthodox or Christian realist perspective came to dominate mainline Protestant theology (on historical sources for the social gospel movement during the 1920s and 1930s, see Horn, 1987: 194–198). A concern for structural issues remained, but the realists were less optimistic about how much social progress is possible, given sinful human nature (Krueger, 1986: 35).

The voice of the Social Gospel continues to be heard within mainline Protestantism (see Krueger, 1986; Tabb, 1986; West, 1986). However, it is more the ideals of the Social Gospel rather than its program that find support. What characterizes the mainline is a diversity of viewpoints that makes unified social action improbable.

ROMAN CATHOLICISM

Since the turn of the century, and especially after the Second Vatican Council, the social teaching of the Catholic Church has become more liberal (Curran, 1985; Pawlikowski, 1986). During the last hundred years papal writings on economic matters, while favoring capitalism over socialism, have become increasingly critical of capitalism. For instance, at the present time the Catholic Church seems to place eliminating poverty ahead of a right to private property. The church has also shifted some of its attention away from the plight of the European working class to the issue of poverty and suffering in the Third World (Pawlikowski, 1986: 15–16). All these changes are reflected in the American bishops' pastoral letter on the economy, which was approved at a national meeting of bishops in November 1986 by a vote of 225 to 9 (Hyer, 1986).

The pastoral letter is quite long; it includes detailed discussions of specific economic problems such as unemployment, but we shall consider only the general principles enunciated by the bishops.

As the Bishops wrote, "the themes of human dignity and the preferential option for the poor are at the heart of our approach . . ." (National Conference of Catholic Bishops, 1986: 93). Indeed, these ideas are repeatedly affirmed in the letter. For instance, the bishops state: "Central to the biblical presentation of justice is that the justice of a community is measured by its treatment of the powerless in society . . ." (p. 21). "The fundamental moral criterion for all economic decisions, policies, and institutions is this: They must be at the service *of all people, especially the poor*" (p. 12). The preferential option for the poor must shape foreign policy as well: "meeting the basic needs of the millions of deprived and hungry people in the world must be the number one objective of international policy" (p. 125).

"Yet charity alone is not a corrective to all economic social ills" (p. 178), the bishops declared, and their letter calls for a "New American Experiment." The original American experiment was the establishment of a democratic state. The new experiment would focus on economic rights rather than civil rights, on economic democracy rather than political democracy. Economic rights include the right to employment, rest, medical care, food, and clothing (pp. 41–42). Quoting from the works of the current pope, the bishops ground their call for structural changes in the need to respect and enhance the dignity of labor, so that work is an opportunity for self-realization (p. 37).

Whereas classical Calvinism and the contemporary Christian Right strongly support capitalism, the bishops have expressed ideas that, if acted on, would significantly restructure the U.S. economy. How much support is there for the bishops' ideas?

STUDY I: SUPPORT FOR CATHOLIC BISHOPS' ECONOMIC POLICIES

Our research on this question has been reported in detail elsewhere (Tamney, Burton, and Johnson, forthcoming). We shall, therefore, just briefly present the relevant findings. The data came from a telephone survey of residents living in "Middletown" in the fall of 1986 (Lynd and Lynd, 1929). Respondents were selected by a computer generated random-digit-dialing technique (N = 379).

We began the project believing that Catholics would support the bishops' ideas, while Protestant fundamentalists would oppose them. Since Fundamentalism is a social movement, and as such is not to be equated with membership in certain churches, we defined fundamentalism as acceptance of certain beliefs. Specifically, fundamentalism was conceived of as a religious perspective that includes a belief in biblical inerrancy, an understanding of history in terms of a battle between God and Satan, a pessimistic view of human nature, and a belief that God is controlling the person's life. This is a constellation of beliefs that downplays the purely human and understands everything as a religious matter. Responses to four questions concerning these beliefs were summed to form a Fundamentalism Scale (on the nature of fundamentalism see Ammerman, 1987; Burton, Tamney, and Johnson, forthcoming).

The Fundamentalism Scale was used not only with Protestants but Catholics as well. We do not assume that Protestant fundamentalism and Catholic fundamentalism are, in all respects, the same. We do believe that within both branches of Christianity some adherents more than others allow a greater role for purely human effort—that is, within both branches some followers are less fundamentalist than others.

The questionnaire contained 17 statements meant to reflect beliefs contained in the bishops' pastoral letter (the statements are reprinted in Tamney, Burton, and Johnson, forthcoming). The Likert-type responses to these statements were factor analyzed. The first two factors accounted for the greatest amount of variance in the set of items and also were considered to be the most relevant factors for our purposes. The first factor contained questions that concern making important changes in the economic institution, such as having the government guarantee a job to everyone willing to work, having goods and services distributed more or less equally, and obliging employers to provide jobs people enjoy. Social acceptance of these beliefs would mean restructuring the U.S. economy. The second factor reflected a traditional religious belief about the obligations of the community to help the poor. There was no statistically significant correlation between the two scales based on these two factors ($r = .09$, N.S.).

Of especial interest to us was the restructuring morality. This code has to do with giving more economic power to the lower classes, broadening understanding of human rights to include economic rights, and transforming economic life into opportunities for self-development. As expected from an analysis of previous studies, support for restructuring was greater among those with lower household incomes, with less education, who were politically liberal, who were younger, and who were black (Tamney, Burton, and Johnson, forthcoming). In addition, among white respondents, support for restructuring was higher among fundamentalist Protestants and non-fundamentalist Catholics. After controlling for the aforementioned non-religious variables, the religious type-fundamentalism interaction effect remained.

The attitudes of Catholics were not too surprising. Non-fundamentalist Catholics may be less traditional in their ideas and thus more open to what are new Catholic beliefs about economic matters. The surprise was that economic restructuring found favor among fundamentalist Protestants. However, after looking into the history of fundamentalism, the relationship became understandable.

The association of fundamentalism and economic liberalism is not new. Since the last century the Prohibition and Populist movements included fundamentalist beliefs and economic liberal proposals. From its inception in 1869 until about the time of World War II, Prohibition party platforms included liberal economic proposals (Storms, 1972; on revisionist interpretations of the prohibition movement, see Massa, 1987: 86–87). Similarly, Populists sought to redistribute economic and political power (Wright, 1974: 260; Cherny, 1981: 158–159), and, as the life of William Jennings Bryan illustrated, fundamentalist beliefs sometimes reinforced populist sentiments.

It is suggested that the programs once espoused by the Prohibition and Populist parties are still found associated with fundamentalist religious beliefs. We suggest two reasons for this. First, there is a common historical influence—that is, the nineteenth-century evangelical movement. Second, both parties and fundamentalism appealed to similar people—that is, the relatively powerless.

We concluded our first study, then, by suggesting that support for economic change exists among two religious groups—non-traditional Catholics and fundamentalist Protestants.

STUDY II: FUNDAMENTALISM AND ECONOMIC RESTRUCTURING

Actually, in a study done before the research on the bishops' proposals, we had found that fundamentalists tended to be economically liberal (Johnson, Tamney, and Halebsky, 1986; see also Hertzke, 1988: 142–144). Yet to find that fundamentalists favored economic restructuring was still unexpected. It is true that the aforementioned studies found a weak relationship between fundamentalism and economic liberalism; but this relationship existed after controlling for other significant variables. Yet the question remained as to whether there is really a positive relationship between fundamentalism and economic liberalism. Another test of this relationship was carried out using a new set of data.

The sample was randomly selected from people who lived within the Standard Metropolitan Statistical Area of the Lynds' (1929) "Middletown" in the fall of 1987. Those selected were then interviewed only if they were 60 years old or older (N = 400). The primary purpose of the study was to examine family relations among the elderly. Since fundamentalism was a theological movement within white Protestantism, only white Protestants in our sample were included in the analysis (N = 299). The respondents were interviewed over the phone.

Fundamentalism was measured using three questions: (1) "Do you believe every word of the Bible is true?" (no, not sure, yes); (2) "Eventually Jesus Christ will personally and visibly return to the earth to defeat the anti-Christ" (strongly diagree, disagree, uncertain, agree, strongly agree); and (3) "All religions, such as Christianity, Buddhism, and Islam, have something good in them" (strongly agree, agree, uncertain, disagree, strongly disagree). Scores for the first question were weighed so that the range for each question was 1 to 5. The three questions were significantly related to each other as expected (the correlations ranged from .20 to .36). Thus the scores from these questions were added together to form the Fundamentalism Scale.

Two Likert-type questions were used to measure economic restructuring: (1) "The American government guarantees everyone such things as freedom of speech and freedom of religion; in the same way the government should guarantee a job to everyone willing to work" (strongly disagree to strongly agree); and (2) "To solve the problems of poverty and unemployment, we must create a society in which goods and services are distributed more or less equally among all people" (strongly disagree to strongly agree). These two items had the highest factor loading on the previously discussed restructuring factor (Tamney, Burton, and Johnson, forthcoming). The correlation between the two questions was .56 (significant at the .01 level). Scores from these questions were added together to measure economic restructuring.

Previous research has suggested that economic liberals have lower income, are less educated, are self-defined political liberals, and are younger (see Tamney, Burton, and Johnson, forthcoming, and their earlier studies noted in that paper). Standard questions for these variables, as well as sex, were included in the 1987 study. In addition, we used a question that asked how well the respondent's income and assets met financial needs. It was thought that this question might be a better measure of economic condition than household income among elderly people.

Table 4.1 shows the correlations between the Economic Restructuring Scale and the other variables discussed. For the most part the results are as expected. Age was not significantly related to support for economic change, but the sample included only elderly people. What was surprising was that among the three religious questions, only the one about biblical inerrancy was significantly related to the Economic Restructuring Scale. For the remainder of the analysis, then, we did not use the Fundamentalism Scale but focused on the relationship between a belief in biblical inerrancy and support for economic restructuring.

Table 4.1
Correlations with the Economic Restructuring Scale (Middletown Sample)

Independent Variable	Pearson r	(n)	Significance Level
Fundamentalism	.21	(281)	.001
All Religions Good	.02	(291)	NS[a]
Jesus Will Return	.07	(288)	NS
Biblical Inerrancy	.28	(288)	.001
Household Income	-.35	(236)	.001
Satisfaction With Income	-.19	(289)	.001
Education	-.32	(292)	.001
Age	.06	(290)	NS
Sex[b]	.16	(293)	.003
Political Conservatism	-.18	(272)	.001

[a]NS means not significant at the .10 level.
[b]"1" is male, "2" is female.

A regression analysis was done with the Economic Restructuring Scale as the dependent variable. All the variables significantly related to this scale (see Table 4.1) were used as independent variables. The beta values for sex and income satisfaction were not significant at the .10 level of confidence. A second regression was performed excluding these two variables. The results are in Table 4.2. Those supporting economic restructuring tended to be poorer, politically liberal, less educated, and biblical literalists. These variables accounted for 19 percent of the variance in Restructuring Scale scores.[1]

Table 4.2
Results of Regression Analysis with the Economic Restructuring Scale as Dependent Variable (Middletown Sample)

Independent Variable	beta	Significance Level
Household Income	-.22	.002
Political Conservatism	-.20	.001
Biblical Inerrancy	.14	.040
Education	-.14	.045

In a recent study we found that fundamentalism was related to economic beliefs only among the less educated (Burton, Johnson, and Tamney, forthcoming). Thus we repeated the analysis reported in Table 4.2 for two subsamples varying in education levels. The results are in Table 4.3. Among those with 12 years of schooling or less, supporters of economic restructuring tended to be poorer, less educated, political liberals, and believers in biblical inerrancy (results similar to those for the total sample). Among those with more than 12 years of schooling, such support was significantly related only to political conservatism, and of course the relation was negative.[2]

As in our previous studies, then, we found a positive relation between fundamentalism and support for economic restructuring. However, two caveats are necessary: (1) it was not fundamentalism in general but biblical inerrancy in particular that was related to the Economic Restructuring Scale, and (2) this relationship only held for the less educated.

Table 4.3
Results of Regression Analyses with the Economic Restructuring Scale as the Dependent Variable by Educational Level (Middletown Sample)

A. Twelve Years of Schooling or Less

Independent Variable	Beta	Significance Level
Household Income	-.27	.001
Political Conservatism	-.19	.01
Biblical Inerrancy	.23	.01
Education	-.16	.04

B. Thirteen Years of Schooling or More

Independent Variable	Beta	Significance Level
Household Income	-.11	NS
Political Conservatism	-.41	.001
Biblical Inerrancy	-.02	NS
Education	.16	NS

STUDY III: A NATIONAL STUDY OF THE RELATIONSHIP BETWEEN FUNDAMENTALISM AND SUPPORT FOR ECONOMIC RESTRUCTURING

There were questions on the 1987 General Social Survey of the U.S. population that allowed us to examine the relationship between fundamentalism and economic beliefs. The measure of fundamentalism was based on questions concerning biblical inerrancy and sinful human nature. In 1987 two alternative questions were used to inquire about the Bible. The first question was: "Which of these statements comes closest to describing your feelings about the Bible?" The responses were: (1) "The Bible is the actual word of God and is to be taken liberally, word for word"; (2) "The Bible is the inspired word of God but not everything in it should be taken literally, word for word"; (3) "The Bible is an ancient book of fables, legends, history, and moral precepts recorded by men." The alternative question was: "Here are four statements about the Bible, and I'd like you to tell me which is closest to your own view." The responses were: (1) "The Bible is God's word and all it says is true"; (2) "The Bible was written by men inspired by God, but it contains some human errors"; (3) "The Bible is a good book because it was written by wise men, but God had nothing to do with it"; (4) "The Bible was written by men who lived so long ago that it is worth very little today." A respondent was considered a literalist if the person chose the first response to either question. All others were placed in a non-literalist category.

Regarding human nature, respondents were asked to place themselves into one of seven categories on a continuum from "Human Nature is basically good" to "Human nature is fundamentally perverse and corrupt." Respondents were divided into two groups: those who believed human nature is corrupt, and those who did not so believe.

The responses to those two topics were combined so that a high score indicated biblical literalists who believed human nature is fundamentally perverse and corrupt.

Only one question on the GSS related to economic restructuring. This read as follows:

Some people think that the income differences between the rich and the poor ought to be reduced, perhaps by raising taxes of wealthy families or by giving income assistance to the poor. Others think that the government should not concern itself with reducing this income difference between the rich and the poor.

Here is a card with a scale from 1 to 7. Think of a score of *1* as meaning that the government ought to reduce the income differences between rich and poor, and a score of *7* meaning that the government should not concern itself with reducing income differences. What score between *1* and *7* comes closest to the way you feel?

One advantage of using the GSS data was that we had enough cases to study black Protestants, a group not considered in our Middletown research. The mean scores for the economic restructuring question for the religious groups in our sample were: religious nones–4.17 (N = 130), Catholics–4.42 (433), black Protestants—5.12 (196), white Protestants—4.03 (930). Religious nones were excluded from further analysis.

Table 4.4 contains the correlations between our measure of support for economic restructuring and the independent variables, previously discussed, for the total national sample and for three religious subsamples. First, we shall consider the total sample. As expected, supporters for restructuring tended to be fundamentalists, poorer, less educated, women, political liberals, and blacks. However, the relationships with race and sex were quite weak. Moreover, economic restructuring was unrelated to age and, more importantly, was only slightly related to one of the fundamentalist indicators, namely a belief that human nature is inherently corrupt.

Considering the three religious subsamples, the results differed by subsample. As would be expected, given the size of the subsample, the relationships described in the previous paragraph were are also true for the white Protestant subsample. Among Roman Catholics, support for restructuring was greater among fundamentalists and political liberals. The same was true for the black Protestants. While each of the two fundamentalist variables was significantly related to economic restructuring support among Catholics, this was not true for black Protestants; however, the pattern was the same for both subsamples.

For each religious subsample a regression analysis was performed, with the restructuring question as the dependent variable and the variables significantly related to this question within each subsample as the independent variables (see Table 4.5). Again, the results are similar for Roman Catholics and black Protestants, although the significance levels are lower for the latter subsample. Among white Protestants, all the variables significantly related at the zero-order level of analysis to restructuring support were also significant in the regression analysis.

Since in the analysis of the 1987 Middletown data the relationship between belief in biblical inerrancy and economic restructuring support varied by educational level, the analyses reported in Table 4.5 were done separately for those with a high school degree or less schooling and those who continued their education beyond high school.[3] The results are in Table 4.6. The black Protestant subsample of respondents who had gone beyond high school was too small for analysis.

Among less-educated black Protestants, the results were similar to those reported in Table 4.5. Among Catholics, the results differed by educational group; among the less educated, fundamentalists tended to support

Table 4.4
Correlations with Economic Restructuring (National Sample)

Independent Variable	Total (N)	Roman Catholics (N)	Black Protestants (N)	White Protestants (N)
Fundamentalism	.14 (1723)	.17 (416)	.12 (188)	.11 (906)
Biblical Inerrancy	.15 (1742)	.14 (421)	NS (910)	.16 (914)
Sinful Nature	.04 (1769)	.11 (429)	NS (194)	NS (922)
Household Income	-.20 (1659)	NS (414)	NS (178)	-.23 (860)
Education	-.12 (1785)	NS (433)	NS (195)	-.17 (927)
Age	NS[c] (1785)	NS (433)	NS (193)	NS (927)
Sex[a]	.05 (1792)	NS (433)	NS (196)	.08 (930)
Political Conservatism	-.17 (1689)	-.12 (410)	-.12 (173)	-.18 (890)
Race[b]	.06 (1792)			

a"1" is male, "2" is female.
b"1" is white, "2" is black.
c"NS" means the correlation was not significant at the .05 level.

Table 4.5
Results of Regression Analyses with Economic Restructuring as Dependent Variable by Religious Subsample (National Sample)

Religious Subsample	Independent Variable	Beta	Significance Level
Roman Catholics			
	Political Conservatism	-.13	.01
	Fundamentalism	.15	.01
Black Protestants			
	Political Conservatism	-.11	.16
	Fundamentalism	.14	.06
White Protestants			
	Political Conservatism	-.16	.01
	Biblical Inerrancy	.11	.01
	Sex	.07	.04
	Household Income	-.18	.01
	Education	-.07	.06

economic restructuring; among the more educated, such support was related only to being more politically liberal. The fact that fundamentalism was not significant among educated Catholics resulted, at least in part, from the near absence of fundamentalists among such Catholics. There were 105 relatively educated Catholics in the sample; only 10 of them had scores higher than zero on the Fundamentalism Scale. Among white Protestants, the results were similar for both educational groups; the only major difference was that while among the less educated sex was unimportant, among the more educated women tended to favor economic restructuring.

It is possible that fundamentalist beliefs in themselves are not important. Conceivably, some other religious variable might be what is important. As a partial check of this possibility, the analyses reported in Table 4.6 were repeated with an additional independent variable, frequency of prayer. For the most part the results were similar to those reported in Table 4.6. Frequency of praying was never significant; however, among more educated, white Protestants including prayer frequency resulted in the biblical inerrancy variable no longer being significant. Given the overall results we conclude that it is religious beliefs, per se, that are critical in understanding economic attitudes.

Table 4.6

Results of Regression Analyses with Economic Restructuring as Dependent Variable by Religious Subsample and Educational Level (National Sample)

Religious Subsample	Independent Variable	H.S. Grad or Less		Beyond H.S.	
		Beta	Significance Level	Beta	Significance Level
Roman Catholics		(N=291)		(N=104)	
	Political Conservatism	-.07	.20	-.29	.01
	Fundamentalism	.17	.01	.05	.58
Black Protestants		(N=138)		(N=28)	
	Political Conservatism	-.12	.15		
	Fundamentalism	.14	.10		
White Protestants		(N=624)		(N=187)	
	Political Conservatism	-.16	.01	-.17	.01
	Biblical Inerrancy	.10	.01	.13	.06
	Sex	.03	.41	.21	.01
	Household Income	-.15	.01	-.23	.01
	Education	-.07	.10	.01	.84

To summarize our results from the national study regarding fundamentalism: (1) among white Protestants, a belief in biblical inerrancy, and not the fundamentalism measure, was positively related to support for economic restructuring; this was true for both educational categories; (2) among Catholics the fundamentalism measure was positively related to support for restructuring; however, this was not true among more educated Catholics; and (3) among black Protestants the Fundamentalism Scale was positively related to the restructuring variable; because of a lack of cases, we do not know if this is true among more educated, black Protestants.

DISCUSSION AND CONCLUSION

There is one major finding that is the same in all three of our studies. Among white Protestants, those who believed in biblical inerrancy were more likely to support economic restructuring.

Since the populations studied and the measures used varied among the three studies just discussed, it is difficult to know what to make of seemingly inconsistent results. For example, while the 1987 Middletown study found belief in inerrancy to be related to economic restructuring only among the less educated, for the national sample this relationship was true for both educational groups. Again, in the 1986 Middletown study support for economic restructuring was higher among the less fundamentalist Catholics, but the opposite was true in the national survey. More research is needed on these issues.

Our work suggests there are three types of religious people who are somewhat disposed to economic restructuring: fundamentalist Catholics, black Protestant fundamentalists, and white fundamentalist Protestants. We conclude that justification for significant economic change can be found in these quite different traditions—that is, Catholicism with its roots in a continental communal theology, the black experience of oppression and black churches' call for justice, and American Populism with its roots in a tradition of Protestant dissent. These traditions can be used to argue for and to justify economic change. However, it is not known if these diverse traditions can be used to justify the same specific economic program. Moreover, it remains to be seen whether any one organization can effectively mobilize discontent rooted in such diverse belief systems.

NOTES

1. Protestant churches were classified as liberal and conservative. A measure of conservative church affiliation was added to a regression analysis that included the variables in Table 4.2. The affiliation variable did not significantly affect the

economic score. Another regression analysis was done using income, education, political conservatism, and the Fundamentalism Scale as independent variables. The Fundamentalism Scale had no significant impact on support for economic restructuring.

2. Regression analyses as described in Table 4.3 were done with frequency of church attendance added to the list of independent variables. For neither education category was this new variable significant.

3. For white Protestant subsamples, however, variables with insignificant betas (see Table 4.5) were not used.

5
Knowledge and Attitudes of Catholic College Students Regarding the Creation/Evolution Controversy

Alfred R. Martin and Ted G. Jelen

For most of the twentieth century, the dispute between adherents of the theory of evolution and believers in special creation has been a prominent social and political issue in the United States (Numbers, 1982; Nelkin, 1978, 1982). Despite widespread acceptance of evolutionary theory within the scientific community, fundamentalist religious opposition to the teaching of evolution in public schools has persisted since even before the 1925 Scopes "Monkey Trial" and the level of political activism has increased greatly in recent years.

Having initially failed to get the teaching of evolutionary theory banned from the classroom (the case of *Epperson v. Arkansas*, 1968), modern adherents of special creation have attempted to have their religious ideas reborn as a "science" (so-called creation science, which uses scientific terminology but is not based on scientific methodologies) and have pushed at the grass-roots level and in the courts, state legislatures, school boards, and local churches (Nelkin, 1982:93–102; Broad, 1981; Lewin, 1982a, b) to have this "science" taught in public schools alongside evolutionary science as a "two model" system that encourages "balanced treatment" of creationism and evolution in the classroom (Hoover, 1981).

Opposition to the teaching of evolutionary science has long existed in the United States. Scott (1987: 21–39) has identified three periods of antievolution sentiment in U.S. history. During the first period, the teaching of evolution was explicitly prohibited by many state laws such as the Tennessee law allegedly violated by John T. Scopes in 1925. The second period, following the Scopes Trial (which largely turned public opinion against the creationists), was characterized by an uneasy coexistence in which creationism and evolution were both sometimes taught in public schools (although the coverage of evolution in textbooks actually quietly declined after 1925).

Finally, the third period, largely born of the activism of George McCready Price and Henry Morris, is the present age of "creation science" in which biblical literalism is passed under the guise of science as a means of forcing its inclusion into public school science curricula. These "evolving" states of creationism no doubt reflect the changing responses of fundamentalist activists to increasing knowledge and appreciation of evolution by the scientific community and to emphasis on church/state separation by the courts is interpreting the First Amendment.

The prospect of including "creation science" in public school curricula is not just a threat to the quality of biology education. Other sciences coordinate with evolutionary biology such as geology, physics, astronomy, and even linguistics have come under creationist attack as well. Despite a vast body of scientific evidence to the contrary, creationists are insisting that all the fossil beds were laid down in a single universal flood lasting a year (Morris, 1968: 54–87, 1970: 84–106, 1972: 96–99, 1973a: 13–25; Kofahl, 1980: 85–98; Kitcher, 1983: 128–134), that the speed of light has been slowing (Setterfield, 1983), and that the galaxies, sun, and planets show evidence of being only a few thousand years old (Whitcomb, 1973: 43–51; Morris, 1973b: 89–94; Kofahl, 1980: 109–120; W. T. Brown, 1981). They have rewritten the second law of thermodynamics (the "entropy" law) to preclude the possibility of evolution (Morris, 1970: 111–139, 1972: 13–20, 1975; Patterson, 1983). Evidence that languages develop into other languages is eschewed by creationists as an evolutionary doctrine inconsistent with the Tower of Babel story (Bruce, 1977; Futuyma, 1983: 5).

While many scientists and educators have tended to dismiss creationist arguments and demands as unworthy of serious attention, others—extremely alarmed by the certain detrimental effects they would have on public education—have studied the arguments put forth by the creationists and have criticized the non-scientific nature of their beliefs (Eldredge, 1982; Futuyma, 1983; Godfrey, 1983; Kitcher, 1983). But the creationists, apparently enjoying a high level of popular support within the current conservative political environment, have continued their political activities. "Balanced treatment" bills have been introduced into several state legislatures and were actually enacted into law in Arkansas and Louisiana. The Arkansas Act was struck down in 1982, the court ruling that "creation science" does not qualify as a science because "it requires supernatural intervention which is not guided by natural law" and is "not subject to investigation by scientific methods" (Lewin, 1982c; Gorman, 1982). The Louisiana Statute, passed in 1981, was eventually invalidated by summary judgment of the 5th District Court. Upon appeal, the U.S. Supreme Court granted certiorari. In this case, *Edwards v. Aquillard* (1987; Lewin, 1987), the creationists changed their strategy and claimed that the purpose and effect of the Louisiana Statute was to advance the secular goal of "academic freedom" (specifically the "freedom" of creationist teachers to teach "creation science" and thus allow a "balanced" view of evolutionary and creationist "evidences"). The Court's opinion, announced in June 1987, ruled by a 7 to 2 margin (under strong dissent by Justice Scalia) that the Louisiana Act was invalid under the "Establishment Clause" of the First Amendment because its effect was to advance religion and that the state's claim of secular purpose was nothing more than a "sham."

Why should a dispute over a scientific theory generate so much intense political activity? Nelkin (1976: 35–36) has identified three attitudinal sources of opposition to evolutionary theory: (1) Among many doctrinally conservative laypersons, there exists widespread disillusionment with science in general. In particular, science is thought by some to weaken belief in transcendent values, and to give rise to a disturbing moral relativism. (2) Many in the creationist movement resent the perceived status and authority of scientists. (3) This authority is thought by some to conflict with more egalitarian and pluralist values. Moreover, science does not claim to offer final or absolute answers to problems. Many people seem uncomfortable with the uncertainty inherent in science, preferring instead the unchanging values of religion. Evolutionary science is thus regarded by some as antireligious and anti-democratic.

While the activist-level dispute concerning creationism has been well-chronicled, few studies concerning mass attitudes toward creationism have appeared (Handberg, 1983; Fuerst, 1984; Harrold and Eve, 1986). The purpose of our brief study is twofold. First, we intend to investigate the impact of science education on attitudes toward the theory of evolution among non-fundamentalist (Roman Catholic) college students. Does exposure to evolutionary theory result in greater acceptance of this theory among students who presumably are not insulated by the effects of religious tradition hostile to evolution? Second, we are interested in whether science education (either directly or through intervening variables) affects attitudes toward "equal time" sorts of measures. Are students exposed to evolutionary theory more or less likely to support the teaching of "creation science" as an acceptable alternative to evolutionary science?

DATA AND METHODS

Data for this study were gathered through 290 self-administered questionnaires given to classes of students at a small Catholic college located in the Midwest. When non-Catholic respondents and incomplete questionnaires are excluded, this design yielded 220 usable instruments. This is a non-probability sample (thus the usual caveats regarding the interpretation of results apply) specifically designed to overrepresent biology majors.

"Academic major" is defined dichotomously to separate biology majors from others. Thus a respondent's major field was coded "2" if he or she indicated a major in biology and "1" if the student indicated another major.[1] Most of the statistical results reported below are based on responses to modified Likert items (see Appendix to this chapter). In addition, students were encouraged to write their own reactions to the questions at the end of the survey. Somewhat more than half of the respondents took advantage of this opportunity.

The analytical technique used here is to construct a recursive path model, based on a series of multiple regression equations. All variables used in the model are responses to single items (see Appendix) with the exception of two computed indicators: "Knowledge of evolution" is a simple additive index of factual statements regarding the theory of evolution.[2] "Source credibility" is a variable designed to determine whether the respondent regards religion or science as the more believable source of information.[3]

FINDINGS

Among our respondents, belief in the evolution of non-human species is rather widespread, with 62.3 percent expressing certainty that "modern animals and plants evolved from other forms of life which lived a long time ago." However, these students were somewhat more skeptical about the evolution of humans, as only 37 percent endorsed the belief that "man evolved from non-human forms of life." Finally, 68.7 percent of all respondents expressed the belief that special creation should be taught in schools along with evolution. These findings correlate closely with those of Harrold and Eve (1986: 61–75) who studied pseudoscientific beliefs among students at a large secular university (the University of Texas at Arlington). Of the students surveyed in the Texas study, 51 percent believed that "evolution explains the history of life" while 48 percent believed that "creation should be taught in public schools."

Johnson and Peeples (1987) report that majoring in biology is moderately related to "understanding science," which in turn is related to acceptance of the theory of evolution. Our analysis essentially confirms Johnson and Peeples' result, and permits a more detailed elaboration.

Figure 5.1 contains the results of a recursive path model, relating both "scientific" attitudes to student attitudes about evolution. Turning first to the causal path associated with scientific attitudes, we are gratified to learn that academic major is positively related to knowledge of evolutionary theory. The student's major field is also related to the source credibility variable. However, specific knowledge of evolution is not significantly related to the student's sense of source credibility. Any relationship between these

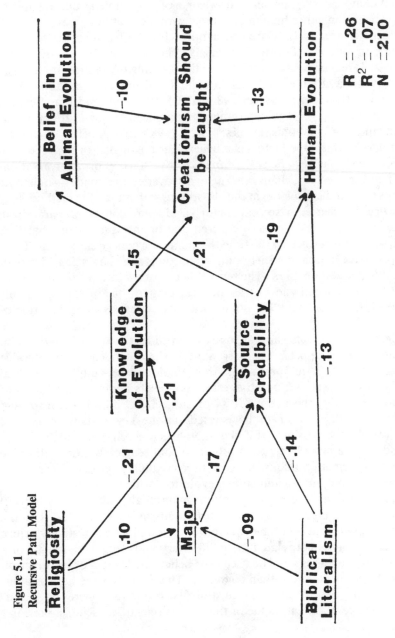

Figure 5.1
Recursive Path Model

Figures are path coefficients; omitted coefficients are not significant at 0.05 level.

two variables is therefore spurious, as even students who appear well informed about evolution may find religion a more plausible source of information than science. Further, knowledge of evolution is not related to specific beliefs in either human or animal evolution, although evolutionary knowledge is negatively related to support for the teaching of "creation science" in public schools. Conversely, the student's sense of source credibility is related to attitudes toward the teaching of creationism through the intervening variables of belief in animal and human evolution. In the Texas study (Harrold and Eve, 1986: 61–75), it was found that "college courses in biology, geology, astronomy and archaeology had little or no effect on students' creationist beliefs." Scott (1987: 21–39) offers several explanations for this. One factor, she believes, is the quality of instruction in college science classes. Scientists may stress "facts" or interpretations (which are subject to change as new discoveries are made—something students may find confusing) in the classroom, rather than the methodology or essence of science. A second factor is poor pre-college preparation in science. Students may already be bored and unimpressed with what they have been told is science by the time they enter the college classroom. Third is a "pervasive notion in society that evolution is somehow scientifically or intellectually questionable." The term "theory of evolution" is often interpreted as an educated guess or as an idea, perhaps one of several equally tenable ideas, which many but not all scientists accept as an explanation of the past.

Religious attitudes also appear to affect attitudes toward creationism and evolution. There appears to exist a very slight tendency for literalist Catholics to select majors other than biology. In addition, Biblical literalism exerts a direct, negative effect on beliefs about the evolution of humans. However, the main effects of subjective Biblical literalism and general religiosity appear to be exerted on the key variable of source credibility. Not surprisingly, Biblical literalists and self-identified religious respondents are more likely than others to find religion a more believable source of information than science. Source credibility, as noted above, affects beliefs about human and animal evolution, which, in turn, affect opinions concerning the teaching of creationism as an alternative to evolution.[4] Both sets of variables seem to have substantially independent effects on the important intervening variable of source credibility. Interestingly, since source credibility is not related to evolutionary knowledge, the impact of a biology major on a respondent's sense of believable sources of information appears to be social rather than cognitive. That is, it may be that social interaction with scientists and science students, rather than increasing scientific knowledge, is the causal factor that makes scientific insights more compelling.

It should also be noted that the predictive power of the model is very unimpressive ($R^2 = .07$). Does this indicate that religious students who are also biology majors experience high levels of cognitive dissonance? When the responses to the open-ended section of the instrument are considered, the answer appears to be negative. Among those who took the trouble to write open-ended comments, two themes predominate. Some respondents took an explicit "two realities" position (see Nelkin, 1978: 60). That is, these students expressed the belief that religion and science are incommensurable fields of knowledge, each of which is authoritative within its own domain. These respondents apparently experience no anxiety about believing two alternative (and potentially incompatible) concepts of the origins of the world. Other respondents expressed what might be termed "pluralist" beliefs (Nelkin, 1978: 134–138), arguing that alternative accounts of the beginning should be presented, with students allowed to "make up their own minds." Several students volunteered the assertion that there is no pedagogical purpose to be gained by suppressing the creationist version.

DISCUSSION

At this point, it seems useful to reiterate some of the limitations of this brief study. Our sample is not fundamentalist or evangelical, nor is it particularly highly exposed to the creation/evolution controversy.[5] Nevertheless, these respondents seem very supportive of the teaching of creationism along with the theory of evolution, and many are rather skeptical of the theory of evolution itself.

Our findings also suggest that evolutionary theory stands at the intersection of religion and science. Both religious beliefs and science education affect attitudes toward evolution and the teaching of creation science. However, the model we have developed seems radically recursive, in that it is unlikely that evolution has any reciprocal impact on either religiosity or attitudes toward science. While students may believe that religion and science are conflictual,[6] Catholic students cope with the perceived inconsistency by a process of compartmentalization. That is, rather than altering either scientific or religious beliefs to bring their belief systems into greater consistency, Catholic college students regard religion and science as completely independent spheres of knowledge. The students in the predominately Protestant Texas study (Harrold and Eve, 1986: 61–75), on the other hand, appear to have resolved the conflict between science and religion by viewing God as the instrument of the evolutionary process. While 62 percent of the respondents in that study believe that "Adam and Eve were created by God," a full 48 percent accept "Divinely directed human evolution."

Our result suggests that the fears of some conservative Christians regarding the "secularizing" effects of science education may be unfounded. Even students who come from a religious tradition not explicitly hostile to evolutionary theory seem to have developed cognitive devices that enable them to defend their faith. While the creation/evolution controversy may seem an irreconcilable conflict to many theologians and scientists, science and religion seem to maintain an uneasy coexistence among young members of the educated laity.

NOTES

1. In order to determine whether we have construed the "major" variable too narrowly, we have experimented with recoding the major field so that "2" includes all science majors (biology, physics, chemistry, biochemistry, health science). The only effect of this recode is to reduce the relationship between major and knowledge of evolution. All other coefficients in Figure 5.1 remain substantially unaffected. Further, in order to determine whether experienced biology majors are more knowledgable about or more accepting of evolution, we have attempted two alternative versions of the model depicted in Figure 5.1. In one case, "class" (e.g., freshman, sophomore, etc.) was included as a separate variable in the model. In the other, a class/major multiplication interaction term was computed and replaced major in the model. Neither of these changes substantially alters the results presented here.

2. The four items comprising the "knowledge" variable are as follows:

- "As I understand it, evolutionists believe that humans evolved from modern monkeys."
- "According to biologists, the process of evolution is totally random."
- "Biologists believe that the giraffe has a long neck because it had to stretch to reach the tops of trees where the best leaves are found."
- "As I understand it, evolution can best be defined as changes in species which always result in increasing complexity and organization with Man as the ultimate goal."

In all cases, a "no" response is considered correct.

3. The "source credibility" variable (which is similar to what Harrold and Eve [1986], refer to as "lifestyle concern issues") was computed as follows: If respondents agreed with the statement: "I believe that scientific viewpoints, such as evolutionary theory, are compatible with the teachings of Christianity," that respondent was coded a "2" (neutral) on the source credibility variable. If the respondent disagreed with the above statement (or was uncertain) and agreed with the statement: "On issues where science and religion seem to be in conflict, I would tend to favor the religious viewpoint," the respondent was assigned a code of "1" (pro-religion). If a respondent disagreed with both statements, he or she was coded

"3" (pro-science). As it happens, the computed "source credibility" variable was nearly perfectly normally distributed, with slightly more than half the sample in the "neutral" category.

4. The coefficients leading from the subjective religiosity and biblical literalism items are almost certainly depressed by their highly skewed marginal distributions. Some 82.5 percent of our respondents considered themselves religious while 85.8 percent rejected a literal interpretation of the Bible. Had we drawn a sample from a more religious variation, these coefficients would almost certainly be higher. See Erbe (1977) for a discussion of the effects of skewed marginals on correlation-based statistics.

5. For example, while slightly over half of our respondents have heard of something called "creation science" or "scientific creationism," only 11.9 percent of them claim to have heard of either Henry Morris or Duane Gish (the two most widely publicized proponents of "creation science"). Similarly, only 15.5 percent of our respondents believe that there exists scientific evidence to support the creationist viewpoint, and only 2.3 percent believe that most scientists must be either atheists or agnostics.

6. About one-fifth (20.9 percent) of our respondents agree that evolution is compatible with Catholic teaching, while only 4.1 percent believe that evolution is compatible with the teachings of the Episcopalian, Methodist, and Presbyterian Churches (mainline Protestant groups, which largely tend to have no theological conflicts with evolution).

APPENDIX

Respondents were asked to answer *yes*, *no*, or *not sure*.

1. I believe I understand what is meant by the term "evolution."

2. As I understand it, evolution is considered by virtually all biologists to be a fact.

3. The term "the theory of evolution" means that scientists do not know for sure if evolution is a fact.

4. I am certain that modern animals and plants evolved from other forms of life which lived a long time ago.

5. I believe that Man evolved from nonhuman forms of life.

6. I was taught in school that evolution is a fact.

7. I was taught in church that evolution is a fact.

8. I was taught at home that evolution is a fact.

9. The Catholic Church accepts the position that Man's physical body is the result of an evolutionary process.

10. The Episcopalian, Methodist, and Presbyterian Churches accept the position that Man's physical body is the result of an evolutionary process.

11. I have heard of something called "creation science" or "scientific creationism."

12. I believe that there is scientific evidence to support the idea that the human body was directly created by God.

13. I have had a biology course in college.

14. I have had a biology course in high school.

15. I consider myself a religious person.

16. I believe that the Bible should be interpreted literally. Every statement is factual and accurate in historical and scientific matters.

17. I have heard of Henry Morris and Duane Gish.

18. I believe that most scientists must be atheists and agnostics.

19. My parents believe that evolution is probably true.

20. I am a Catholic.

21. I believe that scientific viewpoints, such as evolutionary theory, are compatible with the teachings of Christianity.

22. On issues where science and religion seem to be in conflict, I would tend to favor the religious viewpoint.

23. As I mentioned it, evolutionists believe that humans evolved from modern monkeys.

24. According to biologists, the process of evolution is totally random.

25. Biologists believe that the giraffe has a long neck because it had to stretch to reach the tops of trees where the best leaves are found.

26. It seems to me that accepting evolution as fact requires as much faith as believing in special creation as fact.

27. I would like to see schools teach both evolution and special creation when dealing with the subject of origins in science classes.

28. I believe that gaps in the fossil record of life tend to disprove evolution.

29. As I understand it, evolution can best be defined as changes in species that always result in increasing complexity and organization with Man as the ultimate goal.

6
Habits of the Mind?
The Problem of Authority in the
New Christian Right

Kenneth D. Wald, Dennis E. Owen, and
Samuel S. Hill, Jr.

For those who value civility in public discourse, the rise of the New Christian Right has been a source of considerable anxiety. Generally uneasy about the passions aroused by politicized religion, secular elites have expressed particular alarm over the combative political style exhibited by conservative Christian activists. Their concern has grown with stories of the campaign mailing by a North Carolina congressman condemning his opponent, a Southern Baptist divinity school graduate, for failing to support "the principles outlined in the word of God" or the alarming comment from a supporter of another congressional candidate that she was working to "get some of God's people in" because she was "tired of having the devil's people run things" (H. Johnson, 1986; Flalka, 1986b).[1] Claiming a divine mantle with sublime self-assurance, these enthusiasts resemble Garrison Keillor's Sanctified Brethren of Lake Wobegon, a disputatious sect whose elders, Keillor said in one radio broadcast, undertook fierce doctrinal battles "certain without a glimmer of a doubt that God was standing right behind them, smiling and holding their coat."

Certainty and self-righteousness, harmful enough within the bounded world of the religious congregation, are potentially even more dangerous qualities when they suffuse political conflict in the wider society. As Reinhold Niebuhr (1972) reminds us, some of the most brutal and repressive regimes in modern history originated with leaders who possessed an unshakable confidence that they were on the side of the angels. Whether inspired by belief in historical inevitability or a divine mandate, the sense of absolute certainty has encouraged acts of barbarism otherwise too repugnant for sane people to contemplate. Contemporary social science and recent newspaper headlines confirm that religiously based political conflict frequently imposes severe and unmanageable strains on democratic political systems (Powell, 1982: 42–47). Familiarity with this disturbing record has prompted some critics to suggest that the New Christian Right, by mobilizing persons with antidemocratic impulses, threatens the norms of political tolerance and civility. In light of these concerns, this chapter attempts to assess whether the New Christian Right can be represented accurately as the mobilization of authoritarians.

By framing the research question in these terms, we may be charged with exhibiting bias against a particular religious tradition and political preference.[2] Lest we be understood in such terms, note three important qualifications that inform our understanding of the problem. First, theological liberals may exhibit the same unattractive qualities blithely attributed to conservative Christians. The nearly hysterical reaction of liberal groups to the emergence of the Christian Right indicates that rhetorical excess is by no means the exclusive province of religious traditionalists (Hunter, 1983b). On his return from Tehran, one of the former American hostages in Iran found the arrogance, intolerance, and "smug self-righteousness" of nuclear freeze supporters in liberal churches startlingly reminiscent of his fanatical Iranian captors (Kennedy, 1985). Second, if some elements in conservative Christianity seem conducive to antidemocratic politics, other aspects of the tradition may promote respect for democracy and human rights (Griffith et al., 1956: 113). Some scholars regard evangelical Christianity as a major source of democratic sentiment during the founding period and a potential force for democratic renewal today (Helmert, 1956; Neuhaus, 1984). Finally, we recognize that just as democratic political systems may break down from a surfeit of religiously inspired passion, so, too, may they atrophy from the dominance of an amoral technocratic ethic (Tesh, 1984). Precisely because it mounts such a vigorous challenge to the genteel norms of a consensus model of political life, the passionate political commitments of Christian conservatives may invigorate a political system in danger of withering away from lack of conviction and moral sensibility. These qualifications should be kept in mind as the analysis proceeds.

AUTHORITARIANISM VERSUS AUTHORITY-MINDEDNESS

In pioneering research conducted during the 1940s, a group of social psychologists professed to isolate a distinctive personality type that exhibited a disposition toward extremist, reactionary political values. Support for far-right political movements was said to derive from a deeply-rooted personal drive to behave in "an aggressive, domineering, and destructive way toward other people" (Ray, 1976: 307).[3] Though the original research report left open the role of religion in forming or maintaining the "authoritarian personality," subsequent research suggested that certain religious groups—Protestant fundamentalists and those strongly committed to Christian orthodoxy—were most likely to exhibit the traits associated with authoritarianism (L. B. Brown, 1962; Gregory, 1957; Rhodes, 1960). These empirical findings, confirmed by the involvement of several fundamentalist ministers in wartime racist and anti-Semitic mass movements, promoted "a general tendency to equate fundamentalism in religion with fascist tendencies in politics" (Gregory, 1957: 217). Though the political activities of modern-day fundamentalists hardly warrant the "fascist" label, some observers have professed to find the same complex of authoritarian tendencies in conservative Christian political activism.

Evidence about the "authoritarianism" of the contemporary Christian Right is based largely upon the unsystematic observation of the white fundamentalist Protestants who dominate its ranks.[4] Yet it is possible to go beyond anecdotal accounts to identify mechanisms within fundamentalist Christianity that might promote the authoritarian personality type. For example, the child-rearing norms in fundamentalism have traditionally exalted discipline and obedience over creativity and self-expression, precisely the developmental milieu thought most conducive to forming the authoritarian personality (MacNamara, 1985). Similarly, fundamentalist churches have been portrayed as havens for people seeking moral absolutism in response to the severe anxiety induced by the chaos of modern life. These are the same type of people who likely would be attracted to political movements that stress social order and obedience to authority. Through such linkages, fundamentalist churches may incubate traits of character and habits of mind that eventually take form as a personality-based disposition to favor authoritarian solutions to public problems.

Drawing on the insights of scholars who have criticized the authoritarian personality tradition, we wish to offer and test an alternative formulation that distinguishes between the personality type known as "authoritarianism" and a normative or ideological stance that we will label "authority-mindedness." To put it simply, authority-mindedness is an ideological commitment that values authoritativeness and obedience as a matter of principle rather than the outgrowth of a personality disorder. The high degree of authority-mindedness manifested by fundamentalist churches, which stems in the first place from respect for divine authority as revealed by Biblical truth, may predispose adherents to support political movements that similarly promote conformity to transcendent standards.

A palpable respect for authority pervades the world of fundamentalist Christianity. The Bible—inerrant, infallible, verbally inspired, often "God-breathed"—is both an ultimate and operational source of authority. Fundamentalism views scripture as a collection of factual information (in theological terms, a "propositional revelation") given in ordinary language, adjusted to human common sense and consequently capable of an infallible reading.[5] The Bible is taken to be the fundamental fact from which all other forms of knowledge are to take their lead. For example, biology can be properly scientific only if its inquiries begin with a recognition of the truth of Genesis. The same is true for all other areas of life. Ideally anything that one does or believes should have a biblical warrant. Fundamentalism is quite convinced that the biblical revelation is the only world view sufficient to cover the whole of human experience. It is, in the words of a fundamentalist theologian, "true to local reality," superior to alternative world views because it alone "has an apex under which everything fits" (Schaeffer, 1968: 20-21, 1972: 33). As a corollary, fundamentalists are also convinced that all experience can be reduced to a limited number of Biblical principles. There is a goodness of fit between revelation and the rest of reality.

The authority principle determines church practice and the mode of reasoning employed by fundamentalists. In a revealing phrase, members of "Bible-believing" churches are expected to "surrender to the Lord" as a condition of salvation. The authority principle is reinforced in the critical spheres of home and school where the Christian is enjoined to submit to the will of the constituted authority—respectively, the husband and teacher. As Ammerman (1987: 128) noted in her observation of one congregation, fundamentalists extend to all arenas of life the basic rule of authority governing relationships between the pastor and his flock:

The preaching situation thus provides the model for authority: A biblically legitimated expert provides unquestioned and respected leadership for those less able to care for themselves. Because this model of social relationships involves an unequal division of authority and status, believers come to see such a division as valued and right—both inside and outside the church. They come to expect groups to be divided between sheep and shepherds. The shepherds are entitled to deference and rewards, while the sheep are entitled to love and care.

The result is an epistemology that consists almost entirely of arguments from authority. The highest authority, the Word of God, is invoked almost reflexively as a means of confirming statements of fact or opinion. This consistent invocation of authoritative sources may be the single most distinctive quality of fundamentalist Protestantism.

Outsiders who converse with fundamentalists may come away convinced that they have encountered authoritarianism. One quickly finds that since the fundamentalist has the Truth, information can legitimately flow only one way. One's best arguments are likely to be discounted as demonic temptations to be resisted instead of opportunities for deepened understanding.

Perhaps most frustrating of all may well be the fact that the fundamentalist will seem never to take responsibility for his or her opinions. In all things, the fundamentalist is the servant of God and may even from time to time offer the consolation that a particular viewpoint is not what he or she wished, but what God requires. It is as if deniability were built right into the system. We are convinced that such denials ought not to be routinely dismissed. Rather than being an aggressive power-hungry personality seizing on religion as a convenient tool for controlling other people, the fundamentalist is a person who has been socialized into a world view that places a premium on biblical guidance and believes that one's choice is limited to the infallible revelation of God or complete chaos.[6]

Though it may resemble other explanations for susceptibility to right-wing mobilization, the commitment to authoritativeness differs in several respects from these formulations. To reiterate the principal difference, a philosophical preference for authority cannot be reduced to a personal need to dominate other people nor to any other "unconscious" drive or autonomous personality trait—in a word, authoritarianism. Rather, authority-mindedness is a set of values with coherence and integrity, chosen with the same degree of freedom that human beings enjoy in selecting any other world view. We also reject the view that respect for authority represents a form of deficient socialization to democratic norms. Exemplifying this view, Gabennesch (1972: 858) attributed authoritarianism to limited "breadth of perspective" on account of restricted access to educational experiences that would otherwise "broaden, multiply, and diversify the individual's sociocultural perspectives." Like other hypotheses couched in terms of social learning theory, this explanation treats authoritarianism as a type of residual category, something people believe in or exhibit because they have not learned any better (Sniderman and Hagen, 1985: ch. 5). This approach fails to accept the possibility that respect for authority derives from "direct instruction in belief systems within an emotional context which fosters acceptance of an implicit faith in the tenets" (Seaman et al., 1971: 253). That is, individuals may be socialized to regard authority as the critical force holding society together and apply that premise to various spheres of reality. The authority principle is apt to be regarded as especially crucial in the school and home, institutions that fundamentalists like Jerry Falwell regard as crucial for the restoration of social order. We thus hypothesize that authority-mindedness will promote support for social conservatism *independent of personality style or limited exposure to social diversity*.

DATA AND VARIABLES

As part of a 1986–87 survey of Protestant churchgoers in 23 congregations from the Gainesville (Florida) metropolitan area, respondents completed lengthy self-administered questionnaires that explored a variety of social, political, and religious themes. Data from the nearly 700 surveys will be used to measure the relevant political and social orientations identified in the preceding discussion.

One major purpose of the undertaking, measuring respondent orientation toward the New Christian Right, was achieved through construction of a four-point scale. Conceiving NCR orientation as the product of both cultural conservatism and attitudes toward organized Christian political involvement, we cross-tabulated respondents on dichotomous measures of moral conservatism and affect toward NCR groups.[7] The *opponents* (n = 192) scored below the mean on both moral conservatism and approval of NCR groups. We described as *ambivalents* (n = 163) respondents in the off-diagonal cells, those who combined a below-average score on one of the variables with an above-average score on the other. The remaining group, positioned in the top half on both moral conservatism and NCR approval, was subdivided on the basis of past support, financial or otherwise, for the NCR organizations. Respondents from the category who reported having provided tangible assistance to any of the conservative Christian groups were accorded the status of *supporters* (n = 72), the most pro-NCR individuals in the sample, while the term *sympathizer* was reserved for the remainder of respondents (n = 167) who were both morally conservative and positively disposed to the NCR but inactive on its behalf. We will try to identify the independent variables that dictate the placement of individuals into the four NCR categories derived from this set of questions.

Authoritarianism is a key predictor to be employed in the analysis. Once among the most widely used measures in survey research, the California "F" scale has lately fallen into disuse as an indicator of authoritarianism. The scale was abandoned because of well-known deficiencies regarding item direction, content, and tone (Altemeyer, 1981).[8] Rather than rely on one of the many "F" scale clones that have yet to be established as satisfactory alternatives (Ray, 1984), we have instead utilized a revised version of John J. Ray's "directiveness" scale. In addition to balanced wording, lack of religious referents, and satisfactory psychometric properties, use of Ray's 14-item scale was prompted by its embrace of a personality inventory approach consistent with the original concept of authoritarianism and its extensive validation, including reference to behavior in real-world settings (Ray, 1976, 1979).

On the fourth page of a thirteen-page booklet, respondents confronted the item in Figure 6.1. We altered the spelling and wording of some of Ray's items to conform to American usage and also added an explanation to encourage use of the question mark—a modification introduced in response to comments received during pretesting.[9] On the basis of factor and reliability

Figure 6.1
Items Used to Measure "Authoritarianism"

Q-14 As you know, the world is composed of all kinds of people. We'd like to
      know about you as an individual and how your personality is different
      from other people. Please answer each of the following questions by
      circling either "yes" or "no." If a statement fits you sometimes and not
      others, just circle the question mark.

                                                        Is This You?
                                                       (circle answer)

a. Do you always like to get your own way?   YES ? NO

b. Do you tend to boss people around?   YES ? NO

c. Do you like to have things "just so"?   YES ? NO

d. Do you put up with foolish behavior from others?   YES ? NO

e. Do you think one point of view is as good as another? YES ? NO

f. Do you often criticize the way other people do things? YES ? NO

g. Do you like people to be definite when they say things? YES ? NO

h. Does incompetence irritate you?   YES ? NO

i. Do you dislike having to tell others what to do?   YES ? NO

j. Are you uncomfortable taking charge of a situation? YES ? NO

k. Would you rather take orders than give them?   YES ? NO

l. Do you dislike standing out from the crowd?   YES ? NO

m. Do you have trouble making up your mind about things? YES ? NO

n. Would you like to end up as Top Dog?   YES ? NO

analyses, we excluded five of the original items (14c through 14g), reducing
the scale to nine components. The composite measure contained four
positively worded statements and five anti-authoritarian items with the scoring reversed so that a high score indicates greater authoritarianism of personality. The scale ranged from 0 to 18 with a mean of 9.6 and a standardized
Cronbach's alpha of 0.61. The latter figure is less than we had hoped for but
is comparable to Ray's experience with a larger number of items and high
enough to reveal significant relationships if they are present in the data.

The construct of "authority-mindedness," which we have proposed as an
alternative to authoritarianism in explaining NCR support, was represented
by two measures—one religious, the other essentially secular in tone. The
religious authority-mindedness scale (see Figure 6.2) consisted of eight

Figure 6.2
Items Used to Measure "Authority-Mindedness"

A.   Religious Authority-Mindedness

4. Part of being a good Christian may involve helping other people but it is more important to develop a close relationship with God.

5. Christians can disagree about what the Bible means. (R)

6. God blesses those who love and obey Him with success in life.

7. You can easily tell if people are saved by how they lead their lives.

8. A true Christian is absolutely certain what he or she believes.

11. If enough people were brought to Christ, most social problems would take care of themselves.

12. To me, the things of this world are not very important. What really matters is what happens after death.

13. If you want to be right with God, how important is it for you to do good for other people?

B.   Secular Authority-Mindedness

15. There are two kinds of people in the world: the weak and the strong.

18. A person either knows the answer to a question or he doesn't.

20. There is only one right way to do anything.

NOTE: The item number refers to the original questionnaire. For all questions except #13, the response options were Agree Strongly, Agree Somewhat, Neither Agree Nor Disagree, Disagree Somewhat, and Disagree Strongly. Question #13 presented the options of Very Important, Somewhat Important, or Not Important.

items, statements that emphasized the clarity and certainty of Christianity (questions 5 and 8), promoted faith over works as the road to personal and social salvation (4, 11, 13), identified visible signs of grace (6, 7), and endorsed otherworldliness (12). The seemingly disparate items in the scale (mean = 18.1, alpha = .78) are linked by a common willingness to "trust in the Lord" that would be unthinkable save for a deity whose beneficence and support could be counted on without question. For that reason, we interpret a high score on this scale as a sign of certainty of faith and respect for religious authority. The three items listed in the bottom part of Figure 6.2, derived from Martin and Westie (1959), were used as a composite measure of authority-mindedness without religious reference. The secular "authority-mindedness" scale had a reliability coefficient of 0.73 and a mean of 4.7 with a distribution from 0 through 12. It was strongly though by no means perfectly correlated with its religious counterpart (Pearson R = .61). Though both measures demonstrate a positive wording bias, we believe that the impact of "yea-saying" can be controlled by the inclusion of socioeconomic status measures, the principal correlates of acquiescent response set.

Our argument about the sources of NCR support depends on a distinction between the personality syndrome known as authoritarianism and a respect for constituted authority that we treat as a coherent world view. Fortunately for us, the measures of these concepts have proven to be statistically independent. The authoritarianism scale is very weakly related to religious authority-mindedness ($r = -.10$, $p < .01$) and almost completely unrelated to the secular measure of respect for authority ($r = -.01$, $p = .35$). The relative contribution of the three scales to NCR support will not be confounded by shared variance among them.

Not wishing to suggest that authoritarianism and authority-mindedness are sufficient to account for attraction to the New Christian Right, we plan to include predictors associated with four major alternative explanations. The "resource mobilization" perspective emphasizes the accessibility of the NCR's target population to mobilization through immersion in church-based networks; the concept will be represented by measures of conservative religious values and frequency of church attendance. In the so-called culture and socialization model, the NCR has also been portrayed as a movement that draws on the antimodern values of traditionalist subcultures. Such resistance to modernity is thought to be concentrated among a variety of groups defined by gender, race, age, occupational standing, marital status, family size, region, community size, and education. These variables will be included as proxies for socialization to traditional norms, representing limited exposure to cultural diversity. The "status politics" framework suggests the appeal of the NCR to persons who feel that social change has diminished the respect society accords to groups that reflect traditional values. We include a direct measure of respondent dissatisfaction with the social respect received by such groups. The final explanatory framework, which interprets the NCR as a front for economic conservatism, is represented by ideological self-designation, partisanship, and party choice in presidential elections.

Prior research has confirmed the contribution of each of these factors to mobilization by the Christian Right. We include them mostly as a way to guard against spurious relationships between the dependent variable and the three principal measures of theoretical interest. If "authority-mindedness" results simply from lack of exposure to broadening experiences, as some scholars maintain, its explanatory power should dissipate in face of controls for socialization in traditional subcultures. But if it is, as we believe, a genuine ideological commitment evinced by persons of varying social backgrounds, then it will demonstrate predictive power in a multivariate analysis. The controls are also useful to check the problem of acquiescence in the two authority-mindedness scales. To the extent that acquiescence is a function of limited education, the measures of socioeconomic status should help to correct that weakness in the scales.

ANALYSIS

Discriminant function analysis provides a means of isolating the combination of variables that best accounts for the classification of respondents according to some criterion variable. In this case, we wish to determine which predictors have the largest impact on respondent scores on the NCR orientation index. That can be determined from Table 6.1, which presents information on the 447 respondents who provided complete information on the 18 independent variables and the classification measure.[10]

The analysis provided two significant functions and a third (not shown) that made marginal contributions to separating respondents into NCR categories. Taken together, the three functions proved a powerful classification tool with more than 60 percent of respondents correctly classified by the three functions. The performance was even better at the extremes where 70 percent of opponents and supporters were accurately predicted to fall into their respective observed categories.

The first function, with a canonical correlation of 0.75, neatly corresponded to the NCR index in arraying opponents, ambivalents, sympathizers, and supporters along a continuum. While the correlates of this function speak to a variety of theoretical formulations, our particular interest is with the measures of authoritarianism and authority-mindedness. To put it simply, the religious "authority-mindedness" scale is one of three major forces that predict scores on the NCR index. The secular counterpart ranks among a tier of secondary influences. By contrast, authoritarianism is fairly useless in discriminating among respondents on the NCR index. Indeed, the sign indicates that authoritarianism is *negatively* related to NCR support although the very modest magnitude of the coefficient should preclude us from making too much of that finding. The big news is that authoritarianism does not help us understand why some people enroll in the Christian Right while authority-mindedness, in both its forms, does.

The second function, notably weaker than the first, distinguishes principally between the active supporters of the NCR (who have a low score)

Table 6.1
Discriminant Analysis of NCR Index

VARIABLES	Function #1	Function #2
Religious authority-Mindedness	.68	.51
Secular authority-Mindedness	.35	.29
Authoritarianism	-.11	.10
Theological conservatism	.65	-.07
Church attendance	.39	-.13
Education	-.30	.11
Occupational Prestige	-.19	.10
Gender (1 = female)	-.02	.25
Marital status (1 = married)	-.02	-.05
Race (1 = white)	-.04	-.45
Family Size	.03	-.14
Age	-.13	.23
Region (1 = South)	.15	-.21
Community size	.04	-.06
Partisanship	.29	.04
Ideological conservatism	.58	-.10
Presidential vote, 1984 (1 = Mondale)	.38	-.05
GROUP CENTROIDS:		
NCR Opponents	-1.32	-.21
NCR Ambivalents	.02	.47
NCR Sympathizers	1.08	.08
NCR Supporters	1.73	-.58
Canonical R	.75	.33
x^2	434.1*	73.5*

Table entries are structure coefficients, representing the correlation between discriminating variables and each function.

*$p < .001$

and the ambivalents who anchor the positive side of the continuum. Once again, religious authority-mindedness and, to a lesser extent, the secular variant of that approach, are strong influences in the function and authoritarianism plays a trivial role. In substantive terms, respect for authoritativeness is more likely to manifest itself in ambivalence toward the NCR than in support. This initially puzzling result seems to be more heavily influenced by race than anything else. Nonwhite respondents, who value religious authority, make up a disproportionate share of NCR ambivalents—hardly surprising given the appeal of the Christian Right's moral conservatism and the repulsion of its conservative economic agenda. The low canonical correlation for the function (0.33) should remind us that this tendency is clearly less important than the general finding that authority-mindedness promotes a positive orientation toward the NCR.

Because we have explored the impact of the other variables elsewhere (Wald, Owen, and Hill, forthcoming), we will only briefly note here that the four alternative theoretical approaches fared well in the major function. As predicted by resource mobilization theorists, conservative religious values and high levels of churchgoing accentuated receptivity to the NCR. We have elsewhere shown how religiously conservative environments incubate social and political traditionalism (Wald, Owen, and Hill, 1988). Socialization to traditional culture, at least in the form of low education and occupational prestige, similarly promoted a positive disposition regarding Christian conservatism. The muted impact of these variables and the insignificant contribution of the other indirect measures of the modernity syndrome make "culture and socialization" the least strongly supported of the hypotheses for NCR support. The status dissatisfaction scale operated as expected to facilitate identification with the contemporary Christian Right as did conservative self-identification and Republicanism, measures derived from another theoretical tradition.

After this barrage of findings, it should be reiterated that authority-mindedness is arguably the major influence on Christian Right activism. Despite its status as a favorite variable in the repertoire of Christian Right analysts, authoritarianism makes a negligible contribution to orientations toward the movement and, ironically, actually correlates with opposition rather than support.

DISCUSSION

Those who "know" that the NCR is authoritarian in spite of this evidence are apt to challenge our findings with charges of deficient measurement. While the dependent measure is subject to criticism, its predictable relationship to the other variables seems to preclude that avenue of attack as well as the charge of an unrepresentative sample. Perhaps the authoritarianism measure itself is flawed. The "directiveness" scale, a personality inventory rather than an attitude scale, permits clever authoritarians—those who recognize the social undesirability of admitting a desire to dominate others—to mask their true feelings by selecting options that portray themselves as benign. While plausible, this argument is deficient on several counts. Ray (1984) has validated the measure with behavioral indicators and has also demonstrated its freedom from the influence of social desirability. Moreover, "closet" authoritarians who disguised their domineering attitudes to not seem to have similarly hidden their philosophical commitment to certainty in religion and life, an orientation every bit as culturally disfavored as authoritarianism. The moderate reliability of the authoritarianism measure does not suffice as a reason to impeach the findings.[11]

Rather than seek out weaknesses in the authoritarianism scale to explain the findings, we think it is important to understand why Christian fundamentalists would fail to score distinctively on it. The items in the scale, which might otherwise tap into the personality dimensions of some respondents, are likely to reveal the ideological components of the fundamentalist respondent's world view. To illustrate, we found that a majority of fundamentalists selected the non-authoritarian response of "no" to the following items from the directiveness scale:

Do you always like to get your own way?

Do you tend to boss people around?

Would you like to end up as Top Dog?

Fundamentalists may reject these statements on the grounds that one is always required to submit to the will of God, not to have one's own way, or to exercise personal power. The idea is to hold one's own sinfulness in check and let the Holy Spirit provide direction. Even when fundamentalists answer in a manner that is regarded as indicative of authoritarianism, the reason may have little to do with personality traits. The following items, both answered in the negative by a majority of fundamentalist respondents, illustrate the limits of the psychological interpretation:

Do you dislike standing out from the crowd?

Do you have trouble making up your mind about things?

In scoring a negative answer as authoritarian, the scale assumes that non-conformity and decisiveness stem from a desire to dominate or direct other people. From the fundamentalist perspective, these items suggest something altogether different. A witness for the Lord who is enjoined *not* to be conformed to the world but to a higher standard will certainly stand out from the crowd. By living according to a revealed blueprint, the Bible believer is relieved of difficulty in making up his or her mind. It does not require a resort to the authoritarianism model to explain why fundamentalists answer these questions as they do.

CONCLUSION

The findings largely vindicate our argument about the processes involved in bringing fundamentalists to the New Christian Right. Rather than accept the authoritarianism model, we suggested that authority-mindedness explained the attraction. The distinction is largely a matter of how one perceives the basis for NCR mobilization. The authoritarianism model treats the NCR as a magnet for persons who are characterologically incapable of dealing with others in a democratic fashion. We have also rejected the argument locating support for the NCR among populations lacking exposure to modernity and acceptance of the broadened cultural perspectives that accompany it. NCR supporters appear to have developed a preference for strong authority relationships that does not depend on having been cocooned in some premodern environment.

In reporting these findings, we are registering a dissent from the perspective that has dominated scholarly analysis of the Christian Right and earlier movements seeking moral reform. Such movements are commonly portrayed as relentlessly anti-modern, vengeful efforts to restore a Golden Age that never was and never can be by people who are incapable of coping with complexity. To judge by the survey data, the NCR appeals to people who have experienced modernity, who may even have mastered some of its aspects, but who nonetheless mount an ideological critique of it. In that sense, NCR supporters resemble the Moslem fundamentalists who call for modernization without Westernization. While accepting the tools of modernity, the NCR objects to some of the cultural baggage that has accompanied the process of economic development. In particular, NCR supporters challenge moral relativism by asserting the validity of strong faith claims and pressing for a respectful attitude toward legitimately constituted authority. Neither an outgrowth of a distinctive personality style nor the residual of constricted socialization, these claims are the product of an ideological commitment fostered by involvement in powerful institutions that promote a distinctive world view.

The results suggest a need to rethink our approach to the New Christian Right. The movement should be comprehended as a political force that offers a coherent world view. One may dislike the political agenda, particularly the insistence that the United States acknowledge a socially normative revelation that is clearly sectarian and anti-pluralistic, but there is no empirical basis to dismiss it as mental aberration nor the consequence of isolation from the currents of modernity.[12] Indeed, we are struck by the widespread concern about the lack of any public moral consensus among social critics outside the NCR fold. The liberal Protestant, Parker Palmer (1981), fears that Americans have decided that the public world is not worth their attention. The sociological tradition inspired by Robert Bellah claims that even Americans who do commit themselves to a world outside their own skins lack a moral language capable of supporting the ways they actually live. Bellah sees the dominant cultural style as one leading to the walling up of each individual in the privacy of his or her own heart, making decisions solely on the basis of cost-benefit analysis serving only the isolated self (Bellah et al., 1985). Philosopher John Wikse (1977) suggests that we are creating a culture of "idiocy" in which each individual seeks to be an autonomous universe—autism as a model for maturity. Christopher Lasch (1978) sees Americans turning to narcissistic self-aggrandizement in the absence of a public order capable of providing an arena for more genuine accomplishments and worth. Thus the NCR is not idiosyncratic in its sense of what our problems are or where they lie. Its pessimistic assessment of our possibilities—either submission to the authority and revelation of the fundamental deity or the war of all against all—will tend to limit its appeal and also cloud the social insights contained in its views. Such are the appropriate grounds of criticism.

NOTES

1. It may be some consolation that both the North Carolina incumbent and the Indiana challenger lost decisively.
2. Conservatives have long maintained that social-psychological analysis of the right wing constitutes a subtle form of character assassination. Treating a political movement as the outgrowth of potentially pathological states of mind relieves the analyst of the task of dealing substantively with its arguments and principles. When the tables are turned, as in Rothman and Lichter's (1982) psychologically informed analysis of Jewish leftists, liberals may appreciate the charge of reductionism.
3. This approach was criticized for failing to consider the possibility that similar motives might produce the phenomenon of "left-wing" authoritarianism.
4. In a multitude of studies that examine the mass base of the Christian Right, adherence to fundamentalist Christianity (in terms of belief or denominational membership) has emerged as the most consistent predictor (see Wald, 1987: ch. 7). This is not to deny that the movement has enlisted support from other Protestants, Mormons, Catholics, Jews, and secularists who share the social concerns of the NCR. Notwithstanding this qualification, the center of gravity of the movement is firmly located in the fundamentalist world.
5. Fundamentalism characteristically denies that it interprets scripture, insisting rather that it acknowledges what is clearly there.
6. Fundamentalists invariably argue that unless there is an authority available to the world *from outside the world*, all possibility of coherent and persuasive moral argumentation is destroyed. It is only the authority of God—tell us what is right—that allows us to assign any moral praise or blame whatsoever. If God is not objectively there, if God is not infinite and personal (in the sense of having characteristics normally attributed to persons, especially the capability of entering into relationships), if God's self-revelation in the Bible is not acknowledged as universally authoritative, then there is no basis from which one could condemn even the Third Reich. The force of this line of reasoning seems so compelling to fundamentalists that it is occasionally used as proof for the existence of God: We need

God, therefore he exists. The fact of God's existence, for the fundamentalist, means that we must be "mindful" of the Lord in all things. We must bring the totality of our living into conformity with divine will. There are no secular enclaves where Christianity is irrelevant. For fundamentalism, then, God serves primarily as a source of order. The fundamentalist deity is the the giver of law and first principles, the might fortress against ambiguity, uncertainty, relativism, and chaos.

7. For validation of these measures, consult Wald, Owen, and Hill (forthcoming).

8. Even if the measure could be exonerated from those criticisms, the inclusion of a "supernaturalism" subscale would unfairly bias analysis in the direction of a positive tie between authoritarianism and religious fundamentalism.

9. Prior to this addition, a significant number of pretest respondents had omitted answers to these items. Debriefing indicated that they did not know the meaning of the question mark and they suggested that we clarify by providing instructions. Perhaps this modification accounts for the very low rate of non-response (4.6 percent) to the entire scale.

10. The missing cases were distributed relatively equally among the four groups defined by the NCR index. As a further check on the impact of missing values, the analysis was rerun without the discriminating variable that accounted for the largest number of lost cases. The results were indistinguishable from the those reported for the 447 cases with complete information.

11. Controlling for attenuation, the correlation between authoritarianism and NCR support does not rise appreciably. If anything, it appears that the two authority-mindedness measures are more strongly affected by imperfect reliability and would exert even greater impact on NCR support with higher alphas.

12. To do otherwise recalls Carlyle's complaint about Victorian cynics: "Show our critics a great man, a Luther for example, they begin to what they call 'account' for him; not to worship him, but take the dimensions of him,—and bring him out to be a little kind of man!" (quoted in Himmelfarb, 1988: 228). While we certainly do not regard the NCR as heroic, we think that reductionism is a strategy for rejecting the movement out of hand rather than confronting its arguments and claims.

7
The Catholic Vote from 1980 to 1986: Continuity or Change?

Henry C. Kenski and William Lockwood

The Roman Catholic church is the largest religious denomination in the United States, with a membership equal to one-fourth of the adult population (Penning, 1986). When broader categories that combine various Protestant denominations into larger groupings are utilized (mainline Protestants, for example), the size of the Catholic population is still striking and second in size only to white evangelical Protestant denominations with 33 percent (Wald, 1987). Catholics historically have been at the very heart of the Democratic electoral coalition, both in number and reliability. For decades, since the New Deal, "loyalty to the Democratic party has been something on the order of a theological commitment for a large share of America's Catholic community" (Dionne, 1981: 308). Until the 1970s, Catholics provided more than one-third of the Democratic presidential vote, although constituting only one-quarter of the population (Axelrod, 1970).

Some scholars and contemporary political analysts, however, suggest that Catholic voting behavior has undergone significant change in recent decades. The key questions are whether there has been a change and, if so, how much in what electoral arenas, and whether more recent Catholic voting behavior in the Reagan era is characterized by continuity or change. Parsimony, manageability, and data availability lead us to concentrate on two important areas: (1) presidential voting, and (2) House voting. Although these electoral arenas are our major focus, a deeper appreciation of Catholic political behavior is also tapped by use of data on party orientation, ideological and issue orientation, and select statewide voting results for various offices in 1984 and 1986.

To accomplish our goal, an overview of party identification is presented, followed by a similar effort for ideological and issue orientation. After

a broad partisanship and ideological/issue orientation portrait that
  s the Catholic voter to both the electorate overall and to white Pro-
  ......as well, a review of the literature on major propositions involving
Catholic voting behavior is put forth. It is followed by a historical overview
of presidential and House voting patterns, particularly Catholic and white
Protestant differences, and an analysis of Catholic voting in recent
statewide elections for president, Senate, and governor. After these various
overviews, a brief description of our data and methods is provided, particularly the use of log-linear models. The final and major segment of this
chapter presents findings on Catholic presidential and House voting
behavior from 1980 to 1986. Our first task, however, is to examine party
identification.

PARTY IDENTIFICATION

Party identification is a most important variable that contributes to opinion formation and influences voting behavior even though the relationship
between party identification and electoral choice has declined since 1964
(Abramson, 1983). Wattenberg's thesis (1986) about the decline of U.S.
political parties, especially party identification as a cue in voting behavior,
however, is persuasive. Voters are less influenced by party identification
than they have been in the past, and elections are now more candidate
oriented and media oriented. Despite its diminished value, party identification remains important and is still one of the best predictors of how an individual will vote.

A very extensive literature and lively debate exist about the role of party
identification in voting behavior that merit a separate paper that we have
written elsewhere (Kenski and Lockwood, 1987). For purposes of this
chapter, we simply seek to place Catholic voters on the spectrum of party
identification change. A very comprehensive multi-variate study of group
support patterns over time by Stanley, Bianco, and Niemi (1986) examined
the partisanship of individual group members with multi-variate methods.
Their general findings indicate that the Democratic party is no longer so
dependent on a few groups as it was in the 1950s, but is now almost equally
dependent on six groups. In contrast to earlier studies (Axelrod, 1974;
Petrocik, 1981), which noted a decline in Catholic Democratic party identification by 1972 and 1968, respectively, Stanley et al. (1986: 972) concluded that "except for the special circumstances of 1960, being Catholic
stimulated a Democratic identification to about the same degree until 1980."
The probability of a Catholic being a Democratic identifier in 1952 was .56
and the third highest of the six groups, exceeded only by native southern
whites at .75 and Jews at .70 but ahead of union households at .54, working

class at .54, and blacks at .53. By 1984, Catholics were in a three-way tie for fourth with native southern whites and the working class at .42, and all were topped by blacks at .64, Jews at .59, and union households at .46.

It is instructive in the Stanley et al. study (1986) that five of the six core Democratic groups manifested the political dealignment syndrome, underscored by a decline in partisan identification. The only core group in the coalition to experience a partisanship increase was blacks from .59 in 1952 to .65 in 1984. The partisan decline was most pronounced for native southern whites (.75 in 1952 and .42 in 1984), while Catholics, the largest Democratic core group, experienced a noticeable decline as well from .56 in 1952 to .42 in 1984.

Table 7.1 presents data for selected years from 1952 to 1986 from the American National Election Studies (ANES) of the University of Michigan, the largest and most continuous electoral data sets available, to identify changes in party identification in the nation overall, as well as changes in Catholic Democratic identification compared to white Protestants. Important political, economic, and social differences clearly exist for various Protestant denominations, particularly for evangelical and mainline groups. Considerations of parsimony and manageability, however, necessitated our use of either a larger white Protestant aggregate or an overall Protestant aggregate in this short chapter. In much of our initial analysis, we follow in the footsteps of other scholars (Dionne, 1981; Greeley, 1978 and 1985; and Lopatto, 1985) who disaggregate Protestant data into white and black voter categories. The rationale for this decision is twofold. First, as Lopatto (1985: 38) points out, the proportion of black Americans voting Democratic in presidential elections the past few decades has consistently registered around 90 percent. "Therefore, there is little variance from election to election to be explained." Second, "there is good reason to believe that this affinity for the Democratic party among black voters is based mainly on considerations involving race and the unique problems that the American black population has faced over the last few decades" (pp. 38–39).

Several prominent features in the data in Table 7.1 emerge for the nation overall. First, the overall level of *Democratic identification has declined over time* and registered 40 percent in 1982, 1984, and 1986. Second, *Independents have recorded the largest percentage improvement* the past 32 years, increasing their proportion of the electorate from 22 percent in 1952 to 33 percent in 1986. The high point for Independents was the 1970s, when 35 percent of the voters identified themselves as Independents from 1972 through 1976 with the apex being 37 percent in 1978. Third, *Republican identification has improved slightly over time*, with some 29 percent viewing themselves as Republican in 1984 and 25 percent in 1986. Overall, the biggest changes were the Democratic decrease and the Independent increase rather than any major surge in Republican identification.

Table 7.1
Party Identification by Religion, Select Years from 1952 to 1986 (in percentages)

Year	Party Identification	Nation	White Protestants	Catholics	Catholic Demo. Edge
1952	Democrat	47	43	56	+13
	Independent	22	21	26	
	Republican	27	34	18	
1960	Democrat	47	39	64	+25
	Independent	21	22	20	
	Republican	30	38	16	
1964	Democrat	56	46	59	+13
	Independent	21	21	24	
	Republican	22	31	17	
1968	Democrat	48	37	54	+17
	Independent	28	30	32	
	Republican	23	32	15	
1970	Democrat	45	36	51	+15
	Independent	31	31	32	
	Republican	23	32	17	
1980	Democrat	41	34	43	+9
	Independent	35	34	32	
	Republican	22	29	25	
1982	Democrat	40	36	54	+18
	Independent	30	30	28	
	Republican	24	32	16	
1984	Democrat	40	33	44	+11
	Independent	29	27	31	
	Republican	29	38	23	
1986	Democrat	40	31	44	+13
	Independent	33	34	33	
	Republican	25	33	22	

Source: American National Election Studies, Center for Political Studies, University of Michigan.

Levels of support for party identification among white Protestants are marked by a decline in Democratic identification from 43 percent in 1952 to 31 percent in 1986 and increases in both Independent and Republication identification. Independents jump from 21 percent in 1952 to 27 percent in 1984 and 1986, while Republicans improve from 34 percent in 1952 to 38 percent in 1984, but slip back to 33 percent in 1986. White Protestants were

9 percent more Democratic than Republican in 1952 but this turned to parity in 1986 with Independents (34 percent), Republicans (33 percent), and Democrats (31 percent).

The data in Table 7.1 also underscore the Catholic Democratic edge in party identification compared with white Protestants. It has moved considerably since 1952 with a high of + 25 percent in 1960 (Kennedy's victory), a low of + 9 percent in 1980 (Reagan's triumph), and a + 13 percent edge in the recent 1986 midterm election. Democratic party identification for Catholics has decreased over time from 56 percent in 1952 to 44 percent in 1984 and 1986. Still, a *plurality of Catholic voters remain Democratic and are more likely to identify as Democratic or Independent than as Republican.* The strong majority or plurality dominance that Democrats had among Catholics from 1960 to 1968, however, has gone with the political wind. Catholics today are less Democratic without embracing Republican identification to any great extent.

The *political dealignment has affected both white Protestants and Catholics*, but it is the latter that retains a plurality edge for Democratic identification. The volatility in party identification is reflected in the fact that in 1980, 1984, and 1986 some 43 percent, 44 percent, and 44 percent of Catholics, respectively, thought of themselves as Democrats. This jumped dramatically to 54 percent in the recession-ridden election of 1982, underscoring that short-term forces like recessions can result in considerable movement in party identification that can affect groups differently. White Protestants moved from being 29 percent Democratic in 1980 to only 32 percent in 1982, while their Catholic counterparts mushroomed from 43 to 54 percent. Thus the + 9 percent Catholic Democratic partisan edge in 1980 jumped to a + 18 percent advantage in 1982. The Catholic advantage slips though to + 11 percent in 1984 and + 13 percent in 1986. Given these data, however, it would appear that a major future economic downturn could easily result in a Catholic Democratic party identification majority. Such a change would have important implications for electoral outcomes, as party identification still counts for something in an era of party decline.

IDEOLOGICAL AND ISSUE ORIENTATION

That Catholics are more liberal in self-identification and on most issue positions than white Protestants is well documented, beginning with the seminal work of Andrew Greeley (1977, 1978) and confirmed by other scholars (Abramson, Aldrich, and Rohde, 1986; Penning, 1986; Wald, 1987; and Kenski, 1988). On ideological self-identification, for example, CBS/New York Times exit poll data in 1986 reveal that Catholics approximate the nation and are somewhat more liberal and moderate than white Protestants. Some 17 percent of all American voters saw themselves as liberal compared to 48 percent as moderate and 35 percent as conservative. Similarly, 17 percent of Catholic voters viewed themselves as liberal compared to 51 percent as moderate and 32 percent as conservative. The corresponding figures for white Protestants were 12 percent liberal, 47 percent moderate, and 41 percent conservative (Kenski, 1988). Recent research by Greeley (1985) and Gallup and Castelli (1987) also underscore Catholic liberalism on select economic issues. Looking at General Social Survey data from 1980 to 1984, Wald (1987) found that Catholics approximated the overall national distributions favoring increased spending on health, education, urban areas, and the environment. Although clearly more liberal on domestic issues than either evangelical Protestants or mainline Protestants, Catholics were not as liberal as black Protestants, Jews, or respondents with no religious preference.

On social issues, the stereotype of Catholics as conservative needs to be avoided. They are slightly more conservative than both the nation overall and white Protestants on issues like legalized abortion (38 percent opposed in the 1985 CBS/New York Times exit poll, compared to 28 percent for the nation overall and 23 percent for white Protestants). Even here caution is urged, as a recent study by Kenski and Lockwood (1988) analyzed GSS data for 1984 and found that Catholic opinion on abortion varied by circumstances. A majority of Catholics supported legalized abortion in three circumstances (possible birth defects, woman's health endangered, and rape). In four other circumstances, a majority of Catholics opposed abortion (families wanting no more children, poor families, unmarried women, and abortion for any reason).

Catholics approximate the nation's conservatism on other social issues like capital punishment, school prayer, pornography, and busing. They are more liberal than the nation and Protestants generally on other social issues like women's rights, gun control, civil rights for minorities and homosexuals, and decriminalization of marijuana (Gallup and Castelli, 1987). Gallup and Castelli point out that "the strong Catholic support for women's rights and minority rights is one of the most overlooked social phenomena in the nation today" (p. 115).

Catholics are also more liberal on foreign policy questions than the nation and white Protestants. A 1984 CBS/New York Times exit poll survey asked a question about whether we should negotiate a freeze with the USSR first or strengthen our defense before we negotiate. Overall, voters were evenly split with 50 percent for each of the choices. Catholic voters, however, opted for negotiating a freeze with the USSR over strengthening defense first by a 56 to 44 percent margin, while white Protestants endorsed strengthening defense first by 58 to 42 percent (Kenski, 1988). Gallup and Castelli (1987: 89) have found that "the new change in attitudes toward war and peace among Catholics triggered by the Vietnam War is one of the most significant public-opinion shifts in recent decades." Catholics are not pacifists, but favor the discreet use of force. They strongly favor arms control and weapons reduction as well as reduced military spending, and are also opposed to the Reagan administration policy in Central America (Gallup and Castelli, 1987).

The overall profile is one of ideological moderation, moderate to liberal views on select government spending issues, a concern about the economy, but a reluctance to increase taxes to balance the budget (Kenski, 1988). On social issues, Catholic voters are slightly more conservative than the nation on legalization of abortion, approximate the nation's conservatism on issues like capital punishment and pornography, but are more liberal than the nation on issues like women's rights and minority rights. Finally, Catholics are more liberal than the nation on foreign policy, and policy solutions that require more defense spending on increased military force do not have much appeal. An emphasis in arms control, however, is a strong political plus. Catholic voters in the 1980s still appear to be, in Franklin Roosevelt's classic phrase, "a little bit left of center" (Greeley, 1978: 292).

REVIEW OF THE LITERATURE

Our literature review on Catholic voting focuses on the presidential and House levels, with different views offered in both electoral arenas. An analysis of the presidential voting literature, for example, uncovers five schools of thought. All of the scholars examined accept the fact that a majority of plurality of Catholics voted Republican in three of the last four presidential elections (1976 being the exception), but they differ in the emphasis used to interpret it. We label the *five schools of thought* as follows: (1) Democratic erosion over time, (2) Democratic erosion but persistent Democratic strength, (3) Democratic erosion and Republican gains, (4) electoral convergence, and (5) electoral volatility at the presidential level.

The most definitive and continuous work on presidential voting is a seminal article and continual communication updates by Robert Axelrod (1970, 1974, 1978, 1982, and 1984). His focus is on the components of the Democratic coalition, the poor, blacks, union members, Catholics, southerners, and residents of central cities and he takes into account the factor of size, turnout, and loyalty. His most recent research (1986) emphasizes *Democratic erosion* and notes that once again in 1984, as in 1980, the Democrats did not do nearly as well with the largest groups in their coalition: union families, Southerners, and Catholics. The Democratic coalition did well, however, among the poor, blacks, and city dwellers, groups that were relatively small and contained no more than 12 percent of the population. Axelrod's findings on Catholics suggest a lessening of Democratic loyalty over time. In 1984, for example, they were 6 percent more Democratic than the nation overall. Although this was better than their 3 percent loyalty edge in 1980, it was far from the substantial margins given the Democratic ticket in 1960 (+32), 1964 (+14), and 1968 (+18).

The *Democratic erosion but persistent Democratic strength* perspective is advanced by Greeley (1985: 36) who minimizes the importance of the 1984 Reagan victory with the observation that "one election does not a trend make." He argues for a longer time perspective and stresses that "about half of American Catholics voted for Democratic presidential candidates in the fifties and half voted for Democratic presidential candidates in the late seventies and early eighties (for Carter against Ford, and for Carter against Reagan)" (p. 30). He concedes that Catholic presidential voting fluctuates more than Protestant voting but emphasizes that "at all times, the proportion voting Democratic in presidential elections are higher among Catholics than among Protestants" (p. 38). Hoffman (1985) also stresses the basic Democratic orientation of Catholic voters at the presidential level, even against the basic backdrop of Democratic erosion in recent elections in his examination of GSS data. Unlike Greeley, however, he is more interested in locating the sources of erosion in Catholic support for the Democratic ticket. Hoffman concludes that party identification is the key, as Republicans have been more successful since 1968 (with the exception of 1976) in capturing Catholic voters who see themselves as Independents.

At the other end of the spectrum are those scholars who emphasize *Democratic erosion and Republican advances*. Petrocik (1987), for instance, uses both ANES and Market Opinion Research data to argue that a definite change has occurred among various groups at the presidential level. For Catholics, he contends that they were unusually supportive of Reagan but "their Republican vote was not unprecedented" (p. 367). His data show Republican voting low among Catholics in 1960 (19 percent) and 1964 (27 percent), but Republican advantages in 1972 (67 percent), 1980 (57 percent), and 1984 (65 percent). In 1976 it was 48 percent. He does note, however, that in each election the Catholic Republican vote was always 10 percent or more lower than that of white Northern Protestants (p. 366). Reichley (1985a) also emphasizes Democratic erosion and Republican gains, particularly in the 1980 and 1984 elections. Overall, he sees this as a weakening of traditional Catholic political allegiance to the Democratic party, and with future Republican opportunities. His emphasis on Republican gains is less decisive than Petrocik, and Reichley feels that thus far Catholics have not come down decisively on the Republican side.

Another scholarly view emphasizes *electoral convergence*. Ladd (1985a), for example, notes that the strong historical religious divisions in presidential voting, with Protestants inclined to suport Republicans and Catholics the Democrats, are eroding and the two religious groups are converging on presidential voting. He observes that in 1960 Catholics were 28 percent less Republican than the nation overall and Protestants were 12 percent more Republican. By this measure, they were 40 percentage points apart in presidential support. In 1964, the intergroup difference was 21 percent, with a steady decline to the present. The intergroup differences between Protestants and Catholics, Ladd points out, were the smallest in history in the 1980 (6 percent spread) and 1984 elections (4 percent spread).

A final school of thought embraces the notion of *electoral volatility* at the presidential level. Dionne (1981) sees a weakening of Catholic loyalty to Democrats, but without embracing the Republicans with enthusiasm. He sees substantial electoral shifting at the presidential level, which is not mirrored in the persistent Democratic domination of House elections. He finds contrary to Ladd, however, that differences between Protestants and Catholics are still salient, particularly if one disaggregates Protestants to focus on white Protestants, a procedure recommended by Greeley (1978) nearly a decade ago. By including the substantially more Democratically oriented black Protestants in an overall Protestant category, Ladd may have artificially reduced the intergroup spread and found a spurious convergence trend. Dionne (1981: 316) by contrast discovers a 17 percentage difference between Catholics and white Protestants that is much closer to "the old religious divide."

Another scholar emphasizing electoral volatility is Lopatto (1985), who has used the ANES Michigan data for a comprehensive study of religion and presidential voting from 1960 to 1980. Overall, Lopatto views Catholic voters as having changed from a disproportionately working class group to one of the most economically successful religious denominations. Generally they have been attracted to Republican candidates on economic issues, but not on foreign policy grounds. As to the latter, Catholics have shifted from the strong anti-communist views of the pre-Vatican II church to the moderate-to-liberal views of the institutional church in the 1970s and 1980s. As such, Catholics are "more open to diplomacy and compromise as an alternative to the use of military force in dealing with our international adversaries" (Lopatto, 1985: 164). A proper combination of issue appeals is, therefore, necessary to win Catholic support, particularly young Catholics in whom both the economic and foreign policy orientations previously mentioned are heightened. Lopatto demonstrates the decline in appeal of mainstream liberals like Muskie, Kennedy, and the late Hubert Humphrey (particularly in the 1968–1972 time period) for Catholic voters.

Since 1968, the respective Democratic tickets have had little appeal for Catholic voters, save for Carter in 1976. Even here, Carter ran behind Humphrey's 1968 record. Lopatto stresses that "the key variable here seems to be the exact nature of the candidate pairing" (p. 88), that majorities must be built anew in every successive election, and "thus the ability to define political issues may be more important than ever in this era of electoral instability" (p. 167). A ticket that would appeal to Catholics appears to be one with a strong leadership image combined with one of foreign policy moderation. The emphasis of the 1988 Democratic candidate Michael Dukakis on economic management, competence, traditional values, and foreign policy moderation constitutes a judicious balance of the necessary political elements particularly attractive to Catholic voters.

The literature on House voting produces three schools of thought: (1) continuity, (2) Democratic domination with Republican gains, and (3) electoral parity. In analyzing voting for the House of Representatives, where personality and candidate image are less critical and incumbency is a more salient political factor, most scholars and analysts find that the Catholic allegiance to the Democrats is strong, but disagree on the degree of commitment. Greeley (1985: 37) makes the strongest case for *Democratic continuity* and finds that "about three-fifths of the Catholics in the country, regardless of what they say their political affiliation is, routinely vote for Democratic congressional and senatorial candidates." Dionne (1981: 323) also emphasizes persistent Catholic Democratic support at the congressional level, and even suggests that "if Jimmy Carter had won just those Reagan-voting Catholics who supported Democratic congressional candidates, he would have won a substantial Democratic majority."

Reichley (1985b), on the other hand, detects *Democratic domination with Republican gains* at the House level. He suggests that Catholics are still pro-Democratic in House voting, but cites the 55 percent Catholic Democratic vote outcome in 1984 in the CBS-New York Times exit poll as a manifestation of some erosion of support. Reichley's contention is not that Catholics are voting Republican at this level, but rather that "the time when Democratic candidates could count on almost automatic backing from solid majorities of Catholic voters seems irretrievably passed" (p. 32).

Finally, Petrocik (1987: 370) presents a picture of *electoral parity*. He uses Market Opinion Research surveys and goes so far as to argue that the Catholic House vote achieved parity between the two parties with the Republicans receiving 53 percent of it in 1986. These empirical claims need to be tested against other findings. Our testing begins with a historical overview of Catholic presidential and House voting, as revealed in ANES data from 1952 to 1986, followed by observations based on supplemental statewide data for other political offices in 1984 and 1986.

HISTORICAL OVERVIEW

The data on presidential elections are presented in Table 7.2 and are clearly subject to candidate images and short-term forces. They underscore though that Republicans are far more successful in capturing the presidential vote than their party identification support would suggest, winning six of the past nine elections. In these elections, only once did a majority of white Protestants support the Democratic candidate and that was Lyndon Johnson in 1964. Catholics, by contrast, have recorded higher levels of support for the Democratic nominee in six of the nine elections, the exceptions being 1972, 1980, and 1984. In all nine elections, Catholics were considerably more supportive of the Democratic ticket than white Protestants and the Catholic Democratic edge ranged from a low of 10 percent in 1980 to a high of 45 percent in John F. Kennedy's narrow 1960 victory. While Catholics are not solid and consistent Democratic voters at the presidential level, they are continually more Democratic than both white Protestants and the nation overall. Thus, in 1984, for example, the Catholic Democratic vote was only 45 percent, but this was higher than the 41 percent national Democratic vote or the 28 percent white Protestant Democratic vote. Still, the Democrats no longer have the strong edge among Catholics that they held in the Franklin Roosevelt and Truman eras, and while the Catholic vote leans Democratic it can not be taken for granted and must be cultivated anew in each presidential contest.

If the presidential vote is marked by volatility, voting for the House of Representatives is less so. The data appear in Table 7.3. The Republicans had an edge in 1952, but the Democrats have dominated House voting since 1954. Democratic support reached a high of 68 percent in the Johnson landslide of 1964 and an impressive 60 percent in the 1974 Watergate midterm contest. A majority of white Protestants voted Democratic only in the strong Democratic years of the 1958 recession, 1964 presidential landslides, and the 1974 Watergate contest. They also voted slightly Democratic in the 1978 midterm that was not marked by salient short-term forces. Overall, white Protestants tend to vote Republican at the House level, but at lower percentages than their presidential balloting. Catholics, on the other hand, have voted Democratic in every congressional election since 1952, with a high of 78 percent in 1960 and 72 percent in 1974, and lows of 55 percent in 1952 and 58 percent in 1980 and 1984, respectively. In the recession-ridden 1982 contest, Catholic Democratic support jumped to an impressive 66 percent. In 1986, contrary to the findings of Petrocik, nearly two out of three Catholics voted Democratic (65 percent), suggesting support for Greeley's emphasis on Democratic continuity.

Table 7.2
Presidential Vote by Religion, 1952 to 1984 (in percentages)

Year	Party of Presidential Vote	Nation	White Protestants	Catholics	Catholic Demo. Edge
1952	Democrat	42	34	50	+16
	Republican	53	61	43	
	Other	*	*	0	
	Undecided	5	5	7	
1956	Democrat	39	33	48	+15
	Republican	53	60	44	
	Other	0	*	0	
	Undecided	8	6	9	
1960	Democrat	44	30	75	+45
	Republican	50	64	23	
	Other	*	*	0	
	Undecided	5	5	3	
1964	Democrat	71	58	75	+17
	Republican	22	33	18	
	Other	*	*	0	
	Undecided	7	9	7	
1968	Democrat	38	21	47	+26
	Republican	39	53	31	
	Wallace	12	11	9	
	Other	*	*	0	
	Undecided	11	15	12	
1972	Democrat	28	18	31	+13
	Republican	61	73	56	
	Other	1	1	1	
	Undecided	10	9	12	
1976	Democrat	48	39	53	+14
	Republican	48	58	43	
	Other	2	1	2	
	Undecided	3	2	3	
1980	Democrat	39	30	40	+10
	Republican	50	60	48	
	Other	10	9	9	
	Undecided	2	1	3	
1984	Democrat	41	28	45	+17
	Republican	57	69	53	
	Other	1	1	1	
	Undecided	1	2	1	

Source: American National Election Studies, Center for Political Studies, University of Michigan.
*Less than 1 percent.

Table 7.3
House Vote by Religion, 1952 to 1986 (in percentages)

Year	Party of House Vote	Nation	White Protestants	Catholics	Catholic Demo. Edge
1952	Democrat	49	42	55	+13
	Republican	51	58	45	
1956	Democrat	53	46	61	+15
	Republican	47	54	39	
1958	Democrat	60	52	72	+20
	Republican	40	48	28	
1960	Democrat	54	43	78	+35
	Republican	45	56	21	
1962	Democrat	58	47	75	+28
	Republican	42	53	25	
1964	Democrat	68	58	72	+14
	Republican	31	42	28	
1966	Democrat	57	47	68	+21
	Republican	42	53	32	
1968	Democrat	56	43	61	+18
	Republican	43	57	39	
1970	Democrat	56	48	57	+9
	Republican	43	52	42	
1972	Democrat	56	47	66	+19
	Republican	44	53	34	
1974	Democrat	60	52	72	+20
	Republican	38	47	28	
1976	Democrat	55	46	62	+16
	Republican	42	51	36	
1978	Democrat	58	51	64	+13
	Republican	41	49	35	
1980	Democrat	54	45	58	+13
	Republican	45	54	39	
1982	Democrat	56	47	66	+19
	Republican	42	51	33	
1984	Democrat	53	44	58	+14
	Republican	44	53	38	
1986	Democrat	59	49	65	+16
	Republican	39	50	34	

Source: American National Election Studies, Center for Political Studies, University of Michigan. Not available in 1954.

What is evident is that Catholics remain highly Democratic at the House level, with respectable but lower levels of support than they recorded throughout most of the 1950s, 1960s, and 1970s. Still, *the Democratic Catholic edge* relative to white Protestants emerges in all congressional elections since 1952, with highs of 28 percent in 1962 and 25 percent in 1960, and lows of 9 percent in 1970, 13 percent in 1952, 1978, and 1980, 14 percent in 1964 and 1984, and 16 percent in 1986. Compared with white Protestants, Catholics are quite Democratic in House voting. Having presented this overview, we are struck by what may be significant differences between white Protestants and Catholic voters, and want to be sure that these differences are real and will not disappear with the introduction of control variables, an issue of concern in both our data and methods and findings sections of this chapter.

Although constraints of data availability lead us to focus on voting for two offices, the presidency and the House, some observations can be made on Catholic and Protestant differences for statewide voting in both 1984 and 1986 (Kenski, 1988). The data used are the NBC News 1984 and 1986 exit polls, and appear in Table 7.4. This table focuses on Protestant and Catholic differences and the extent of split-ticket voting. Owing to the form in which the data are published, the Protestant category is an overall one that combines black and white respondents. Such a data aggregation tends to increase the Democratic percentage for Protestants and to reduce the Protestant and Catholic differences.

Because of the paucity of gubernatorial races in a presidential year, the 1984 office comparison is between the statewide presidential and Senate vote in eight states. As the data demonstrate, the Democratic presidential candidate fared poorly and lost the Protestant vote to Reagan in all eight states, including his home state Minnesota where he registered his highest Protestant support percentage (45 percent). Mondale also lost the Catholic vote in six of the eight states, carrying only Minnesota (53 percent) and Massachusetts (52 percent). In all eight races, the Catholic Democratic percentage exceeded the Protestant one from a high of 14 percent in Massachusetts (52 to 38 percent) to a low of 1 percent in Illinois (38 to 37 percent).

Senate and gubernatorial races are, of course, affected by incumbency. The test of a group's partisan strength is its willingness to vote for its historically preferred party's candidate even when paired against a popular incumbent of the other party. Catholics voted for the Democratic candidate in six of the eight contests, and defected to popular Republican incumbents twice (Minnesota and Virginia). Protestants, by contrast, gave the Democrats the edge in only one of the eight races, voting for a popular Democratic incumbent in New Jersey. Once again, the Catholic Democratic

Table 7.4
Split-Ticket Voting Patterns for Protestants and Catholics in 1984 and 1986 (percent of Democratic votes)

1984		PRESIDENT			SENATE			OUTCOMES	
STATE	INCUM-BENT	PROT.	CATH.	INCUM-BENT	PROT.	CATH.	PROT.	CATH.
Massachusetts	R	38	52	Open	45	61	RR	DD
New Jersey	R	28	37	Demo	51	64	RD	RD
Illinois	R	37	38	Repub	42	52	RR	RD
Michigan	R	34	39	Demo	47	56	RR	RD
Minnesota	R	45	53	Repub	38	43	RR	DR
N. Carolina	R	37	40	Repub	47	52	RR	RD
Texas	R	28	48	Open	33	54	RR	RD
Virginia	R	32	36	Repub	26	30	RR	RR

1986		GOVERNOR			SENATE			OUTCOMES	
STATE	INCUM-BENT	PROT.	CATH.	INCUM-BENT	PROT.	CATH.	PROT.	CATH.
New York	D	62	69	R	38	37	DR	DR
Pennsylvania	Open	40	64	R	37	53	RR	DD
Illinois	R	37	48	D	58	71	RD	RD
Iowa	R	46	57	R	33	45	RR	DR
Florida	Open	40	42	R	51	52	RD	RD
California	R	32	43	D	44	54	RR	RD

Sources: NBC News 1984, 1986.

edge appeared in all eight races from a high of 21 percent for a Texas open seat (54 to 33 percent) to a low of 4 percent in Virginia (30 to 26 percent), where the Republican incumbent won handily.

An examination of the 1984 outcomes suggests that Protestant voters are Republican inclined (even when black Protestants are included in the data) and voted Republican for both the presidency and Senate in seven of the eight states, splitting the ticket only in New Jersey. Catholics, on the other hand, tended to split their tickets in six of the eight states, voting straight Democratic only in Massachusetts and straight Republican only in Virginia.

In 1986 data exist for six states in which there was both a gubernatorial and a Senate race, an office pairing that constitutes a sensitive measure of ticket splitting. In the gubernatorial races, Catholics gave the Democrats a majority in only three of the six races (two incumbent and one open seat). Protestants by comparison voted Democratic in only one of the six match-ups, giving their support to popular New York Democrat Mario Cuomo. Again, the Catholic Democratic edge over Protestants appeared in all six contests from a high of + 24 percent in the open seat Pennsylvania clash (64 to 40 percent) to a low of + 2 percent in the open seat Florida encounter (42 to 40 percent). All Senate races had incumbents (four Republican, two Democrat). Catholics gave Democrats a majority in four of the six elections, while Protestants supported the Democratic incumbents in only two. The Catholic Democratic edge over Protestants occurred in five of the six races. It was highest (+ 16 percent) in Pennsylvania and lowest (− 1 percent) in New York.

The gubernatorial-Senate pairing is probably the most sensitive indicator of the willingness of a particular voting group to split the ticket. In 1986 Protestant voters (black and white combined) split their tickets in three races and voted straight Republican in three. Catholic voters, on the other hand, may not be as Democratic as some have assumed as they split their ticket in five of the six contests, voting straight Democratic only in Pennsylvania. Future research should definitely focus on both the Senate and gubernatorial arenas for a comprehensive assessment of voting behavior for various groups.

DATA AND METHODS

In order to provide a rigorous test for Protestant and Catholic voting differences, our analyses for the most part will use the large Protestant category (blacks and whites combined) to make it more difficult to find statistical differences between the two religious categories. In the cross-tabulations that provide the data for our analyses we contrast Catholics with Protestants controlling various other known correlates of voting behavior and differences in yearly marginal distributions. Jews are not included as there are too few cases for reliable parameter estimations when distributed across multiple categories of religion, year, and control variables. We recognize that any differences among various individual Protestant denominations will not be detected because of this aggregation but, again, there are too few cases to use the separate denominations in multi-way cross-tabulations.

The data we utilize are the 1980, 1982, 1984, and 1986 American National Election Studies conducted by the Center for Political Studies of the Institute for Social Research at the University of Michigan. The data for each of the four surveys were collected just after the fall national elections. The data sets are especially useful for the present research because sampling frames were selected and questionnaire items were constructed in the same manner as each survey was administered.

The data analysis technique we use is the fitting of standard hierarchical log-linear models (L. A. Goodman, 1970, 1972; Feinberg, 1980), which assume that variables need only be measured nominally. Such qualitative data are certainly characteristic of the variables we have selected from the ANES surveys. Log-linear models are described in terms of the combination of one-way (a single variable), two-way (the association between two variables), three-way (the interaction among three variables), or n-way (the interactions among n variables) marginals, which most closely reproduce the observed cell frequencies in a n-way table. Each model produces "expected" or "fitted" cell frequencies that are compared to the observed frequencies with the likelihood-ratio chi-square statistic, L^2. The L^2 for a particular model is compared to the chi-square distribution for its appropriate degrees of freedom. A model is considered to "fit" the data if the probability of obtaining its L^2 is greater than .05. We refer to a "preferred" model as one that fits and, also, does not exclude any marginal relationships with L^2 probabilities less than .05. Except when noted, the preferred models presented below were chosen from a backward elimination variable-selection algorithm (Benedetti and Brown, 1978).

When discussing particular log-linear models we refer to the variables involved with bracketed letters. For example, if the letter "P" is assigned to presidential vote, "R" to religion, "Y" to year, an "B" to race, the model [PR] [PB] indicates that there is an association between religion and presidential vote and between race and presidential vote but religion and race are independent, given presidential vote. The model [PR] [PB] [RB] includes, in addition, an association between religion and race and corresponds to the hypothesis of no three-way interaction among the variables religion, race, and presidential vote. The model [PRB] indicates that the three-way interaction is present.

FINDINGS

We look first at the presidential vote. The ANES estimate for 1980 was 50.8 percent for the Republican Reagan, 39.4 percent for the Democrat Carter, 8.3 percent for the Independent Anderson, and 1.4 percent for other candidates. In 1984 the ANES estimates were 57.7 percent for Reagan, 41.4 percent for the Democrat Mondale, and 0.9 percent for other candidates. Table 7.5 presents the results from the hierarchical log-linear analysis of presidential vote, year, and religion. There are 2,051 cases in the table, of which Protestants and Catholics reporting presidential preferences in the

1980 sample total 839 while there are 1,212 similar cases from the 1984 sample. We use the conventional "odds" and "odds ratios" to describe the relationships among variables. The top panel of Table 7.5 displays the observed frequencies. The odds on voting "Democrat" are calculated by dividing the Democrat frequency by the frequency for another category of the party vote variable. Odds of 1.0 represent the point at which there would be even odds on voting for a particular party compared to the other. Since Reagan easily won both elections, the observed odds on voting Democrat as opposed to Republican are, of course, less than 1.0. The observed odds on voting Democrat are smaller for Protestants than Catholics. The odds ratio for religion and party vote can be calculated by dividing the Catholic odds by the Protestant odds (although less rounding error occurs if it is calculated from the appropriate four cells of the table).

The odds on Catholics voting Democrat in 1980 were 1.1 times higher than the odds for Protestants. By 1984 this observed odds ratio had grown to 1.4. This suggests a possible three-way interaction of presidential party vote [P], religion [R], and year [Y] with Catholics increasing their Democratic voting preference. The botton panel of Table 7.5 presents the expected frequencies under the preferred model [PR] [RY] ($L^2 = 4.18$; d.f. $= 2$; $p = .12$). There is no three-way interaction and, in addition, no association of presidential party vote and year. The nature of the religion by year association [RY] is that there are significantly (in a statistical sense) more Catholics than Protestants in the 1984 ANES sample than the 1980 sample. The finding that is the primary focus of the present research is that there is a constant odds ratio for the religion by party vote association [PR] over the two elections. Catholics' support for the Democratic party in the 1980 and 1984 presidential elections remained consistent with the Catholic odds on voting Democrat 1.3 times higher than the odds on Protestants voting Democrat.

Results in Table 7.5 also indicate that Catholics were less likely to vote for Anderson in the 1980 election as opposed to voting Democrat. We performed a parallel set of analyses to that reported here with multi-way tables including Anderson in 1980 and structural zeros for 1984. The results for the vast majority of our control variables from those analyses are essentially the same as reported below, but since there are so few Catholics who voted for Anderson in the 1980 ANES sample we simply do not have enough respondents to distribute across multiple categories of some control variables, and we continue to feel comfortable with the reliability of parameter estimates. Therefore, we will not present further results from analyses that include the Anderson category.

Despite the assertion of some that the party that controls the executive branch controls the tenor of political discourse and governmental public

Table 7.5
Observed and Expected Frequencies of Presidential Party Vote by Religion and Election Year*

		Party of Presidential Vote			Odds on Voting Democrat			
Year	Religion	Republican	Democrat	Anderson	Democrat: Republican	Odds Ratio	Democrat: Anderson	Odds Ratio
Observed Frequencies:								
1980	Protestant	333.00	248.00	40.00	0.74	1.12	6.20	0.73
	Catholic	108.00	90.00	20.00	0.83		4.50	
1984	Protestant	523.00	311.00	0.00	0.59	1.43	0.00	
	Catholic	204.00	174.00	0.00	0.85		0.00	
Expected Frequencies Under Preferred Model:								
1980	Protestant	351.47	229.52	40.00	0.65	1.29	5.74	0.79
	Catholic	107.24	90.75	20.00	0.84		4.54	
1984	Protestant	504.53	329.48	0.00	0.65	1.29	0.00	
	Catholic	204.76	173.25	0.00	0.84		0.00	

*See text for a description of the preferred model in the bottom panel.

policy, the party that controls the Senate and/or the House of Representatives has considerable influence. Therefore, it is important also to analyze the Catholic vote for these races. There are not enough cases to feel confident about results from analyses of the Senate party vote with the ANES data but the House vote can be examined. We are fortunate in that we now have two more years of observations, 1982 and 1986, with which to investigate any over-time changes. Prior to the addition of control variables to the analyses, there are a total of 3,319 Catholics and Protestants reporting candidate preferences for House of Representatives contests of which 747 come from the 1980 ANES sample, 638 from 1982, 1,046 from 1984, and 888 from 1986.

The top panel of Table 7.6 presents the three-way cross-classification of religion by House vote [H] by year. An important difference from the presidential vote table is immediately apparent. The observed odds on voting Democrat are all greater than 1.0 (although very close to 1.0 for Protestants in presidential election years) reflecting both that, in the aggregate, respondents reported more Democratic House votes than Republican in the ANES samples and that the Democratic party did have a majority in the House of Representatives throughout the 1980s. The observed odds on Catholics voting Democrat are 1.36 to 1.76 times higher than the odds for Protestants. When this odds ratio is computed from expected frequencies of the preferred model [HR] [HY] [RY] (L^2 = 1.10; d.f. = 3; p = .78) it is a constant 1.51 for all four elections. As with the religion by year by presidential party vote results, we find a statistically significant religion by year association [RY] with the distribution of Catholics compared to Protestants in the ANES samples highest in 1984, then lower in 1986, lower still in 1982, and lowest in 1980. Unlike the presidential party vote analyses we find a significant party of House vote by year association [HY] with the overall sample odds on voting Democrat lower in presidential election years and higher in the off years. The odds on voting Democrat increased by a factor of 1.1 from 1980 to 1982, decreased by a factor of 0.9 from 1982 to 1984, and increased by a factor of 1.3 from 1984 to 1986. Clearly, the Reagan success in 1980 and 1984 helped the Republican party in the House of Representatives contests. Despite these marginal shifts in the relative numbers of Catholics and Protestants over the four elections and the carryover that Reagan popularity had on party of House vote in the presidential years, the important finding here is that Catholic support for Democrats in the House of Representative contests has remained constant in the 1980s.

Through the first four national elections of the 1980s our results indicate that, in aggregate, Catholics are unwavering in their tendency to support Democrats over Republicans. They remain a major part of the Democratic coalition. Yet individual Catholics may possess other characteristics that, as

Table 7.6
Observed and Expected Frequencies of House of Representatives Party Vote by Religion and Election Year*

Year	Religion	Party of House Vote		Odds on Voting Democrat	Odds Ratio
		Republican	Democrat		
Observed Frequencies:					
1980	Protestant	270.00	290.00	1.07	1.36
	Catholic	76.00	111.00	1.46	
1982	Protestant	229.00	257.00	1.12	1.76
	Catholic	51.00	101.00	1.98	
1984	Protestant	361.00	363.00	1.01	1.55
	Catholic	126.00	196.00	1.55	
1986	Protestant	279.00	371.00	1.33	1.46
	Catholic	81.00	157.00	1.94	
Expected Frequencies Under Preferred Model:					
1980	Protestant	273.67	286.33	1.05	1.51
	Catholic	72.33	114.67	1.59	
1982	Protestant	224.91	261.09	1.16	1.51
	Catholic	55.09	96.91	1.76	
1984	Protestant	359.88	364.12	1.01	1.51
	Catholic	127.12	194.88	1.53	
1986	Protestant	280.54	369.45	1.32	1.51
	Catholic	79.46	158.55	1.99	

*See text for a description of the preferred model in the bottom panel.

aggregate categories in their own right, may predispose individuals to specific party voting patterns. It is important to assess the stability of our findings when these other characteristics are taken into account. In the remainder of this section we summarize results from the hierarchical log-linear analyses of four-way cross-classifications of religion by party vote (both presidential and House) by year by a series of control variables. Rather than present separate tables of expected frequencies from these analyses (which consume considerable space but reveal little information about statistically significant associations that cannot be summarized in the text), we instead present Table 7.7, which indicates the strength of the religion by party vote association after control variables are successively

Table 7.7
The Effect of Various Control Variables on the Relationship between Religion and Party of Reported Vote for Presidential and House of Representative Elections, 1980 to 1986

		ODDS RATIO FOR RELIGION by PARTY VOTE ASSOCIATION	
	CONTROL VARIABLE	Presidential Vote	House Vote
	none	1.30^a	1.51
[R]	Race	1.77	1.81
[U]	Union Household	$1.00/1.22^b$	1.46
[C]	Church Attendance	1.30	1.53
[I]	Family Income	1.34	1.53
[A]	Age	1.30	$varies^c$

[a]Values are interpreted as: "The Catholic odds on voting Democrat are (value) times higher than the odds for Protestants."
[b]See text for description of comparative models.
[c]Three-way interaction with age. See text for explanation.

introduced one at a time. The first row repeats the odds ratios without control variables, which we have discussed above. The values in Table 7.7 should only be considered significant at one decimal point, but we have presented them with two decimal points to emphasize the fact that the relationship between party vote and religion is barely affected by the majority of the control variables.

Perhaps the most important variable to control for is race [B] because blacks, like Catholics, are considered a major part of the Democratic coalition. In fact, previous researchers have taken black Democratic support as a given in their analyses and simply removed blacks from their samples (Greeley, 1978, 1985; Dionne, 1981; Lopatto, 1985). As there are few black Catholics, that research strategy is unlikely to have altered findings in the earlier research. It is not replicated in the present research even though our variable selection yields only 8 black Catholics in the 1980 analyses, 7 in 1982, 13 in 1984, and 7 in 1986. With respect to the party of the presidential vote the preferred model includes the four two-way associations [PR] [PB] [RY] [RB], which fits relatively well ($L^2 = 7.45$; d.f. $= 7$; p $= .38$). Based upon the expected frequencies from this model, blacks are 5.8 times more likely to be Protestant than are whites. Again, we find that there are 1.3 times more Catholics than Protestants in the 1984 compared to the 1980 sample. Blacks, as expected, were overwhelmingly Democratic in their party preference, being nearly 24 times more likely to vote for Carter or Mondale than Reagan. After controlling for race, the religion by presidential party vote association [PR] becomes stronger with the odds ratio increasing to 1.8.

Turning now to the effect controlling for race has on the religion and House vote association we see very similar findings from the preferred model [HR] [HB] [RB] [RY] [BY] ($L^2 = 15.34$; d.f. = 16; p = .5). We find the same marginal changes in the number of Catholics and Protestants over the four elections that we discussed above. (This religion by year association [RY] is a part of all the preferred models for both presidential and House party votes, regardless of the control variable involved. Consequently, we will not discuss it again.) The odds on blacks voting Democratic are smaller than in the presidential vote, although they are still very high compared to the odds for whites (11.0). It is not that blacks are less Democratic at the House than the presidential level, but rather that other components of the Democratic coalition are more likely to register their partisanship at the House level. We find the same result that controlling for race increases the odds ratio of religion and party vote to 1.8 and this ratio is constant over the four elections. Together these results for party of presidential and House vote indicate the strength of the likelihood for both blacks and Catholics to vote Democratic. If the racial distribution were equalized for Catholics and Protestants, Catholics would be more Democratic in their voting patterns than they are. This finding reinforces our historical trend data, wherein white Protestants were contrasted to Catholics.

Another important part of the Democratic coalition has been organized labor. The hierarchical long-linear analysis of presidential party vote, religion, year, and union household [U] yielded the preferred model [PU] [RY] [RU] [YU] whose fit is $L^2 = 8.46$; d.f. = 7; p = .29. The fact that union membership had decreased in the early 1980s is revealed by the result that the odds that a respondent in the ANES surveys was living in a non-union household was 1.2 times higher in 1984 than in 1980. There is a strong association between party vote and union household status [PU], with the odds on voting Democrat for members of union households being 2.1 times higher than the odds for non-union household members. There is also a strong association of religion and union household [RU]. The odds that Catholics live in a union household are 1.7 times higher than the odds for Protestants.

After controlling for union household membership, the association between religion and party vote [PR] under this preferred model is no longer statistically significant. Using conventional levels of statistical significance we would be forced to conclude that the religion and party vote association is explained by Catholics being more likely to live in union households. However, the L^2 change to remove this association (.0536) was only slightly higher than the conventional level (.0500). When the religion by party vote association is allowed to be a part of the model, we find that controlling for union environment slightly reduces the odds ratio from 1.30 to 1.22. We removed year from the analysis to investigate the relationships between religion, union household membership, and presidential party vote in the 1980 and 1984 elections separately. The preferred model for the three-way table in 1980 has no significant religion and party vote association (for the partial association, $L^2 = 0.10$; d.f. = 1; p = .76). In 1984, however, the partial association is strong ($L^2 = 5.23$; d.f. = 1; p = .02). Thus we are not ready to accept that the religion and party vote association is explained by union household membership, although that appears to be the case in the first Reagan election.

When party of House vote is analyzed instead of presidential vote, we find no ambivalent situation as to the effect of religion on party vote. Here the fit of the preferred model [HR] [HU] [HY] [RU] [RY] is $L^2 = 15.78$; d.f. = 16; p = .47. The partial association of religion and vote [HR] is quite strong ($L^2 = 21.73$; d.f. = 1; p < .001). Although the odds on voting Democrat for union household members are 2.1 times the odds for non-union households and the odds on Catholics living in union households are 1.6 times the odds for Protestants, the odds on Catholics voting Democrat remain at 1.5 times the odds for Protestants.

In the public media arena at least, religious behavior as well as affiliation have been important matters of concern during the 1980s. Therefore, we controlled for self-reported religiosity with church attendance [C]. We trichotomized the variable into three categories: those who never attended, those who occasionally attended (from a few times a year to once or twice a month), and those who regularly attended (almost weekly or more often). For the presidential party vote analysis the fit of the preferred model [R] [RC] [RY] is $L^2 = 22.83$; d.f. = 14; p = .06). Catholics have higher levels of regular church attendance as has been reported elsewhere (Hout and Greeley, 1987). The expected frequencies from this model indicate that the odds on Catholics attending occasionally rather than never are 1.5 times the odds for Protestants, while the odds on Catholics attending regularly rather than occasionally are 1.9 times the odds for Protestants. But religiosity is not found to have an effect on presidential party voting preferences. The odds on Catholics voting Democrat remain 1.3 times higher than the odds for Protestants.

Controlling for church attendance along with the cross-classification of religion, House party vote, and year yielded one of only three preferred models in our analyses with significant three-way interactions. The fit of the preferred model [HCY] [HR] [RC] [RY] is $L^2 = 15.09$; d.f. = 17; p = .59. The three-way interaction [HCY] indicates that the effect of church attendance on House party vote is different in different election years. Surprisingly, while the three-way interaction is certainly statistically significant ($L^2 = 16.09$; d.f. = 6; p = .014), both of the partial associations for attendance by House vote [HC] and attendance by year [CY] are not ($L^2 = 0.84$; d.f. = 1; p = .656 and $L^2 = 5.53$; d.f. = 6; p = .477, respectively). To illustrate the nature of the interaction, the reader is reminded that for each category of church attendance, there are six contrasts with which House party vote odds ratios can be calculated, one for each pair of years. Since it makes more sense to focus on change over the evolving history of the 1980s, we generally report only on the three odds ratios for the consecutive elections.

For regular church attenders, the odds on voting Democratic increased from 1980 to 1982 by a factor of 1.2, decreased from 1982 to 1984 by a factor of 0.8, and increased from 1984 to 1986 by a factor of 1.7. In essence, the highly religious were more likely to vote for Republican House members in presidential election years than in the off-year elections. One would be tempted to explain this finding as statistical confirmation of the public support for Reagan by the fundamentalist Christian right, but we are focusing on the House vote here and we found no statistically significant effect of church attendance on presidential party vote. The odds on voting Democratic for occasional church attenders were 1.1 times higher in 1982 than in 1980, 1.1 times higher in 1984 than in 1982, and 1.1 times higher in 1986 than in 1984—a small gradual increase in Democratic support. For those who never attend church, the odds on voting Democratic decreased from 1980 to 1982 by a factor of 0.7, decreased from 1982 to 1984 by a factor of 0.8, and decreased further from 1984 to 1986 by a factor of 0.8. Petrocik and Steeper (1987) have reported that more frequent church attendance for voters overall is associated with increased Republican party identification during the 1980s, a finding that Hout and Greeley (1987) would dispute for Catholics. In a very recent and comprehensive study of church attendance in the United States, Hout and Greeley use the Rasch models advocated by Duncan to demonstrate that a latent commitment variable called loyalty produces a strong association between church attendance and Democratic partisanship for Catholics. Our focus, however, is on voting rather than party identification. Here we find that the results substantiate the Hout and Greeley perspective. More frequent church attendance is found to be associated with increasing Democratic instead of Republican House voting during the 1980s for Catholics. Moreover, the constant odds ratio of Catholics being 1.5 times more likely to vote Democratic than Republican reveals no weakening of Catholic support.

The preferred model for the presidential party vote analysis when income is made a control variable is [PR] [PY] [PI] [RY] [RI] [IY] ($L^2 = 17.05$; d.f. = 13; p = .20). We divided the respondents into four categories: under $12,000, $12,000 to $24,999, $25,000 to $34,999, and $35,000 and over. The nature of the year by income association [IY] is that reported incomes were lower in 1984 than in 1980. That is, the odds of being in the higher of any two income categories instead of the lower were smaller in 1984 than in 1980 except for the lowest two categories where there were slightly higher odds (1.1) of being in the $12K to $25K category in 1984 as opposed to 1980. The odds ratios for the religion by income association [RI] show that Catholic respondents were slightly more likely to be in higher income categories than Protestants. The biggest difference is between the lowest two categories where the odds for Catholics being in the $12K to $25K category as opposed to the under $12K category were 1.4 times higher than the odds for Protestants. The analogous odds ratio dropped to 1.1 for both the middle two categories ($12K to $25K compared to $25K to $35K) and the top two categories ($25K to $35K compared to over $35K). Our results confirm previous research on the income and party of presidential vote relationship [PI] that as income increases the odds on voting Republican increase (Dionne, 1981). The odds on voting Republican are 1.8 times higher for the $12K to $25K income category compared to the under $12K category, 1.3 times higher for the $25K to $35K category compared to the $12K to $25K category, and 1.5 times higher for the over $35K category compared to the $25K to $35K category. Only respondents from the under $12K income category voted more Democratic; but since Democratic voting went down in 1984, the odds for Protestants in this lowest category in 1984 are about even on party vote. Nevertheless, after controlling for income, Catholic odds on voting Democrat are still 1.3 times higher than the odds for Protestants. The importance of this unwavering Democratic support among Catholics is underscored further in that the preferred model includes a significant year by party vote association [PY] (although this association is not present when any other control variables are involved) with the odds on voting Democrat in 1984 being only 0.8 times as high as the 1980 odds.

For party of House vote, the results when income is controlled for parallel the results of the presidential vote analyses. The preferred model includes the same two-way associations that were significant in that analyses. The fit of the preferred model [HR] [HI] [HY] [RI] [RY] [IY] is $L^2 = 20.97$; d.f. = 33; p = .948. The higher odds on voting Democrat for Catholics still persist and, again, are constant over the four elections. The lowest income category (under $12K) voted overwhelmingly Democrat in all four elections. Only Catholics among the middle two income categories ($12K to $25K and $25K to $35K) have higher Democratic voting odds in the first three elections. But since the overall House party vote became more Democratic in 1986 (see the discussion of the [HY] association above), both Protestants and Catholics had higher odds on voting Democrat in all but the highest category (over $35K) at the time of that election. Focusing on party identification rather than voting, Petrocik and Steeper (1987) found that a strong effect of income on party identification resulted in Catholics turning Republican when their family incomes surpassed $20,000. Our results fail to support this finding as the preferred models for both the presidential and House vote analyses do not include a three-way interaction of religion, income, and party vote. We also analyzed tables with seven income categories (additional cutoffs at $7,000, $17,000, and $50,000). The results were the same as those reported here.

Recent research by Norpoth (1987) has suggested that by the time of the 1984 national election, the youngest voters had become more Republican in their party identification. Using ANES and New York Times/CBS survey data, he finds that 49 percent of young adults identified as Republican in 1984 compared to 35 percent of young adults in 1960 and 29 percent in 1952. This stimulated our interest whether the age variable would affect our general findings on religion and voting. When we controlled for age [A] in the presidential party vote analysis with six age categories (18 to 29, 30 to 39, 40 to 49, 50 to 59, 60 to 69, and 70 and over), the preferred model was [PR] [RAY], which fit at $L^2 = 27.03$; d.f. $= 22$; p $= .21$. The religion by age by year interaction [RAY] is significant at $L^2 = 12.27$; d.f. $= 5$; p $= .03$). But the interaction is not substantively interesting in the context of our research because it does not involve the party of presidential vote variable. We had already discussed above that the distribution of Protestants and Catholics was different in 1984 than in 1980. The only thing new the three-way interaction tells us is that the joint distribution of religion and age was different in the two elections. Of the three partial associations in that interaction, the age and year association is not even statistically significant ($L^2 = 8.97$; d.f. $= 5$; p $= .11$). The important finding here is that controlling for age does not alter the religion and presidential party vote relationship; the Catholic odds on voting Democrat remain 1.3 times higher than the odds for Protestants.

The last statistically significant three-way interaction we encountered in our analyses occurred when we controlled for age in the religion by party of House vote by year table. The fit of the preferred model [HRA] [HY] [RY] [AY] was $L^2 = 52.74$; d.f. $= 48$; p $= .30$. The interaction involves our dependent variable, party vote, and is very substantively interesting because it is the only case in our research where the relationship between religion and House party vote is found to vary depending upon the category of the control variable. Because the partial association of age and party of House vote is not statistically significant ($L^2 = 2.27$; d.f. $= 5$; p $= .81$), we feel confident that describing the interaction in terms of the last sentence does not mask any of its importance. Only for the youngest age category (18 to 29) are the Catholic odds on voting Democrat less than the odds for Protestants. The odds ratio is 0.9. For the next two age categories the odds ratios are higher than the 1.5 that we have generally found when other variables are controlled for: 1.7 for the 30 to 39 category and 2.0 for ages 40 to 49. The odds ratio is 1.5 for ages 50 to 59, it drops to 1.2 for the 60 to 69 category, and rises sharply to 2.6 for those age 70 and older.

We find only weak evidence to extend Norpoth's finding on party identification to voting. There was no association between age and party vote in the preferred model for the presidential party vote analysis, and the partial association of age and party vote was not statistically significant in the three-way interaction of religion, age, and party of House vote. Among the youngest voters, the Catholic odds on voting Democrat in House of Representatives races is slightly smaller than the odds for Protestants (0.9). We will have to wait and see if this translates into Catholic defections from the Democratic party as the population ages but, given the consistency of the Catholic odds when other variables are controlled for, we have little reason to suspect their voting behavior will soon be indistinguishable from Protestants. Contrary to Ladd's convergence proposition, we find that the odds of Catholics voting Democratic for both the presidential and House races is greater than the odds for Protestant throughout the first four elections of the 1980s.

CONCLUSIONS

First, an erosion of the Democratic support by Catholics has clearly occurred since the 1960s. Basically, however, a plurality of Democrats still identify with the Democratic party and support its House candidates. Catholic voters remain centrist across a large spectrum of ideological views, and still appear to be a little left of center, especially in foreign policy issues. Although considerable research still remains to be done on ticket-splitting and statewide voting for the presidency, governor, and Senate, our preliminary research suggests that Catholics are more likely to be ticket-splitters than Protestants. Presidential voting is more volatile, and Republicans have made inroads in recent years, capturing the Catholic vote in three of the last four elections (1972, 1980, and 1984). Catholic identifiers, like other voters, are clearly influenced by short-term forces like candidate personality and issues in presidential contests, forces that can override partisan attachment. Second, no convergence is emerging between Protestants (particularly white Protestants) and Catholic voters, even at the presidential level. Our use of hierarchical log-linear models clearly underscores greater odds of Catholics than Protestants voting Democratic at both the presidential and House levels, even when testing for complex interactions. An examination of our four most recent elections from 1980 to 1986 reveals an image of continuity rather than change in the Catholic vote.

8
The New Christian Right and the Mobilization of the Evangelicals

Clyde Wilcox

During the 1980 and 1984 elections, the leadership of the New Christian Right was highly visible. Representing organizations that span the interstitial zone between religion and politics, these leaders claimed to speak for a constituency of evangelical and fundamentalist Christians on a range of issues, including social, economic, and foreign policy matters. This constituency, which the leadership of the New Christian Right has targeted for mobilization, has been described, along with the goals of these organizations with respect to this target constituency, as

the approximately 50 million evangelicals in the country and in particular the fundamentalist wing of this community. The aim from the beginning was to mobilize a group of people who had traditionally avoided politics because they saw it as dirty, corrupt business . . . by convincing these people that political involvement was a God-given responsibility (Zwier, 1982: 9–10).

Despite the media attention to the leadership of the New Christian Right, the electoral importance of these groups is unclear. The leaders have made two claims that suggest that these groups are a potent force in U.S. politics. First, they claim success in mobilizing their target constituency in the electoral arena, registering millions of voters in both the 1980 and 1984 elections. Second, the leadership of the New Christian Right claims to speak for the large group of evangelical Christians described above, and suggests that they might mobilize the entire community into conservative political action.

The importance of this constituency for U.S. politics has been stressed by some scholars, such as Menendez (1977), who characterized it as "the sleeping giant" of electoral politics. The prospect of this mobilization of the white evangelical community by the organizations of the New Christian

Right has been greeted by skepticism by other scholars, however, including Lipset and Raab (1981), who suggested that evangelicals are a diverse, heterogeneous group with little potential for concerted political action.[1]

Although there has been much speculation concerning the potential of the New Christian Right to appeal to and mobilize the white evangelical community, to date there has been little systematic research on the topic. This research is needed to answer two sets of questions. First, have the evangelicals been mobilized in the most recent elections, and can we attribute this to the New Christian Right? Second, what is the probability that the New Christian Right can expand its support among the white evangelicals, and start a social or political movement?

PREVIOUS RESEARCH

Research on popular support for the New Christian Right has indicated that actual supporters are not particularly numerous. Shupe and Stacey (1983) found that 16 percent of the respondents to their Dallas/Ft. Worth survey held positive evaluations of the Moral Majority. Buell and Sigelman (1985) found that only 11 percent of the respondents to the 1980 CPS National Election Study met their definition of supporter or sympathizer with the Moral Majority, and Sigelman, Wilcox, and Buell (1987) found that support stayed fairly constant between 1980 and 1984. These studies do not address the potential of the New Christian Right to expand its support to the broader evangelical community.

Other studies, however, suggest the potential for such mobilization. Simpson (1983) and Stockton (1984) found a fair degree of support in the population for the Moral Majority platform, and Kellstedt (1988) found support for a number of Moral Majority issue positions among white evangelical Protestants. Such support for the Moral Majority agenda, particularly among evangelicals, suggests that the Christian Right might be able to mobilize white evangelicals more fully.

A larger literature addresses the connection between religion and politics, particularly among evangelicals. Knoke (1976) explored the impact of religious affiliation on partisanship. After tracing this relationship to historical patterns of immigration and party behavior, he examined recent trends in the partisanship of various religious groups. Of particular import to this study is the partisanship of Southern Protestants, which he asserted were primarily fundamentalist. Knoke noted a steady erosion of Democratic identification among this group for 1952 to 1972, with gains for Republicans only in 1972. Knoke concluded that religious affiliation is one of the most important predictors of partisan identification, even after controls for region and stratification. He suggested that the relationship may be the result of theological factors, group identification that is cultivated by the parties, or by denominational socialization.

Beatty and Walter (1982) explored the impact of denominational affiliation on political beliefs, and found a relationship that persisted after controls for socioeconomic status (SES). They speculated that religion may play an even larger role in the structuring of beliefs of the "disinherited" groups, including presumably the lower SES evangelical and fundamentalist Christians.

Smidt (1988c) using doctrinal measures to operationalize a group of evangelical Christians in the 1980 CPS National Election Study, found evidence that this group was mobilized into greater electoral participation in 1980. Comparing several hypotheses (none of which posit a role for the New Christian Right), Smidt concluded that the evangelicals were mobilized by economic issues in 1980. He noted that the evangelicals are a potentially vital group to both parties in the 1980s. Smidt (1987) using both 1980 and 1984 National Election Study data, reported that the mobilization of evangelicals in 1980 was followed by a sharp decline in evangelical participation in 1984, particularly in the South.

Although this research has described in some detail both the New Christian Right and the evangelical Christian community, little research has examined the connection between these two groups. Yet this connection is important for both practical political reasons and for theoretical reasons. The practical political import of the connection is obvious. The relatively small size of the New Christian Right is of little substantive import if it speaks for a larger, potentially sympathetic constituency that is ripe for mobilization.

The connection between the New Christian Right and the evangelical community is also interesting for theoretical reasons. Evangelical Christians are a group that seems ripe for a social or political movement of the type described by Smelsner (1963) as "value oriented." Smelsner suggests that "disinherited peoples" (a category in which he explicitly places fundamentalists) are generally susceptible to value-oriented movements, if there exists a viable means of communication. The television preachers who speak for and in some cases head the organizations of the New Christian Right have a readily available communication network (Hadden and Swann, 1981), one that is supplemented by the rise of direct mail.

Despite this evidence that the evangelicals may be ripe for mobilization, however, there are also theoretical reasons to expect that this mobilization may be difficult. The theology of the evangelicals, particularly among the fundamentalist wing, stresses the need to keep oneself separate from the world. In the past, this has resulted in even lower levels of political participation than the demographic profile of the evangelicals would predict. Moreover, despite Knoke's observation on the changing partisanship of the

Southern Protestants, they remain nominally Democratic. Most of the literature on movements of the Right has found that Republican identification is the best predictor of support for these movements, and the leadership of the New Christian Right is firmly associated with the Republican party. Doctrine and partisanship, then, should pose some barriers to the mobilization of a group that otherwise fits well the theoretical portrait of one ripe for political mobilization.

OPERATIONALIZATION OF GROUPS

The 1980 and 1984 CPS National Election Studies contain items that allow scholars to identify the two groups important to the analysis of this problem: supporters of the New Christian Right and their target constituency, evangelical Christians. Because the political implications of evangelicalism differ for white and black Americans, I have limited this analysis to whites. Respondents were asked to rate a number of social and political groups on an imaginary thermometer, ranging from 0° (extreme coolness) to 100° (extreme warmth). Supporters of the New Christian Right are those individuals who assign a thermometer score that is at least 10° warmer than their mean thermometer rating of all other groups in the survey.[2] This operational definition results in the classification of approximately 11 percent of the white population as supporters of the Christian Right in both 1980 and 1984.

Operationalization of the evangelicals poses a difficult choice.[3] The surveys included two items that permit the identification of these groups on the basis of their theological beliefs, rather than by denominational affiliation. Responses to items on the inerrancy of the scripture and on a "born-again experience" allow us to identify evangelicals among mainline Protestant denominations, as well as among Catholics. This operationalization identifies 206 evangelicals in 1980: 71 are supporters of the New Christian Right, and the remaining 135 constitute the target constituency of the New Christian Right. Using these definitions, the New Christian Right commanded the support of over one-third of the white evangelicals in 1980. Approximately the same percentage of evangelicals supported the Christian Right in 1984, with 202 white evangelicals constituting the target constituency—17 percent of the white population.

This doctrinal definition of the target constituency of the New Christian Right is superior to one based on denominational affiliation for two reasons. First, it enables us to identify those respondents who are predisposed to the message of the New Christian Right by their doctrinal beliefs but are members of mainline Protestant denominations or are Catholics. In many areas of the Midwest and South, mainline denominations such as the nationally liberal Methodists have congregations who are strongly evangelical, even fundamentalist. Moreover, the leadership of the New Christian Right has explicitly targeted conservative and evangelical Catholics for their message. Second, it enables us to eliminate those who belong to an evangelical denomination but who do not themselves hold the doctrinal beliefs that are associated with evangelicalism.

While this definition is superior to one based on denominational affiliation, it is limited to terms of longitudinal utility: to examine the mobilization of evangelicals over time, we need to compare the results of our analysis of the 1980 data with that of earlier surveys, notably 1972 and 1976. Since these doctrinal items do not appear in these earlier surveys, we are forced to rely on a denominational definition for longitudinal analysis. Respondents who report affiliation with denominations classified in the CPS survey as "Neo-Fundamentalist" are identified as fundamentalists or evangelicals. This denominational definition identifies 213 evangelicals in 1980, approximately 18 percent of the sample. The doctrinal definition of evangelicalism will be used throughout most of the analysis that follows, although the denominational definition will be employed for the longitudinal analysis. The differences between the groups identified by these two operational definitions are discussed in Wilcox (1986b).

MOBILIZATION OF VOTERS

The evangelical community seem predisposed to low rates of participation by two factors. First, evangelical doctrine stresses keeping oneself pure and separate from the world, and has traditionally portrayed political activity as a worldly undertaking. This doctrine has been particularly important among the fundamentalist wing of the evangelical community. Doctrinal separatism has been linked to depressed levels of turnout in empirical analysis (Jelen, 1987).

Second, the evangelicals have lower levels of education and income than the rest of the white population. Research on the determinants of voter turnout has suggested that the voting act is highly associated with socioeconomic status. Table 8.1 suggests that on these variables the supporters of the New Christian Right and their target constituency, the white evangelicals, display lower levels of education, income, and occupational status in 1984. In the 1980 data (not presented), evangelicals reported lower levels of SES, while the supporters of the New Christian Right were indistinguishable from the rest of the population.

In addition to SES, turnout is also strongly related to past participation. Voting is somewhat of a habit, and those who have voted often in the past are more likely to do so in the future. In 1980 the white evangelicals were

Table 8.1
Predictors of Participation

	Supporters	Target	Others
Education 1984			
< High School	23%	29%	15%
High School	37%	43%	35%
Some College	26%	19%	28%
College+	14%	10%	22%
Occupation, Head of Household 1984			
Worker	47%	48%	36%
Sales & Clerical	21%	26%	23%
Managerial	20%	11%	16%
Professional	12%	14%	26%
Income 1984			
$0-$12,999	22%	29%	19%
$13,000-$22,999	22%	33%	25%
$23,000-$29,999	33%	22%	29%
$30,000+	23%	15%	29%
Voted in All or Most Past Elections (1980)			
	72%	59%*	70%

Percentage of each group falling into given categories. Starred entries are significantly different from the rest of the population at .05.

significantly less likely than the rest of the population to report having voted in most or all past elections, although the supporters of the New Christian Right were no different from other whites. Unfortunately, this item was not included in the 1984 survey.

The popular portrait of this target constituency of the New Christian Right as being historically disenfranchised seems accurate, but the picture is cloudy concerning the actual supporters of the New Christian Right. In 1980 they resembled the population in education, occupational prestige, and income, and were actually slightly more likely to report voting regularly in the past. In the 1984 data, Moral Majority supporters reported significantly lower levels of education and occupational prestige than other whites.

It is possible that this represents actual change in the composition of support for the New Christian Right. In 1980, when the organizations were less well known, only the better educated respondents may have known enough about the movement to support the Moral Majority. By 1984, after four years of constant media exposure, support may have increased among the less well educated, and declined among those well-educated respondents who were exposed to the consistently negative media coverage afforded to Falwell and the Moral Majority.

The data in Table 8.2 show that the supporters of the New Christian Right and their target constituency both voted in 1980 in greater numbers than the rest of the population, although the differences are not significant. In 1984, however, the turnout rate for white evangelicals dropped precipitously, at the same time that reported vote among non-evangelicals was increasing. Turnout figures alone, however, do not tell us anything about mobilization.

Mobilization can best be examined by comparing turnout rates while holding constant past voting history and demographic variables. Among those who had voted in no or only some previous elections, the supporters of the New Christian Right and their target constituency turned out in 1980 at a rate about 10 percent higher than the rest of the population. Unfortunately, no questions on past turnout were included in the 1984 survey.

Table 8.2
Participation of the New Christian Right and the Evangelicals

	Supporters	Target	Others
Validated Vote			
1984	68%	59%*	71%
Self Report — Participation			
Voted 1984	75%	69%*	81%
Voted 1980	79%	75%	74%
Voted (Recall) 1976	86%	92%	87%
Voted in 1980, When:			
Voted in No or Some Past Elections	44%	33%	31%
Voted in Most or All Past Elections	91%	97%	90%
Turnout, 1984, Adjusted for Demographic Characteristics	78%	72%	73%
Turnout, 1980, Adjusted for Demographic Characteristics	79%	79%	74%
Turnout, 1980, Adjusted for Demographics and Vote History	78%	80%*	72%

Percentages of each group falling in each category. Starred entries are significantly different from the rest of the population at .05.

To fully examine the turnout of these groups, however, we also need to hold constant demographic variables that we know are associated with turnout. Turnout figures will take on more significance when the differences on SES, age, and region are controlled.

Multivariate analyses of covariance were performed on turnout for supporters of the New Christian Right and their evangelical constituency for 1980 and 1984. The control variables included education, income, region, age, and age-squared.[4] Multivariate analysis of covariance produces an estimated mean score for subgroups if the effects of demographic variables are removed. The results indicate that, with demographic variables controlled, both the supporters of the New Christian Right and the evangelicals voted at a rate that is higher than the rest of the population in 1980. A second analysis, including the demographic variables and past vote as covariates, suggested that the evangelicals voted at a significantly higher rate in 1980 than the rest of the population, after controls for demographic variables and vote history. In 1984 the supporters of the Moral Majority again voted at a higher rate than their demographic profile would predict, but the turnout of evangelicals was indistinguishable from that of other whites.

This analysis suggests that the target constituency of the New Christian Right did vote in 1980 in numbers that are greater than would be predicted by demographics and past participation levels, a finding that offers tentative support for the Moral Majority claim of mobilization. The analysis does not tell us, however, when these evangelicals were mobilized, or the extent to which the New Christian Right is responsible for this mobilization. A reasonable alternative hypothesis is that this group was initially brought into the electoral arena by the candidacy of Jimmy Carter in 1976, who, as a Southern Baptist and confessed born-again Christian, was viewed as one of their own. These evangelicals would then have stayed in the electorate for the 1980 election. This alternative view would minimize the role of the organizations of the New Christian Right in the mobilization of this target constituency.

TURNOUT OF DENOMINATIONAL EVANGELICALS

To examine the trends in participation of evangelicals over time, we must examine data from previous CPS National Election Studies. This analysis must rely on the denominational definition of evangelicalism, however, since the belief items did not exist in the previous studies. Moreover, our analysis is limited to the years 1972–84, owing to a change in question wording between 1968 and 1972.[5] This time period should provide us with sufficient data points to identify any recent upturn in participation of the evangelicals, however.

The denominational definition identifies a different subset of respondents than does the doctrinal definition. Compared to evangelicals identified by doctrinal beliefs, the denominational evangelicals are even lower in education and income, more male, and more Southern. They are more Democratic, and have a lower turnout rate in both the 1980 and 1984 elections. These differences remain fairly constant between 1980 and 1984, and there is no reason to believe that these differences have not been constant over the period studied. They should therefore pose no real threat to inference concerning trends. Other studies of political trends among evangelicals have employed a version of the denominational definition (Kellstedt, 1986).

Table 8.3 presents the turnout figures for the denominational evangelicals in the three presidential elections since 1972. This rate climbs sharply in 1976, then drops slightly in 1980. This appears to confirm the alternative hypothesis that evangelicals were drawn into the electorate by the candidacy of Jimmy Carter in 1976, and were not newly mobilized in the 1980 election as the leadership of the New Christian Right suggests. Table 8.3 also presents the turnout figures adjusted for demographics and for past levels of turnout. This analysis again suggests that the real increase in evangelical turnout occurred in 1976, not in 1980. Unlike the unadjusted figures, however, this analysis suggests that turnout for evangelicals continued to increase in 1980, then declined in 1984.

Table 8.3
Turnout History, Denominational Fundamentalists

	1972	1976	1980	1984
Turnout				
Evangelicals	61%	66%	65%	65%
Others	78%**	75%*	75%**	78%**
Turnout, Adjusted for Demographics				
Evangelicals	68%	70%	74%	70%
Others	71%*	71%	71%	75%*
Turnout, Adjusted for Demographics and Vote History				
Evangelicals	68%	71%	75%*	n.d.
Others	71%	71%	69%	n.d.

Turnout rate of each group in each survey. * indicates differences from the rest of the population significant at .05. ** indicates differences significant at .01. n.d. indicates no data available.

Although the adjusted figures might tend to support the contention by the leadership of the New Christian Right that their organizations were influential in mobilizing the evangelical community, this contention merits closer analysis. In all three sets of figures, the biggest increase in the turnout rate of evangelicals was in 1976. Moreover, the unadjusted turnout in 1980 was slightly *lower*, not higher, than in 1976. The increasing adjusted turnout rate for 1980 is a function of the somewhat lower SES and participation history of the evangelicals included in the sample, not any real increase in activity.

It seems, then, that the evangelical community has been mobilized into the electoral arena in the past eight years, but that this mobilization has little to do with the organizations of the New Christian Right. The real increase in participation among this target constituency of the New Christian Right claimed success in mobilizing the evangelicals, but in 1976 when a Southern born-again Baptist headed the Democratic ticket. The evangelicals voted for Carter in 1976 at a rate higher than other whites. The evangelical warmth toward Carter remained a force even in 1980, when the mean feeling thermometer rating assigned to Carter by the evangelicals was nearly 20 points higher than the mean score assigned by other whites after controls for region and partisanship. Indeed, a closer examination reveals that the increase in turnout in 1976 came primarily among Southern evangelicals.

The evangelical community stayed in the electorate in 1980, which pitted a regional favorite son against a popular conservative candidate, but their participation was not caused by support for the New Christian Right. Among the evangelicals in the survey, the turnout rate for those who supported the New Christian Right was the same as that for evangelicals who did not support the New Christian Right in both 1980 and 1984, after controls for demographics.[6] Moreover, support for the New Christian Right as measured by the relative feeling thermometer is not related to either turnout or mobilization among evangelicals (R = .02 and .03, respectively.) After the 1980 election, with Carter no longer on the ticket, Southern evangelical participation dropped sharply (Smidt, 1987).

If the New Christian Right is not responsible for the increased turnout among evangelical Christians, its potential political importance is still not negligible. If the New Christian Right can expand its support among the evangelical community, it could comprise a potent electoral force. If the supporters of the New Christian Right could expand its base to 50 percent of the evangelicals, it would comprise nearly 20 percent of the population, and a somewhat higher proportion of the electorate. The next section will explore the prospects for this expansion of support.

MOBILIZATION OF THE EVANGELICALS: AN ANALYSIS OF THE PROSPECTS

This analysis will focus on the limitations to the mobilization of the evangelicals by the New Christian Right based on distributions of political beliefs. Although it is possible to further mobilize a group through manipulation of symbols and images, it is difficult to build a social or political movement without some congruity of beliefs. I will first present the political beliefs of the supporters of the New Christian Right and their target constituency, then examine issue groups within the evangelical community to identify subgroups most sympathetic with the issue positions of the New Christian Right.

Table 8.4 presents the percentage of both groups that selected a conservative response to each item in 1984. Although evangelicals share with supporters of the New Christian Right a conservative orientation on social,

Table 8.4
Political Beliefs of the New Christian Right and the Evangelicals

	Supporters	Target	Others
Social Issues			
Abortion (never)	31%**	20%**	9%
Women's role	34%**	21%**	12%
Gov't help women	41%**	32%	30%
School prayer	90%**	90%**	70%
Economic Issues/ Government Role			
Government services	49%**	33%*	36%
Guaranteed job	60%**	45%	46%
Medical insurance	55%**	49%*	40%
Government too powerful	69%*	57%	55%
Race Issues			
Civil rights too fast	54%**	39%*	29%
Bussing	90%	86%	88%
Minority aid	53%**	46%*	35%
Foreign Policy			
Central America	38%**	28%	25%
Detente — USSR	63%**	49%**	39%
Defense spending	54%**	40%*	33%
Isolationist	19%	28%*	20%

Percentage of respondents in each category choosing conservative alternatives on item. * indicates mean values for group are significantly different from rest of population at .05.

race, and foreign and defense policy issues, they are indistinguishable from other whites on economic issues (perhaps reflecting the concerns of their location on the economic ladder). It appears, then, that should the New Christian Right limit its appeals to social issues and defense policy, it may find the evangelicals sympathetic, but if they persist in staking positions on economic issues, the evangelicals will be somewhat less likely to respond.

One likely prerequisite of a political movement is the dissatisfaction with government performance on salient issues. On a series of items evaluating government performance, the supporters of the New Christian Right were significantly more negative toward all government institutions in 1980 than were the rest of the population. This negative evaluation of government performance was not shared by the white evangelicals, however. These items were not included in the 1984 survey.

Moreover, on a scale constructed of feeling thermometer items in the 1980 survey rating Congress, the Supreme Court, the federal government, and federal employees, the supporters of the New Christian Right displayed significantly lower levels of affect than the rest of the white population, while the target constituency were significantly *warmer* toward government.

One possible reason for the discrepancy between these two groups in their evaluations of government may lie in their differing perception of the position of the government on salient issues. Table 8.5 reveals that while the supporters of the New Christian Right saw the government as significantly more liberal than did the rest of the population, this perception was not shared to any significant degree by the white evangelicals.[7]

Of course, the evangelicals are not a monolithic group with uniform patterns of political beliefs; some share the conservative orientation of the New Christian Right on economic issues as well. To get a better feel for the prospects for expansion of the New Christian Right, I have identified the issue groupings within the evangelicals, which enabled me to assess the similarity between the various groupings and the supporters of the New Christian Right. The issue groups within the evangelical community were identified by cluster analysis, with standardized issues as the variables by which the respondents were clustered.[8] Five issue groups were identified in this analysis, and are discussed below.[9] The number of cases involved is small, and inferences should be taken as suggestive, not definitive. The data contain some clear patterns, however (see Table 8.6).

The first group I have called the Rightists. They were distinguished by their conservative responses to nearly all of the issues in the survey. This group also had a demographic profile similar to that of the supporters of the New Christian Right, and were mainly Republicans. Not surprisingly, they were the warmest cluster toward the New Christian Right.

Table 8.5
Evaluations and Perceptions of Government

	Supporters	Target	Others
Government Evaluation Scale 1980	53*	59*	56
Perceptions of the Positions of the Federal Government — 1980			
Guarenteed Job	3.1*	3.8	3.8
Minority Aid	2.6*	3.0	3.0
Women's Role	2.8*	3.0	3.2
Abortion	1.7	1.5*	1.7
Defense Spending	3.3*	3.8	3.8
Detente	2.9	3.0	3.0
Perceptions of the Positions of the Federal Government — 1984			
Guarenteed Job	4.2**	4.4	4.6
Government Services	3.9**	3.6	3.6
Minority Aid	3.6**	3.9	3.9
Gov't Improve SES Women	4.1**	3.9*	3.3
Central America	3.3**	3.1	2.9
Defense Spending	5.0*	5.1	5.2
Detente	4.5	4.1**	4.6

Mean positions of each group on each item. * indicates group significantly different from the rest of the population at .05. ** indicates differences significant at .01.

The second group I call the Liberals. They were the mirror image of the Rightists on the issues, for on nearly every item, including social issues, they were more liberal than other evangelicals. Their liberalism on social issues extended even to abortion, although they were conservative on school prayer. They had lower levels of education and occupational prestige than other evangelicals, were younger, and were strong Democrats. It should come as no surprise that this group was one of the coolest toward the New Christian Right, rating it at an average of 14 degrees below individual means for all groups in the survey.

The other three groups fall between these two extremes. One cluster was clearly identified as Moderates. This group was not readily characterized on demographic variables, resembling other evangelicals in its demographic profiles. The Moderates were also quite cool to the Moral Majority, however, rating at an average of 14 degrees below their mean for all social and political groups.

The Economic Conservatives were moderate on most issues except those concerned with economic matters. Note that these evangelicals were conservative on spending for social programs and liberal on spending for programs

Table 8.6
Political Beliefs of Issue Groups among Evangelicals, 1980

	Rightists	Liberals	Race	Economic	Social
Social Issues					
ERA	C	L	*	*	C
Equal Role/Women	C	L	*	*	*
Society Discriminates Against Women	*	L	*	*	*
Abortion	C	C	*	C	C
School Prayer	C	L	C	C	C
Race Issues					
Civil Rights Too Fast	C	L	C	L	C
Bussing	C	*	C	*	*
Minority Aid	C	L	C	*	*
Economic Issues					
Gov't Services	C	L	L	*	L
Guar. Job	C	L	L	*	C
Inf./Unemp.	*	L	L	C	*
Env. Regs.	L	*	L	C	*
Nuclear Power	*	L	L	C	*
Tax Cut	C	L	*	C	C
Federal Gov't Power	C	L	*	C	C
Foreign and Defense Issues					
Defense Spend.	C	*	L	*	*
Detente	C	*	L	C	L
Relative Support for New Christian Right					
	-13	-22	-17	-15	-14
	n=26	n=20	n=35	n=14	n=40

Entries indicate differences from other whites. L = significantly more liberal than other whites. C = significantly more conservative than other whites. * = not significantly different from other whites. Relative support for New Christian Right is feeling thermometer minus the respondents average feeling thermometer rating for all other groups in 1980 survey.

favored by conservatives: they generally opposed government spending. Their social issue positions indicate a libertarian streak—they were liberal on abortion and school prayer. This group had the highest socio-economic profile, with professionals with high incomes greatly overrepresented. They were young and urban, located mainly outside the South. They seemed to fit a pattern similar to what might be expected of evangelical Yuppies. This group was fairly cool toward the New Christian Right, rating it at 11 degrees below its mean. It was also the most secular cluster, with fairly low levels of church attendance and personal religiosity.

A final group I have called the Race Conservatives. These evangelicals constituted the smallest subset in the analysis, and were distinguished by their strong conservatism on race issues and their low affect toward minorities (not presented). They were moderately liberal on social issues and cautious doves in defense. Their economic positions were generally conservative, although their liberalism on guaranteed jobs makes it possible to read their responses as a reaction to government aid to minorities—opposition to spending on social programs and government services might be an extension of their strong conservatism on the minority aid item. This cluster was primarily composed of non-Southern women, with low levels of education and high levels of religiosity. They were moderately cool to the Moral Majority.

Of the five groups of evangelicals discussed above, two are clearly poor targets for mobilization by the New Christian Right. The Liberals are cool to the New Christian Right, and do not share its conservative orientation. The Race Conservatives are also not likely targets, with their pattern of liberal foreign policy attitudes and moderately liberal social issue positions. Their only concentration of conservative beliefs is race issues, where the New Christian Right has been careful not to pitch its appeals. These two groups constitute approximately 18 percent of the white evangelicals in the survey. The Moderates are likewise unlikely converts, given their moderate positions and negative affect toward the Moral Majority. They constitute another 35 percent of the target constituency.

One group is a likely target for the New Christian Right. The Rightists share with the supporters of the New Christian Right a conservative orientation toward the whole range of issues on the survey, from social and economic issues to race and foreign policy issues. They also share with the supporters of the New Christian Right a strong Republican identification. This group constitutes 36 percent of the white evangelical community.

The economic conservatives share their economic orientation with the supporters of the New Christian Right and its leaders. Their other attitudes are more moderate, however, and their demographic portrait resembles more closely the group popularly called "Yuppies" (i.e., professional, urban, educated) than supporters of the New Christian Right. The leadership of the New Christian Right has staked clear positions on economic and foreign policy issues, but has not stressed them in more recent times. If the New Christian Right continues this recent policy of stressing social issues and downplaying economic and other issues, then this group is an unlikely target for mobilization.

Table 8.7 presents the turnout rates of the five issue groups among the white evangelicals in the 1984 election. Turnout is highest among the Rightists and the Race Conservatives, and lowest among the Liberals. Each of these groups participated at about the level that their socioeconomic status and age would predict. Table 8.7 also shows the vote choice of the various subgroups. The Rightists predictably voted for Reagan in 1984 in overwhelming numbers, as did the Economic Conservatives, while the Liberals and Moderates were more likely than other evangelicals to support Mondale. Somewhat surprising is the strong support for Mondale among the Race Conservatives. This seems to be due to the strong Democratic partisanship of this group, although the small number of cases makes any inferences very tentative.

What, then, of the possibilities of the New Christian Right to mobilize the white evangelical community into conservative and Republican political action? The 1984 survey does not contain the types of items that would allow us to answer this question directly, but some indirect inferences might be offered. Among the issue groups of the evangelicals, those most likely to be mobilized seem to be the Rightists, which constitute 6 percent of the population. They share with the supporters of the New Christian Right a common demographic portrait, Republican partisanship, and conservative beliefs on nearly all of the issues in the survey. Mobilization of this group would leave the leadership of the New Christian Right with the support of 17 percent of the white population.

The only other group that is a possible candidate for conversion to the New Christian Right's fold is the Economic Conservatives. Although fairly moderate on social issues, the conservative outlook on economic issues of this group makes the positions of the New Christian Right in this area seem attractive. Their demographics, combined with their more moderate positions on social issues, however, make them unlikely candidates to be wooed to the fold while the New Christian Right continues to stress its social agenda.

Table 8.7
Political Behavior of Issue Groups among Evangelicals

	Rightists	Liberals	Race	Economic	Social
Voted 1980	86%	86%	65%	50%	73%
Voted for Reagan	84%	44%	62%	71%	56%
	n=26	n=20	n=35	n=14	n=40

Percentage of each group falling into categories

Should the New Christian Right succeed in mobilizing the Economic Conservatives as well, their support would rise to nearly 20 percent of the population. The Moral Majority would still not be aptly named, but they would be a sizable minority—capable of constituting an important influence on the Republican party.

CONCLUSION

Three questions have been addressed by the analysis in this chapter. First, have the evangelical Christians been mobilized into higher levels of political participation? The answer to this question is yes. Although they report a history of low levels of participation, and have low levels of SES as well, the evangelicals voted in greater numbers in 1980 than the rest of the white population. Moreover, those with little history of past participation were more likely to have voted in 1980 than their non-evangelical counterparts. This mobilization did not endure, however. When Carter was no longer on the ticket, evangelical turnout dropped to a level significantly lower than that of other whites.

Second, are the organizations of the New Christian Right responsible for this mobilization? Here the answer seems to be no. Evangelical turnout increased most markedly in 1976, before the efforts of the New Christian Right, at the time when Jimmy Carter, a Southern evangelical, headed the Democratic ticket. The absolute turnout rate of evangelicals appears to have been lower in 1980 and 1984 than it was in 1976. Moreover, in both the 1980 and 1984 data, support for the New Christian Right was not related to turnout among all evangelicals or among those who had low levels of past participation.

Finally, what are the prospects for the organizations of the New Christian Right to expand their support among their target constituency? Here the prospects are somewhat mixed. Among the issue groups that constitute evangelical Christians, one is clearly a likely candidate for mobilization, sharing with the supporters of the New Christian Right a conservative orientation in all issue areas. A second group could possibly be mobilized on economic issues, although the Moral Majority has traditionally stressed social issues and recently focused on foreign policy. Should the Christian Right manage to mobilize one or both of these groups, it would constitute between 17 and 20 percent of the white population, and a slightly higher proportion of the electorate—much of which would be concentrated in the strategic South. In this event, the New Christian Right would be a potentially significant force in electoral politics.

ACKNOWLEDGMENTS

I would like to thank Elizabeth Cook for helpful comments. The data were made available by the Inter University Consortium for Political and Social Research. All interpretations are my own.

NOTES

1. It should be noted, however, that Lipset and Raab's analysis included blacks and whites. Although blacks are more likely than whites to hold evangelical beliefs, the political implications of their evangelicalism are quite different. Inclusion of blacks in the analysis therefore exaggerates the diversity among evangelicals.

2. Although researchers have long known about the positivity bias in feeling thermometers, only recently has the practice of adjusting feeling thermometer responses been employed. See Knight (1984), Wilcox (1987b), and Wilcox, Sigelman, and Cook (1989).

3. There has been a good deal of discussion in the literature on the proper way to operationalize evangelicals. Most doctrinal definitions include as their core an item on biblical interpretation and one on the "born-again" experience. Other, more complete definitions have been proposed (Kellstedt, 1984), but have not been used in national surveys. Others have employed denominational definitions (Kellstedt, 1986). Still others have relied on doctrinal self-identification (Wilcox, 1987c, 1989; Smidt, 1988b).

4. These variables have been identified as significant predictors of turnout in numerous studies. See, for example, Wolfinger and Rosenstone (1980).

5. Prior to 1972, most Southern Baptists were classified as Baptists in national election studies, lumped together with the more liberal American Baptists. Kellstedt (1986) has argued that all frequently attending Baptists could be termed evangelicals, including Northern Baptists.

6. Note that this statement uses all evangelicals as its base. Moral Majority supporters who were not evangelicals actually had a somewhat higher turnout than those who were.

7. The 1984 data present a somewhat more mixed picture. The evaluation of government items was not included in the survey, and the supporters of the New Christian Right perceived the government to be more conservative on some items, and more liberal on others.

8. Issue groups were identified by the SAS FASTCLUS clustering procedure. This program first computes Euclidian distances between respondents over a set of variables (in this case issue items), and then clusters respondents by the nearest centroid sorting method. All respondents are assigned to a cluster by this procedure, but outliers may be identified and excluded from the analysis. The method produces clusters in which all distances between respondents within clusters are smaller than all distances between respondents in other clusters.

9. The 1980 analysis produced similar results. Instead of a moderate cluster, however, a cluster of social issue conservatives emerged. See Wilcox (1984) for details of this analysis.

9
The Moral Majority as a Political Reference in the 1980 and 1984 Elections

Jerry Perkins

The presidential elections of 1976, 1980, and 1984 have stimulated a renewed interest in the relationship between religion and politics. In the first of these elections Jimmy Carter's commitment to born-again, evangelical doctrine was widely discussed. Not since Kennedy's Catholicism had there been so much concern for a candidate's religious characteristics. In the 1980 election, religion was again potentially important, but there was a shift in emphasis from candidate characteristics to the relevance of religion for ideology and public policy. Conservative religious groups were organized and vocal. The Religious Roundtable, Christian Voice, the National Christian Action Coalition, and, most notably, the Moral Majority led an assault on a perceived immorality of liberal government and the politicians who occupied it. Issue and candidate scorecards were compiled and distributed in congressional politics. In the presidential contest no official recommendation emerged, but the message was clearly anti-Carter and pro-Reagan. In the 1984 election the theme was extended and acknowledged on the TV debates when Walter Mondale attacked Jerry Falwell and raised the church-state issue.

Given the proclivities of right-wing religious groups to issue scorecards, it seems appropriate to assess popular response to these efforts. We already have some analysis. Substantial proportions of the population had not, in 1980, heard of the Moral Majority; the distribution of those that had was biased against Falwell's group (Benson, 1981; Tamney and Johnson, 1983; Shupe and Stacy, 1983; Buell and Sigelman, 1985).

Beyond the ratings we might also ask about the groups in the population that might provide support for the Moral Majority. Existing studies on the 1980 election period are not entirely consistent in their findings, but they suggest the potential bases as membership in a fundamentalist church

(Shupe and Stacey, 1983), religiosity (Buell and Sigelman, 1985) the impact of religious television, cultural fundamentalism, a desire for politics dominated by Christianity (Tamney and Johnson, 1983), religious fundamentalism, and political conservatism (Perkins, 1983b).

In terms of electoral choice, what difference does the Moral Majority make? The literature does not directly answer this question, although there are suggestions of some influence. Existing studies of the 1980 election do not uniformly identify the independent religious variable as Moral Majority support. For example, some use denomination (Miller, 1978; Ladd, 1986) instead of opinion about the Moral Majority. Others use religious beliefs as indicators (Wald and Lupfer, 1983; Smidt, 1983; Perkins, 1983a). One study finds no relationship between fundamentalist political opinion and presidential voting (Johnson and Tamney, 1982). Another finds no link between support for the Moral Majority and evaluations of the Reagan administration (Tamney and Johnson, 1983). Yet another combines evaluations of evangelicals in politics with religious beliefs and illustrates a positive effect between Republican voting and fundamentalist/pro-Moral Majority orientation in the 1980 senatorial election (Miller and Wattenburg, 1984). The same study also argues that the 1980 presidential choice shows some religious influence, although controls for partisanship and ideology reduce such a relationship to one that is minuscule.

The assumptions and operations of existing research either omit significant considerations or are uneven on some major points. With regard to omission, we need a comparative benchmark in looking at popular response to religious groups in politics. Responses have apparently been negative, but are there other more negative groups? How does the Moral Majority fare when compared with other groups? Further, how divided is opinion on the Moral Majority relative to opinion on other groups, which is to ask how politically divisive evangelicals in politics are.

With respect to that which is uneven, some studies do not control for race. The well-known Democratic habits and religiosity of blacks surely suggest that the problem should be cast as ethno-religious rather than simply as religious. To not control for race, in effect, may obscure the influence of conservative religious groups on the white population. In evaluating objects such as the Moral Majority the same potential race effect is possible. It is known, for example, that blacks in 1980 gave higher marks to "evangelicals in politics" than whites (Perkins, 1983b), but they were also far more Democratic in votes than whites.

Miller and Wattenburg (1984) avoid the race problem but create two other potentially misleading effects. From a conceptual point of view we perhaps should separate religious beliefs, such as adhering to biblical inerrancy, from religious reference objects, such as opinion about the Moral

Majority. We might expect some interrelationship between the two, but they certainly are different considerations. In assessing the impact of religion on voting particularly, we ought to weight religious beliefs apart from religious political movements while simultaneously being sensitive to interactive effects between the two.

Finally, controlling for known predictors of the vote such as partisanship may be a good idea, as Miller and Wattenburg have done, but we must also be sensitive to the possibility that variables such as religious attitudes are potential causes of political ideas. To run simple controls may therefore obscure indirect effects on the vote. Religious beliefs, in effect, may be mediated indirectly through their impact on partisanship or ideology.

The intent of this chapter is twofold. First, 1980 and 1984 ratings on various groups in politics are employed to provide a comparative assessment of evangelical groups. The two time points allow us to examine not only relative ratings but also how evangelical groups fare as they age and presumably become better known in 1984. Second, the relationship of evaluations of the Moral Majority and the vote is examined. In so doing, a simple model is created to assess any potential effects relative to other important indicators. The model will also be applied to 1980 and 1984 data in an attempt to detect change over time.

A MODEL

Numerous variables are involved in a comprehensive understanding of religion and voting behavior. Denominational membership, religiosity, education, income, section of the country—all have some potential effect on voter perceptions (Chalfant, Beckley, and Palmer, 1981). This chapter does not examine all potentially important variables. Instead, perceptions of evangelical groups such as the Moral Majority are placed within a limited context of variables that appear compelling at this point in our political history. The general idea to be pursued is that the Moral Majority can provide cues to relevant groups and funnel votes to the Republican party.

Insofar as a group gains public notority, it can represent a reference point for key identifiers in the population and act as a guide for voters by setting an agenda of choice on candidates and issues. Responses to the group and its agenda can be positive, negative, or indifferent. The importance of group relevance can be episodic, as perhaps was the case in the 1980 senatorial elections where a combination of short-term forces negatively affected many liberal Democratic candidacies; or a group may have durable appeal, guiding voters across a series of elections, as in the presumed effects of parties and partisanship (Campbell et al., 1960). Also, group references can reinforce one another, as is the standard suggestion about Protestantism and Republicanism (Chalfant et al., 1981).

Whether durable or episodic, groups in the political arena seek contact with those who might be favorably disposed and seek to reinforce or deflect their long-standing behavioral patterns. Thus the religious Right has sought to elevate a moral agenda that appeals to the more fundamentalist believers among Protestants and Catholics, both of whom have some historical connection to Democratic, liberal politics. In their attempt to weigh against the evils of liberalism, however, support for the evangelical right can also come from those of conservative and Republican identifications who may not be particularly religious in motivation.

In terms of appeal, the Moral Majority would seem most likely to gain the attention of those of fundamentalist Christian beliefs, not Protestants in general. Along both moral and economic lines, existing evidence suggests that the tumultuous decade of the 1960s set in motion a liberalization of upper-status denominations and the reverse among lower status congregations (Nie, Verba, and Petrocik, 1976). The key variable would not appear to be denominational membership per se, but belief that may be not perfectly associated with congregational memberships. Also there are many who are not church-affiliated but are nonetheless connected to religion and politics through the "popular" noninstitutional religion of media (McWilliams, 1980).

In casting a model, religious belief would appear to be more basic than either denomination or religiosity. There are many of religious convictions who would not react favorably to the Moral Majority (e.g., Unitarian-Universalists). On the other hand, there are some of fundamentalist belief scattered across many religious denominations. While religious belief is set in a matrix of ideology and partisanship, one's spiritual convictions would seem more fundamental. Where issues touching upon religion are important, belief would precede or cause the selection of or changes in one's ideology and partisanship. Receptivity to the appeals of a group such as the Moral Majority would be conditioned by one's belief, partisanship, and ideology. In effect a religious reference group could act as a cue for some people and channel their opinions into votes.

A simple version of the posited relationships is diagramatically represented in Figure 9.1. Religious belief is antecedent to partisanship, ideology, and evaluations of the moral majority; party identification and ideology also are presumed to be antecedent to evaluation. If the Moral Majority is a powerful reference group, all of the basic orientations would flow through evaluations as the Moral Majority acts as a conduit for religious fundamentalists, Republicans, and conservatives. This would seem, in fact, to be Falwellian strategy. At the voting stage, the model also allows some direct effects of PID (party identification) and ideological identification on the vote. Here, given the expected overlapping of Republicanism, conservatism, and support for

Figure 9.1
A Path Model of the Vote

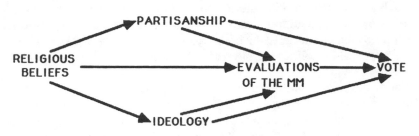

the Moral Majority, the question is how much independent effect of the reference group remains when all three are regressed on the vote.

DATA, METHODS

The variables for the model are taken from the 1980 and 1984 election studies of the Center for Political Studies. Only white respondents are examined, except where otherwise mentioned. Partisanship is the long-standing seven-point indicator that ranges from strong Democrat to strong Republican. Ideology is derived from a seven-point scale ranging from very liberal through moderate to very conservative. The 1984 vote is coded 0 for Mondale and 1 for Reagan; in 1980 the Anderson votes are allocated to one of the two parties on the basis of thermometer evaluations of Carter and Reagan; if an Anderson voter rates one higher than the other, and if the higher is positive, he or she is coded in that party; if, however, there is a tie or neither major party candidate gets a favorable rating, the data are excluded from the analysis.

With respect to group evaluations the "thermometer" questions are used. Each respondent is asked to provide their positive, negative, or neutral feelings about selected groups and politicians on a scale of 0 to 100, with zero representing cold, negative responses and 100 representing warm, positive reactions to the group or institution in question. Among the reference objects on the interview schedule are "evangelicals in politics, such as the Moral Majority." For the purposes of this analysis, all the mentioned groups and institutions—some 34 in 1980 and 24 in 1984—will be employed to establish a comparative benchmark for assessing the importance of the religious right. In turn, the respondents' evaluations of evangelical groups on the thermometer scale will be used as the central intervening variable in the model. It should be noted that the thermometer questions may be "easy" for respondents to answer, and therefore the responses may contain a sizable number of people who really don't have any opinion. The CPS interview schedule does allow individuals to declare that they don't know enough about the group in question to offer an evaluation, but a low proportion of the population actually does this. In the case of the groups and institutions looked at here, the highest proportion of "don't knows" is on the evangelical-in-politics thermometer, but even this percentage is only 5.5 in 1980.

Four questions from the 1980 and 1984 studies permit the creation of a fundamentalist belief index, although the methodology of the survey instrument is not ideal. Two questions assess religiosity by asking if religion is important in one's life, and if so, how much of a role does it play. If the respondent answers the first question "yes," they get the second question and a third on whether they have had a born-again experience and a fourth on biblical literalism. If they say "no" to the first question, the middle two questions are omitted. For two reasons, we cannot simply sum up the responses. Not all respondents are asked all questions. More importantly, the first two questions have to do with religiosity and not necessarily with fundamentalism. The only legitimate approach seems to be a dichotomous measure. If the respondent is highly religious *and if* he or she is born again and believes in biblical literalism, that respondent is classified as being of fundamentalist belief. All others are non-fundamentalists.

For the comparative group ratings, means and standard deviation are displayed. For the model, a staged path analysis is employed. The four variables—partisanship, evaluations, ideology, and religious belief—are regressed upon the vote. The hypothesis is that there with be no direct effect of belief on the vote. Instead, it is assumed that belief is mediated through partisanship, Moral Majority evaluations, and ideology. In turn, it is assumed that belief, partisanship, and ideology heavily influence evaluations of the Moral Majority.

RESULTS

For all groups and institutions addressed in the 1980 election study, Table 9.1 presents the list ordered by means (high to low) and standard deviations. Evangelicals-in-politics do not have high ratings, either in absolute or relative senses. The evangelical mean is low because Americans basically provide migh marks generally for all groups, the overall "mean of the means" being in the high 50s. More important is the Moral Majority's standing in the list ranked by group and institutional means. Only two groups, which have for some time received low marks—radical students and black militants—have lower scores. Such generally "bad" symbols as "big business" do better than the Moral Majority as do "people on welfare."

Table 9.1
Thermometer Ratings of Groups and Institutions in 1980

	Means	Standard Deviation
Older people	83.2	15.9
Workingmen and workingwomen	82.8	16.3
Farmers	79.6	16.4
Whites	77.5	17.8
Young People	76.9	17.7
The Middle Class	76.2	17.1
Poor People	75.2	18.4
Businessmen and Businesswomen	72.9	17.4
People protecting the environment	70.9	21.5
Military	65.1	22.2
Blacks	64.2	20.8
Democrats	63.9	20.4
Conservatives	62.7	18.6
Democratic Party	60.7	23.0
Federal employees	59.5	18.0
Republicans	59.2	18.9
Hispanics	57.8	19.6
Supreme Court	57.7	20.3
Congress	57.4	18.2
Republican Party	57.4	21.6
Political Parties in general	55.6	20.2
Labor Unions	54.4	23.4
Women's Liberation	53.8	25.9
Civil Rights Leaders	53.7	23.4
People who call themselves Independents	52.3	20.9
Big Business	52.2	23.1
The Federal Government	51.8	20.2
Liberals	51.7	21.1
Evangelical Groups, like the Moral Maj.	45.3	25.6
Radical Students	29.7	22.5
Black Militants	29.6	25.0

Our often-maligned institutions such as the Supreme Court, the Congress, and the presumably despised federal government do better than evangelicals. Those arch enemies of purity, the liberals, even beat the Moral Majority as does another source of irritation to the religious right, women's liberation. If the Moral Majority ranks low in overall standing, however, it ranks high in dividing the population. Among all the thermometer objects, only women's liberation has a higher standard deviation, which means that large proportions of the population are thrown in opposite directions.

The 1984 results are substantially the same as in 1980 (see Table 9.2). Some groups posed in the 1980 interview schedule were dropped; others were added. While the absolute rating of the Moral Majority slightly rises, it is still close to the bottom at 45.8. Black militants still fall lower (at 32.5) and a new group, gay men and lesbians, are at the very bottom (30.0). The population remains highly divided on the Moral Majority with only the standard deviations for homosexuals and anti-abortionists exceeding that of evangelicals in politics.

Table 9.2
Thermometer Ratings of Groups and Institutions in 1984

	Mean	Standard Deviation
Older people	78.4	17.5
Whites	74.2	18.0
Middle-class people	73.0	17.7
Poor People	71.8	19.1
The Military	68.7	21.0
Blacks	64.2	20.5
Catholics	63.6	20.9
The U.S. Supreme Court	63.0	19.0
Conservatives	59.9	19.3
Hispanics	59.4	20.5
The Republican Party	58.7	24.0
The Women's Liberation Movement	58.0	23.1
The Democratic Party	57.5	22.7
Liberals	56.0	19.9
Political Parties in General	55.7	17.6
Labor Unions	54.5	24.2
Civil Rights Leaders	54.3	23.9
People on Welfare	52.8	21.7
Big Business	52.3	20.7
Anti-Abortionists	50.3	27.8
People Who Call Themselves Independents	50.3	20.0
Evangelical groups, like the Moral Maj.	45.8	25.2
Black Militants	32.5	23.5
Gay Men and Lesbians	30.0	26.4

As expected, there is a potentially confounding effect of race. In 1980 blacks gave a very high rating to evangelicals in politics with a mean score of 60.3 while voting Democratic; in 1984 the black rating declined to 54.5 but still remained substantially above whites.

Before addressing the controlled effects of Moral Majority references, the potentially confounding impact of race should be illustrated. If we break voters into low, medium, and high support categories for the Moral Majority, while simultaneously controlling for race, the diluting effect on the link between evaluation and the vote can be observed. Figure 9.2 does this. As can be seen from inspection, the slope *for all voters* is moderately but positively related to Republican voting. If, however, blacks are excluded the slope is considerably steeper. Some 70 percent of whites with positive Moral Majority evaluations voted for Reagan; only 58 of the entire sample (including Blacks) did. In effect, the addition of black voters considerably dilutes the correlation between Moral Majority support and Republican voting.

The moderately steep gradient in 1980 for whites suggests a positive bivariate correlation, which does in fact obtain for both 1980 and 1984 (see Table 9.3). Among white voters there is a moderate association between

Figure 9.2
Proportion Voting Republican in the 1980 Presidential Election by Ratings of the Moral Majority (including and excluding blacks)

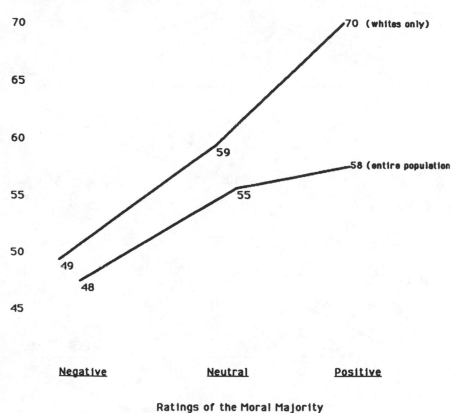

Ratings of the Moral Majority

Table 9.3
Bivarate Correlations (Pearson's r) between the Vote and Model Variables

	VOTE	
	1980	1984
Moral Majority	.17	.24
Religious belief	.05	.15
PID	.62	.71
Ideology	.39	.46

A positive correlation means that a Reagan vote is associated with positive evaluation of the MM, fundamentalist belief, Republican identification, and conservatism.

Figure 9.3
Path Models for the 1980 and 1984 Elections

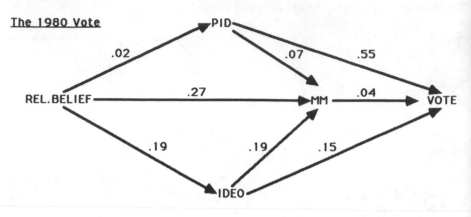

The 1980 Vote

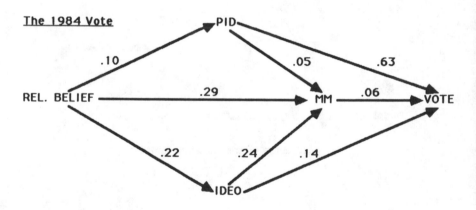

The 1984 Vote

evaluations and voting choice in both elections. High ratings of the Moral Majority are associated with voting for Reagan. In 1980 the correlation is .17; in 1984 it rises to .24. Religious belief is lower in the two years at .05 and .15. While these correlations are not as strong as party identification (.62 and .71) or ideology (.39 and .46), they nonetheless dispel any notions that assessments of evangelical reference groups are not related to the vote. However, the question of whether assessments of the Moral Majority have effects independent of other factors remains to be answered.

The observer must ask how much of the variance in the vote is attributable solely to the white voters' affection for the Moral Majority considered apart from the effects of ideology and partisanship. An examination of the combined model effects confirms what we might expect, but the links are weak (see Figure 9.3). The path between ratings of the Moral Majority and the vote among whites is considerably reduced by controls for partisanship and ideology, but a very small, significant effect remains. The direct effect of religion attitudes is reduced to insignificance. Whatever influence exists passes through evaluation of the Moral Majority. Even here, the impact on the vote is small. Fundamentalist religious attitudes are the most important source of positive evaluations for Falwell's group when run simultaneously with partisan identification and ideology. However, ideology has a substantial impact with conservatives giving high support for evangelical groups apart from their religious convictions.

The generalizations obtain for both 1980 and 1984. If there is any difference between the two points, it would be marginal increases in the paths between the two elections. Religious fundamentalism becomes slightly more related to Republicanism, positive views of the Moral Majority, and conservatism. Similarly conservatism and Republicanism are somewhat more strongly connected to positive view of the Moral Majority. The residual effects of Moral Majority evaluations on the vote are marginally increased between 1980 and 1984.

CONCLUSION

Evangelical groups such as the Moral Majority are highly divisive in U.S. politics. While such organizations have their adherents, they have more detractors, which is perhaps the fundamental reason why Jerry Falwell renamed the group and now downplays its significance. The net effect of the Moral Majority on voting independent of other references would appear to have been minimal, although the anticipated association between high Moral Majority ratings and Reagan voting is present.

It is very likely that the larger U.S. political culture distrusts activity by religious leaders that is too overtly "political." As has been suggested elsewhere, however, this negative reaction to evangelical politics does not tell the whole story. Individuals such as Jerry Falwell may continue to raise specific issues. Americans may not desire candidate endorsement by religious groups but they are more supportive of the role of religion in assessing policy issues of the day (Yankelovich, 1981; Patel, Pilant, and Rose, 1982). To some degree, the evangelical right is in a difficult position. Their arenas of greatest potential success would seem to be local and issue-specific. Yet their own perceptions are that it is national politics and government that is the real problem. The great burning issues of the day such as abortion and school prayer are nationalized and require at least some connection to candidates, coalitions, and parties (Cochran, Perkins, and Havens, 1988). So they may continue even in a negative climate of opinion, although for now a strong reference group is not likely to be offered.

Religious politics may be a significant part of a larger realignment of U.S. politics. Some observers see a replacement of the old economic division with a new "cultural" politics in which traditional values of community and family are challenged by more cosmopolitan, individualistic, progressive values (Shafer, 1985). While the exact ways that cultural conflict affects the party alignment are not yet clear, at least in the short run the traditionalists would seem to be inclined to Republicanism. The voting data for 1980 and 1984 suggest that religious values and religious references may well be a part of the larger defense of tradition. Evangelical groups in politics such as the Moral Majority do seem to have at least a small influence on voter behavior in drawing those of fundamentalist belief to Republican voting. Whether such groups can promote a long-term realignment to Republican identification, however, remains to be determined.

III

Elite Perspectives

10
Coalition Strategies of Religious Interest Groups

Robert Zwier

Religion has invaded the world of politics. In the last two decades we have witnessed the political awakening of the fundamentalists, the prophetic voice of the Catholic bishops, and the judicial thicket of church-state confrontation. Most of the research on religion and politics has focused on the First Amendment decisions, the electoral activities of the New Christian Right, and the impact of religious beliefs on public opinion and voting.

In recent years there has been renewed attention to the role of religious interest groups in the policy-making arena. Paul Weber (1981, 1982a, 1986) has noted that more religious organizations have established Washington offices. Hertzke (1988) has shown how these groups operate and how the legislative process affects them. This chapter attempts to add to our knowledge of the activities of these groups by examining one aspect of their lobbying strategy—that is, forming and maintaining coalitions with other interest groups.

Specifically, this chapter addresses the following questions: How important are coalitions to the religious interest groups? What kinds of coalitions are formed? With whom do the religious interest groups work? Are there any limits on who will be invited to join their alliances? How do these coalitions divide the labor and pool their resources? What are the advantages of joining coalitions? Finally, what are the disadvantages or frustrations encountered in these coalitions?

The theoretical context for this discussion of religious interest groups is the social science literature on coalitions. Although the purpose of this chapter is not to test systematically the propositions of this research, there is a concern to see whether the behavior of religious interest groups fits what we would expect from our reading of the coalition literature, particularly as it addresses questions about why groups join coalitions and which coalitions they join.

This study is based on interviews conducted in the summer of 1986 with 38 representatives of church and other religious interest groups with offices in Washington, D.C. (see the Appendix to this chapter for the list of groups and their representatives). The list was drawn from work by Hertzke (1988) and P. Weber (1986) from the *Encyclopedia of Associations*, and from references made by interview respondents. Access was excellent; only three representatives were unwilling to be interviewed. Unfortunately, two of these were groups aligned with the new Religious Right, so the sample underrepresents that segment of the religious community.

COALITION RESEARCH AND INTEREST GROUPS

The study of coalition formation and maintenance has been an important topic of social science research for several decades. Browne and Franklin (1986) reviewed the field and identified three generations of research. The first, reflected in works by Riker (1962), and Gamson (1961), involved deductive analyses based on game theories and rational decision making. This body of literature developed hypotheses about why people or groups join coalitions, how large the coalitions would be, and how the gains or payoffs would be distributed among the participants. The second generation of research involved empirical attempts to confirm these deductive theories, relying on experimental research or "real world" investigations (cabinet formation in multi-party systems, international alliances, legislative voting, and electoral coalitions). Browne and Franklin (1986) argued that this generation of research in large part failed to confirm the deductive theories of earlier work and concluded that the earlier theories were too restrictive. Thus they called for a third generation of coalition research that would be inductive and descriptive, examining the effects of contextual variables on individual and group behavior.

Most of this literature suggests that coalitions are temporary alliances among rational people or groups who are seeking to maximize gains. Coalition participants are primarily motivated by economic self-interest and they join coalitions that will provide them the most material benefits. A coalition member will contribute resources to the joint effort only as long as he or she continues to receive a payoff proportional to the investment.

Very little coalition research examines the behavior of interest groups. Studies of interest groups suggest that coalitions are one aspect of group behavior, but coalitions have not been the main focus. Case studies of interest groups—Groennings et al. (1970), Berry (1984), Costain (1980), and Keller (1982)—usually mention some kind of cooperative efforts, but none does much to develop or test coalition theories. Textbooks about interest groups typically devote a small section of one chapter to some observations about coalitions, but there is a lack of in-depth or theoretical treatment. The major study of coalition behavior is Hall's (1969) study of business groups in the 89th Congress, which makes a number of common-sense observations about coalition behavior but does little to relate the findings to earlier theory. Furthermore, it is reasonable to suggest that business groups might behave differently from other interest groups, particularly religious groups.

One trend that does appear in these scattered references to interest group coalitions is their increasing importance. Such a trend is noted particularly by Loomis (1986), Keller (1982), and Schlozman and Tierney (1986). Although 80 percent of Milbrath's (1963) respondents said collaborative lobbying was at least moderately important, only 20 percent of the respondents reported that they generally consulted with other lobby groups in planning strategies. More recently Schlozman and Tierney (1986: 150) reported that 90 percent of the organizations in their survey entered into coalitions and that this strategy was mentioned more frequently than most others. These authors (p. 155) also reported that two-thirds of their respondents said that coalition work was more important now than in the past; of all the changes over time, this was the second most significant. Therefore, these authors conclude that "coalition-building is a crucial part of any organization's strategy of influence (p. 278).

Keller (1982: 120) has argued that the major reason for the greater interest in cooperation among groups is the decentralization in Congress as a result of the organizational changes of the 1970s. With the increase in the number and influence of subcommittees, power is more dispersed than before and the number of arenas in which groups must operate has been expanded beyond the ability of single groups to handle.

The literature that concentrates specifically on religious interest groups gives even less attention to coalition behavior. The major studies of religious interest groups—by Adams (1970), Ebersole (1951), and Hertzke (1988)—provide only anecdotal evidence of coalition formation around specific pieces of legislation. Paul Weber (1982a) noted that the average religious interest group belongs to four coalitions and argued that such groups are especially good coalition partners because they bring legitimacy, stability, a larger constituency, and a moral dimension to such cooperative efforts. Fowler (1985) pointed out coalition activity in the battles over prohibition, civil rights, and abortion, but did not tie the references into his theoretical observations. Reichley (1985a) ignored the intergroup phenomenon completely.

JOINING COALITIONS OR WORKING ALONE?

Religious interest groups should be particularly interested in joining coalitions because their small staffs and budgets would make it difficult for them to cover more than two or three policy areas. Another incentive is the fact that many of the mainline liberal Protestant denominations have their lobbying offices in the same building—the United Methodist Building (also known affectionately as the "God-box"). Several other groups have offices within a few blocks.

Do the religious interest groups included in this study join coalitions? Most definitely! Every respondent who was asked about coalition activities reported that the group had worked with others, at least on an ad hoc basis. Robert Dugan of the National Association of Evangelicals summed up the attitude of many: "I would say we never work alone if we can be in coalition."

Why do they join coalitions? The lack of resources was the principal reason. David Saperstein of the Union of American Hebrew Congregations noted the practical argument: "Well, most of us are small operations in the religious community; therefore, by necessity we have to work in coalitions." Catherine Brousseau, formerly of NETWORK, echoed these feelings: "I don't know that we've ever gone alone. The main reason we don't go alone is that we don't have the research staff, so we're always dependent on other people."

The other major reason for joint efforts is the common identity or shared values of these groups. Bill Kallio, formerly of Evangelicals for Social Action, put it this way:

We do consciously want to work with other religious groups because we have a shared value basis and that makes it more effective to form a coalition; we're simply given a mandate by the Board to engage with other Christian organizations that claim to have a common value base.

An interesting question is why groups would sometimes be unwilling to work in coalitions, preferring to work alone. Two groups in particular seemed most likely to work by themselves. The U.S. Catholic Conference (USCC) reflected the bishops' preference to outline their own distinctive position on issues, to make sure that their lobbying efforts reflected the uniqueness of the Catholic tradition. Bryan Hehir noted:

On the whole, the bishops like to have their own position stated, so most of the time we will state our own position and then see how we relate to other groups. We don't sign a lot of group letters; the bishops don't want that. They want their own position laid out. We collaborate, but we collaborate after we set out our own position.

The other group expressing a greater desire to work alone was the United Church of Christ (UCC). Jay Lintner, the UCC representative, pointed out that coalitions can be effective, but then suggested that his group was going to work on its own issues regardless of whether others joined in:

We look at it as a kind of table operation; that is, we come to a common table to decide who is going to be active on the issue and coordinate how we can use some resources, but we do stay with *our* priorities and activate *our* network and work *our* issues.

The USCC and the UCC are among the largest religious groups engaged in policy advocacy. Because they can operate independently, there may be less incentive to become involved in coalitions with their compromising, time commitments, and shared rewards. In addition, Lintner argued that the UCC has a different set of goals from many of the other religious groups. While many groups are content simply to witness to the government, the UCC expresses a greater desire to win, to enact, or to change legislation. Lintner proudly pointed out that the UCC has several of its own staff researchers and that its constituency network was extensive, having 50 state coordinators and contact people in over 300 congressional districts.

For the most part, however, religious groups preferred to work with others. Yet the coalition behavior of religious interest groups was unique. Most coalition theories argue that groups join coalitions to get a fair share of the tangible rewards. Although James Q. Wilson's (1973) concepts of material, solidary, and purposive benefits was designed to explain individual decisions to join groups, they can also help us to understand group decisions about joining coalitions. The common assumption, then, is that groups join coalitions for material rather than solidary or purposive benefits. However, the representatives of the religious groups rarely spoke of material incentives. Instead of focusing on the costs and payoffs, the religious group representatives were more likely to mention the joys of working with like-minded people and groups. It did not appear that these groups were in coalitions primarily to get something for themselves. Rather, they were interested in the *process* of cooperation as much or more than in the *results*. To the extent they were motivated by results, they were seeking policies that would be in the broader public interest rather than in their own self-interest. Coalition theory does not explain such motivations adequately because of its focus on economic self-interest. In contrast to Wilson's (1973: 277) argument that organizations are more likely than individuals to follow Mancur Olson's "logic of collective action," the conclusion here is that these unique organizations are more than willing to contribute to cooperative efforts even when they receive no specific, material benefits for themselves.

COALITIONS WITH WHOM?

The literature on coalitions suggests two major factors involved in the choice of coalition partners. The first is that groups will join minimum winning coalitions, joining with those groups whose combined strength is just enough to win, thus reducing the number of groups who will divide the spoils. This hypothesis has very little relevance to the coalition behavior of religious interest groups. None of the respondents in this study even hinted that such considerations were important to them in their choice of coalition partners. Because the groups worked for legislation that did not result in direct payoffs to themselves, there was no sense of the winners dividing up the pie. Furthermore, with some of the groups, there was little sense of being in the coalitions to win at all. One of the unique features of religious interest groups is that some of them see their mission as making a statement or speaking a prophetic voice to government rather than passing or blocking some legislation. To be sure, everyone who engaged in lobbying would rather win than lose, but the particular character of some religious groups is that they see victory simply in terms of getting a message delivered, of getting policy makers to think about the moral dimensions of proposed legislation.

A second idea suggested by the coalition literature is the spatial hypothesis: groups will join with other groups who are close to them in some dimension, such as ideology. This hypothesis is clearly more relevant to the world of religious groups. When respondents were asked to name the groups they worked with most frequently, they almost always listed groups that shared a common political perspective. Along a religious dimension, however, there is much less support for the spatial hypothesis. Theologically, mainline Protestants have more in common with evangelicals and even fundamentalists than with Unitarians or Jews, yet they were much more likely to join coalitions with the latter groups. This suggests that for religious interest groups, political perspectives are more significant than theology in choosing partners.

Coalition partners are no exclusively other religious groups, although most of the non-religious groups mentioned by these respondents were what we might call "cause groups" seeking broader public goals rather than selfish objectives. This supports the research of Salisbury et al. (1986: 18) who concluded that "the groups in each category (farm organizations, commodity groups, trade associations, externality groups) tend very strongly to find their allies within their own organizational category." Both the religious and the non-religious groups would see some benefit from this pattern. The religious groups would be able to show that a lobbying effort was not just coming from the churches, whom some policy makers might write off as politically irrelevant institutions. For the non-religious groups, join-ing a coalition with church groups might bring added legitimacy to the cause or enable them to tap the institutional structure and membership of the churches.

Most of the respondents could not identify specific criteria they used, suggesting instead that they will work with *almost* any group that shared their position on an issue. Man, reflecting the fluidity of coalition patterns, pointed out how important it was to be on good terms even with those groups on the other side of a particular issue because in future battles the groups might be fighting on the same side. Robert Dugan of the National Association of Evangelicals expressed this sentiment most clearly:

So we will work in coalition with whoever supports the same kinds of causes and that also is a lesson a lot of people haven't learned: that you don't burn any bridges. Because somebody's not with you on one issue, you don't read them the riot act. The Baptist Joint Committee is opposed to us on some things, but on equal access they were terrific allies. Americans United has a different view of separation than I have—they would practically like to see us just about completely secularized—nonetheless we were with them on the Vatican ambassador appointment.

Only one respondent, Gary Ross (1984: 13), who represents the Seventh-day Adventists, seemed particularly deliberate about choosing partners, describing two criteria his organization used in the battle over Vatican recognition: "How were such determinations made? . . . The criteria we apparently used were (1) the potential lobbying effectiveness of the organization in question, and (2) the degree to which we wished to be associated or identified with a particular organization in the media." By lobbying effectiveness, Ross referred to the individual integrity of the Washington representative and the ability to mobilize constituency pressure. In addition, there is an unwillingness to be seen as a partner of cer-tain groups with bad reputations either in the policy-making or the religious community. Ross expanded on this idea in his interview: "My church will weigh very carefully whether it wants to appear in tomorrow's news allied with the scientologists and the ACLU [American Civil Liberties Union]. Even if we agree with them on an issue." Another example involves the Washington Inter-religious Staff Council (WISC) group rejecting the ap-plication for membership of the Church of Scientology. One active WISC participant put it this way: "I consider them to be an unethical group and I don't want us to get entangled with them in any way. We have enough prob-lems with public perceptions without muddying the waters." Some respondents agreed with their organization's reluctance to associate with particular groups, but more were frustrated with the restraints, seeing the decisions from headquarters as a deterrent to lobbying effectiveness.

HOW DO THE COALITIONS WORK?

Coalitions involve a number of groups joining together to pool their resources in the pursuit of some common goal. How does this work among religious interest groups? Is there some specialization of effort or division of labor that occurs? How are decisions made within a coalition? It is useful at this point to consider separately the relatively permanent coalitions—WISC and IMPACT—and the more fluid ad hoc coalitions that form around specific pieces of legislation.

For the most part the coalitions that have some lasting identity grew out of repeated ad hoc efforts over the years. Accounting for the development of WISC, for example, several of the respondents pointed out that their groups had been cooperating informally for years. Mary Cooper (former chairperson of WISC) described an initial WISC gathering:

When we got all the folks gathered in one room, we found out what we had already known, but it became real to us that lots of people were working on the same issues and a lot of them were doing the same sorts of things; and it was sort of silly to have everybody doing their own little piece in their own little shop when we could be helping each other.

WISC was established in 1968, initially including only churches within the National Council of Churches, but quickly expanding to include approximately 35 faith groups from across the religious spectrum. WISC is a coordinator or a facilitator of actions by the individual members; it does not issue statements in its own name. WISC members speak for their own faith groups rather than for the coalition. Unlike many of the established coalitions, WISC has no paid staff; all personnel are representatives of the member faith groups who volunteer their time in this collective effort. There are no dues: instead each group pays a fee to be placed on the WISC mailing list and each group is free to make contributions to cover other expenses.

The primary work of WISC takes place in task forces that have staked out a policy area for concentration. These task forces (about ten of them) are quite fluid, both in terms of membership and agenda. Individual denominations can send a representative to any task force, although, given the small staffs, most faith groups are represented on only a few. Generally the task forces meet twice a month to share information, plan grass-roots and direct lobbying campaigns, write position papers, and provide camaraderie. Joseph Hacala described the efforts of the Foreign Policy and Military Spending task force, which is one of the more active:

We meet every other week, with a regular attendance of about 15 to 20 people. We have a regular lobbying commitment to each other on a Thursday morning. One person takes responsibility for a particular issue. A couple of days ahead of time, he sets up appointments either with the representative themselves or in most cases with aides. We gather at 8:30 on Thursday mornings and the person who is responsible for that issue does a short briefing—what the issue is—perhaps passes out a one-page position paper, indicates why we're seeing the people we're seeing. Then we divide up into teams of two or three or four, and we usually average about a dozen people lobbying and we visit the offices. We keep records of those visits, so we can do follow-up visits later and see how the various representatives have voted on these issues over the years.

WISC and its task forces operate with a consensus style of decision making. Although each faith group has its own statements on issues, there is overwhelming agreement on the basic positions and it is not at all difficult to agree on specific actions. This is due in large part to the fact that WISC represents the liberal Protestants, the Catholics, and the Jewish groups, excluding the more conservative or fundamentalist groups. If there are deep disagreements about issues (for example, abortion and the Middle East), WISC does not work on them. Mary Cooper noted how the group handles disagreement:

We identify who the partners are on the various sides of the issue, and then we say "you folks go in that room and you folks go to another room" and we won't try to work together. We don't spend a lot of time trying to change each other's minds, because by and large we're instructed by the policy of our own organizations and that is what we have to advocate. So there's not much reason to spend time arguing about it.

In situations of disagreement groups could decide to go it alone, but most will seek out other coalition partners from outside the WISC community.

Another established coalition, closely related to WISC, is IMPACT, set up in 1968 by the WISC community to mobilize voter pressure on Congress. IMPACT, unlike WISC, is made up of dues-paying individuals. At its peak, IMPACT had more than 15,000 members, but the 1986 membership was about 11,000. In addition, IMPACT has a full-time staff of five people who coordinate the educational and mobilizing efforts. IMPACT also has affiliates in 20 states monitoring legislation at the state level and promoting letter-writing campaigns to state legislators.

The group has three policy priorities: halting the arms race, securing economic justice, and protecting human rights. The organization produces a variety of written materials for its members, including a monthly newsletter, legislative alerts on specific bills, lengthier policy analyses, and voting report cards for members of Congress.

IMPACT's governing board representing the various faith groups meets twice each year to establish priorities and policies; in the interim a smaller committee appointed by the board provides short-term direction to the staff. These groups operate on the basis of consensus rather than a strict system of majority rule. Like WISC, IMPACT also steers away from divisive issues.

In addition to these formal coalitions, the religious groups have formed many short-term, ad hoc coalitions around specific bills or specific issues areas. Often these ad hoc coalitions would be called together when a representative from one faith group would become interested in an issue and recruit some colleagues into a cooperative effort. Hertzke (1988: ch. 6) provided a good example of this in his case study of the equal access bill: a coalition was formed and maintained largely through the efforts of John Baker of the Baptist Joint Committee.

These ad hoc coalitions divide up the labor among the participants in several ways. For example, some groups would work on direct lobbying of congressional offices, others would stir up a grass-roots letter-writing campaign, and others would do the research and hammer out a joint position paper. Often the congressional contacts would be divided up, depending on which groups have the best access to which members of Congress. There is some evidence, for example, that the representative of the Presbyterian Church would contact the Presbyterian members of Congress, and Lutheran representative would contact the Lutherans, and so forth.

One frequent tactic of coalitions is to write sign-on letters, circulate them around the groups for signatures, and send them to legislators. On rare occasions there are serious disagreements about wording, as each group tries to be consistent with its own official policy statements, but in most instances these letters pass quickly through the circle of coalition members. A certain amount of trust develops over time among the group representatives, so that one person will sign on to a letter without knowing much about the issue but recognizing the special expertise of the person who drafted the letter. The biggest problem with sign-on letters is timing: sometimes the Washington representatives cannot sign on without approval from a denominational board or executive, yet the letter must get to Congress within a few days. In such cases, a group might pass on the letter, knowing that in the cycle of congressional business the same issue might surface again in a few months.

The other favorite tactic involves joint testimony before congressional committees and subcommittees. Several of the respondents reported this kind of activity, arguing that it had two advantages. First, they perceived that a joint statement would have more impact than numerous individual statements by suggesting unity within the religious community. Second, the respondents noted that members of congressional committees appreciated the time that could be saved by having a single witness or panel rather than having several individuals making virtually the same arguments.

These ad hoc coalitions are quite loose in terms of membership and organization. There is no paid staff, no separate budget, no discrete constituency. Individual groups move into and out of these coalitions depending on whether their own purposes are being served. There is no accountability to a governing board, there is no promise of future cooperation beyond the immediate issue, and there are no formal rules for decision making. What binds these coalitions together is the common perspective on a legislative issue and, in many instances, the common fellowship within the Washington religious community.

BENEFITS AND COSTS OF COALITION MEMBERSHIP

The respondents noted several advantages in joining coalitions. First, there was a widespread feeling that collective effort was necessary to keep adequately informed about policy issues. As we have seen, coalitions are formed at least in part to facilitate information sharing among the participants. Mary Cooper spoke of the reciprocal patterns of information exchange within WISC:

The lack of resources would be worse if we were working alone; now at least we have each other's resources. We can save each other's time. I don't have to be an expert on everything because I know there are a lot of experts in this building and I can call on them and they can call on me.

The second perceived benefit of coalition membership comes in terms of advocacy on Capitol Hill. The respondents suggested that joint efforts were more likely to be effective than individual efforts. A coalition represents more resources to investigate and understand issues, more lobbyists to contact more legislative offices, and more constituents to facilitate access to a greater number of legislators. Furthermore, cooperation across faith lines demonstrates a united front that provides more legitimacy to the advocacy. As Carol Franklin of the American Baptist Churches put it: "It also helps when we can walk into an office, and have a Jew, a Baptist, and a Quaker. They at least listen to us."

Finally, many of the respondents pointed to the social benefits of coalition membership. They spoke fondly of working together with those who share a basic faith commitment and whose faith commitment expressed itself in concerns about public policy. William Weiler, representing the Episcopal Church, shared his view of the importance of fellowship: "I think we're very enriched. I've learned a lot as an Episcopalian in working with the more congregational brethren and sisters. I've learned a lot from the Baptists about how they go about their work. I've learned a lot about Quaker silence and working by unanimity." Later in the interview he added: "People in the religious community are very embracing and forgiving. The opportunities we have had to share spiritual pursuits . . . are among my most heartening and joyful experiences."

Many of the respondents felt a particular need for this fellowship, because they had come from jobs—usually pastorates—outside of Washington D.C. and they had few personal friends in the capital. In most cases the denominational headquarters were located in other cities, so there were few close contacts from their own faith groups. Joseph Hacala of the Jesuit Social Ministries spoke about this need for personal ties: "Washington can be a lonely town; it can be a tough town to work in. The successes are very few, particularly right now in terms of the stance of the present [Reagan] administration."

In addition to the perceived benefits of coalition efforts, the respondents expressed several frustrations. The most frequently cited was the fact that each denomination or religious group had its own perspective and its own ego; the Washington offices were restricted in what they could do, how quickly they could do it, and what particular denominational nuances they had to work with.

In this regard, the group representatives most often mentioned an inability to join a coalition effort without going "through channels" to get the approval of the proper authorities. Ron Krietemeyer of the U.S. Catholic Conference spoke of the problem in his organization:

Our system is filled with checks and balances and we're relatively inflexible in our ability to change quickly. On a given strategy, for example, we have to go through a lot of loops to get clearance from the bishops and from the appropriate offices and administrators. It's a good thing from our point of view because it makes sure the bishops' views are not presented carelessly, but it makes dealing with coalitions sometimes difficult because of others expecting us to act very quickly, on the spot, and we cannot do that.

Such comments contrast with the argument by Ebersole (1951) and Duggan (1986) that church representatives are out of step with and unaccountable to their denominations. Many of the representatives in this study went out of their way to suggest their lack of autonomy.

We might also suspect that denominational differences would stand in the way of united efforts. For example, it is unrealistic to expect that separate denominations would pass identical resolutions at their governing assemblies. While there was some evidence that this problem occurs (e.g., difficulties in wording sign-on letters), in large part this potential frustration seemed insignificant. Respondents noted that there was sufficient consensus among the groups to provide a basic direction. What was apparent, however, was the fact that different groups had different priorities concerning issues. Gary Ross (1984: 14) of the Seventh Day Adventists noted the problem: "The price of coalitional activity has another aspect too. When the tables are turned, are we willing to reciprocate by lending *our* support to a cause that may not be primary from our perspective."

One organizational difference that did interfere with cooperation was the split between groups that were primarily interested in grass-roots lobbying and those interested in direct lobbying. Stephen Coates, representing the grass-roots lobby Bread for the World, described this problem:

A frustration for us and a source of conflicts we have with other groups is that we're a grass-roots group and that affects your strategy and your agenda. We're not in a position to pick up an issue overnight and run with it for three weeks and then drop it. We have to do the membership prep work.

Another problem with coalition activities is the time demands on small staffs who soon become overwhelmed with frequent and lengthy meetings. Because of the press of organizational business, there simply is not enough time to put into coalition activities and this frustrates other coalition members who want to get the work done. One indication of this problem came from Coates, who commented on Bread for the World's move from New York to Washington:

There was a great fear when we moved that we would be absorbed by meetings and coalitions. . . . It's possible for almost everybody in our department to spend every day of every week of every month talking about what we're going to do instead of doing something.

Another frustration is the fact that coalitions tend to be driven by congressional deadlines, which leaves little time for in-depth reflection or discussing more theological or theoretical issues. James Skillen of the Association for Public Justice put it this way:

Personally, my main frustration is that almost all of these groups are issue oriented and it means that given the legislative process they are tied to, everything is reaction to whatever comes up before Congress. So it's a kind of day-by-day, week-by-week reaction to the specifics and the details, and there's relatively little time for anybody to step back and say this whole thing is nonsense or this all doesn't add up to anything.

In addition, frustration stems from the different perspectives on the appropriate role of religious groups in policy advocacy. Some see their role primarily in terms of being a moral voice, introducing an ethical dimension in the public debate regardless of whether they "win." These groups look askance at some lobbying tactics, arguing that religious groups must be distinctive in their methods and goals. Other religious groups clearly want to win. There are problems when these two types interact, as Carol Franklin of the American Baptist Churches noted:

One of the ongoing tensions in this community is what is our role as a religious community in Washington. Do we really want to be wheelers and dealers in the midst of the horsetrading or do we want to operate somewhat on the fringes as a moral voice?

A final problem noted especially by evangelical groups was their perception that some groups joined coalitions with them only to gain legitimacy for their own organizations. Bill Kallio, representing Evangelicals for Social Action, commented on this problem:

I also find coalitions many times to be exploitative. It isn't really issue effectiveness that the coalition is built around; there is some other agenda. We have to be sensitive to the fact that some folks might not want to support the common agenda as much as they want to shore up their credibility by having evangelicals involved. That happens very much with us.

DISCUSSION

It is clear from this study that religious interest groups often work in coalitions as they carry out their mission of policy advocacy. It is also clear that the coalition activities of religious groups are distinctive, that their collective behavior is not explained well by traditional coalition theories. Religious groups, because of their small size and limited budgets, are probably more likely to join coalitions than are larger groups. Furthermore, despite some evidence that particular faith groups will contribute to a coalition only to the extent that their own priorities are worked on, there is very little evidence that these groups join coalitions in order to maximize benefits for themselves. Their concern was for solidary and purposive benefits, for fellowship and the good of the larger society rather than their own organizations. Consequently, coalition theories that assume rational actors in pursuit of material benefits do not fit in this case. Only 3 of the 38 respondents in this study gave any indication that the group "counted the cost" of coalition membership. Another important factor is that many of these groups are in Washington not so much to pass or defeat legislation but to make a moral statement. Their foremost concern is not with the results of the policy process (although they would rather win than lose) but with how the process is conducted and with the nature of the debate. Success is defined in terms of whether the moral aspects of public issues have been included in the discussion.

In addition, there is ample evidence that religious groups join coalitions because their convictions lead them toward communal efforts, no matter what the cost or the distribution of benefits. There is a "love thy neighbor" ethic at work within the Washington religious community that is not accounted for by the general theories of coalition behavior.

It is also apparent that the size of coalitions is not an important variable for religious groups. These groups would be more than happy to form "excessive" coalitions because their concern is not in getting more for themselves.

Interest group coalitions represent a fruitful field of study for social scientists. More groups are using coalitions to counteract the decentralization of Congress and to keep up with the diverse set of issues on the congressional agenda. This is clearly true for representatives of the faith groups included in this study, as their organizations enact resolutions on more and more issues beyond those affecting churches directly. This study of the coalition activities of religious interest groups suggests that these groups are distinctive in many ways and that traditional theories of coalition behavior do not adequately explain their activities.

APPENDIX: LIST OF RELIGIOUS GROUPS

American Baptist Churches, USA (Carol Franklin)

American Friends Service Committee (James Matlock)

American Jewish Committee (Hyman Bookbinder)

American Jewish Congress (Marc Pearl)

Americans for Religious Liberty (Edd Doerr)

Americans United for Separation of Church and State (Robert Maddox)

Association for Public Justice (James Skillen)

Baptist Joint Committee on Public Affairs (James Dunn)

Bread for the World (Stephen Coates)

Christian Legal Society (Samuel Ericcson)

Christian Science Committee on Publications (Mason LaSelle)

Christic Institute (Sara Nelson)

Church of the Brethren (Leland Wilson)

Episcopal Church (William Weiler)

Evangelicals for Social Action (William Kallio)

Friends Committee on National Legislation (Edward Snyder)

General Conference of Seventh Day Adventists (Gary Ross)

IMPACT (Craig Biddle)

Interfaith Action for Economic Justice (Anna Rhee, Board Member)

Jesuit Social Ministries (Joseph Hacala)

Justlife (Jack Smalligan)

Liberty Federation (James Boulet)

Lutheran Church–Missouri Synod (Candace Mueller)

Lutheran Council in the USA (Charles Bergstrom)

Mennonite Central Committee (Delton Franz)

National Association of Evangelicals (Robert Dugan)

National Catholic Conference for Interracial Justice (Thomas Reese)

National Council of Churches (James Hamilton)

NETWORK (Catherine Brousseau)

Presbyterian Church, USA (Mary Jane Patterson)

Union of American Hebrew Congregations (David Saperstein)

Unitarian Universalist Association (Robert Alpern)

United Church of Christ (Jay Lintner)

United Methodist Church (Donna Morton Stout)

United States Catholic Conference (Bryan Hehir, Ron Kreitemeyer)

Washington Inter-religious Staff Council (WISC) (Mary Cooper, previous chair)

World Vision (Thomas Getman)

11
The Politics of Armageddon: Dispensationalism among Southern Baptist Ministers

Helen Lee Turner and James L. Guth

Despite the recent outpouring of research on the Christian Right, social scientists have paid little attention to the distinctive theological underpinnings of this movement. Most scholars are unfamiliar with variants of Protestant fundamentalism and, in any case, lack all but the most rudimentary theological items in national surveys, which seldom go far beyond questions on denomination, church attendance, or the importance of religion in one's life. In this situation, then, all conservative Protestants look alike, frustrating scholars' attempts to connect theological views with political behavior.

This chapter explores one component of the world view of political fundamentalism: millennialism. All orthodox Christians believe, in the words of the Nicene Creed, that Jesus will "come again with glory to judge the living and the dead, of whose kingdom there shall be no end." But the meaning of that affirmation has varied. Even within the course of U.S. history, several distinct orientations have emerged. Premillennialists believe that Jesus will return bodily before the millennium, after a series of cataclysmic events. The ensuing thousand years, however, will be filled with righteousness and peace under the earthly rule of Christ. Postmillennialists, on the other hand, argue that Jesus will return to claim an established kingdom after the millennium has already been accomplished through the power of God working in the faithful. Still other Christians are amillennialists, holding that there will not be a literal thousand-year reign, but that Christ's kingdom began with his birth and will be fulfilled in his Second Coming, or that the entire doctrine is really symbolic.

Historians of religion in the United States have noted that a movement's view of the "Last Days" is often associated with either advocacy or rejection of political involvement. For example, both the evangelical Protestant reformism of the 1840s and 1850s and the Social Gospel of the 1890s were driven by postmillennial optimism. By the turn of the century, this doctrine was challenged by revival of premillennial assertions that the world was growing worse and worse and could be rescued (at least for true Christians) only by Christ's return.

The most elaborate, pessimistic, and popular form of this new premillennialism was dispensationalism, which divided history into distinct eras, or dispensations. In each of seven eras, the battle between God and Satan is played out in the lives of human beings. In each, the struggle ends in the failure and judgment of those in league with Satan, generally thought to be the leaders of society, and is followed by the violent introduction of an entirely new era. The present age, which will also end in failure, is that of the church. Dispensationalists are pessimistic not only about the possibility of true progress in the secular world, as traditional premillennialists had been, but also about prospects for the church. Despite tremendous mission efforts, the world could never be won for Christ. Indeed, the church would remain a small, faithful remnant awaiting Christ's return. This theology influenced the "Great Reversal" of the 1920s, a withdrawal of evangelical believers from social and political involvement (Marsden, 1980).

Questions concerning the political implications of millennial doctrines were raised anew by the rise of the Christian Right in the 1980s. Ironically, given the past ties between premillennialism and political quietism, the Right's most vocal leaders were almost without exception premillennialists, and usually dispensationalists as well: Jerry Falwell, James Robison, Jimmy Swaggart, Pat Robertson, and Jim Bakker, to name just a few. Most connected interpretations of biblical prophecy to very specific (and usually very conservative) political notions. Even more astonishing to secular observers were references to apocalyptic theories by national politicans, including President Reagan, Secretary of Defense Caspar Weinberger, and Secretary of the Interior James Watt (W. Martin, 1982).

By 1984 such expressions had engendered heated debate in the secular and religious press. Liberals argued that the most popular dispensationalist vision, advanced by Hal Lindsey's 1970 best-seller *The Late Great Planet Earth*, encouraged militarism in the United States, hostility toward the USSR, uncritical support for Israeli policies, and antipathy to economic and social reform. Lindsey's admirers denied being any less anxious to avoid nuclear war than the liberals, while other evangelicals rushed to repudiate his interpretation of the End Times (W. Goodman, 1984). As *Christianity Today* (1984: 48) observed, the flap was "more of a preelection sideshow than a serious theological debate," but it did "raise questions about what Christians believe and how those beliefs could affect their outlook on public policy." Despite the superficiality of the early exchanges, other authors soon developed these themes in depth, though usually without support from survey data (Halsell, 1986; Mojtabai, 1986).

If eschatological doctrines influence political ideas, that should be apparent among those who take theology most seriously: the clergy. In this chapter, we explore the social and political implications of millennialism, especially dispensationalism, using data from two recent surveys of ministers in the nation's largest Protestant denomination, the Southern Baptist Convention (SBC). We will try to answer the following questions: (1) What are the millennial orientations of Southern Baptist ministers? (2) What are the social bases of the competing millennial perspectives? Are there clear demographic, economic, and educational roots to each? (3) What theological beliefs characterize each perspective? (4) What does each group see as the role of the church in social and political reform? (5) And finally, what are the distinctive political beliefs of contemporary millennialists?

DATA AND METHODS

The data for this analysis are drawn from surveys of Baptist ministers in 1984–85 and 1986–87. Most theological items are from the 1986–87 study, while additional theological and political information comes from the earlier study. The 1986–87 survey included 1,500 ministers in a random sample drawn by the SBC's Sunday School Board. Two mailings brought 694 returns, a 48 percent response rate, once 40 invalid addresses and deceased respondents were excluded. The 1984–85 survey elicited 902 responses from 1,710 ministers (excluding 51 pastors who were deceased or for whom we had incorrect addresses), a response rate of 53 percent after three mailings. Comparison of both samples with Southern Baptist ministers generally (based on profiles in the SBC's *Quarterly Review*) shows that respondents are slightly better educated, from somewhat larger churches, and thus of slightly higher status than the average pastor. Given the modest backgrounds of dispensationalists, they may be a bit underrepresented in the samples, but the traits of the groups we identify should not be seriously affected. Respondents to the two surveys, moreover, are remarkably similar, facilitating use of both.

MILLENNIAL ORIENTATIONS

The millennial views of Southern Baptists have elicited much attention from scholars, who have contended at length over the relative size of the millennial camps, both today and in the past (Barnhart, 1986; Thompson, 1982; T. P. Weber, 1987). Our 1986–87 survey provides the first hard evidence on the issue. We measured the pastors' millennial views by asking: "How would you identify yourself: Postmillennialist, Amillennialist, Premillennialist, Undecided, None of the Above Terms are Appropriate, or Uncertain About the Meaning of the Above Terms." Premillennialist was by far the most popular label, chosen by 435 pastors (63 percent). Next was Amillennialist, with 95 (14 percent), None of the Above, 93 (13 percent), and Undecided, 33 (5 percent). Only 5 ministers (1 percent) were postmillennialists, once a powerful force in U.S. Protestantism. To identify dispensationalists (who should all be premillennialists), we also asked: "Do you consider yourself to be a dispensationalist?" Of the 694 respondents, 213 (31 percent) responded "Yes," 380 (55 percent) said "No," and 101 (14 percent) either did not answer or were not sure.

Although T. P. Weber (1987: 11) sees few behavioral differences between dispensationalists and other premillennialists, even cursory analysis of our data reveals important variations. Therefore, we divided pastors into three groups: dispensationalist and premillennialist ("Dispensationalists"), premillennialist but not dispensationalist ("Traditional Premillennialists"), and neither ("Nonpremillennialists"). The three groups are almost equal in size, with Dispensationalists making up 28 percent of the sample (N = 197), Traditional Premillennialists, 25 percent (N = 172), and Nonpremillenialists, 29 percent (N = 200). About 18 percent (N = 125) could not be classified, having failed to answer one or both questions. We also excluded a few "nonpremillennial dispensationalists," a theological compound unknown to the literature. Although these procedures eliminate one-fifth of the sample, the omission is not troubling. The excluded pastors act like Traditional Premillennialists; indeed, they might have been included there with few changes in our findings.

Most of the analysis of theological orientations below is based on the 1986–87 survey, which, unfortunately, had relatively few political questions. The 1984–85 survey was considerably richer in political variables, but lacked the items on eschatology considered here. As the two surveys included 35 identical questions (including standard demographic variables, educational attainment, theological and ideological items), we used discriminant analysis (Klecka, 1980) to assign ministers in the 1984–85 study to Dispensationalist, Traditional Premillennialist, and Nonpremillennialist categories. (See the Appendix to this chapter for further information on this procedure. In the tables, items from the 1984–85 survey are marked by a double asterisk, **.)

THE SOCIAL ENVIRONMENT OF MILLENNIALISM

Perhaps no aspect of millennial movements in recent U.S. Protestantism has raised more controversy than their social origins. One classic theoretical orientation sees millennarian movements as the protest of the dispossessed and powerless. To date, however, virtually no survey evidence addresses specifically the social correlates of dispensationalism, but there is much theorizing about a closely related phenomenon, fundamentalism. Some scholars locate fundamentalism in the segments of conservative Christianity furthest from the processes and institutions of "modernity" (compare H. R. Niebuhr, 1937; Hunter, 1983a). Others see it as the product of confrontation between tradition and modernity, a result of the process of modernization (Ammerman, 1987). Still others stress the essentially "modern" location of such theological conservatism (e.g., Marsden, 1980: 202). We can, by extension, test these perspectives on millennial views that, most scholars agree, have been among the chief building blocks of fundamentalism.

Our data favor the "remoteness from modernity" thesis, albeit in modified form (Table 11.1). Dispensationalism is most common among ministers with the lowest family income, from farm and blue-collar backgrounds, from rural areas and small towns, working in blue-collar congregations, in the Deep South. Personal dislocation does not seem to produce dispensationalists: their greatest strength (45 percent) lies among ministers brought up in rural and small-town areas who still live there. Nor does age show any consistent relationship with dispensationalism. Traditional Premillennialists are from somewhat more prosperous backgrounds, while Nonpremillennialists exhibit, on the other hand, distinctly "upscale" social traits.

Although social background distinguishes dispensationalists from other believers, another factor, education, may be even more crucial. As Hunter (1983a: 60) puts it, the public school has been "the veritable classroom for the inculcation of the world view of modernity." Dispensationalism is the clearly favored religious perspective of those with limited secular and theological education. The type of education also has some impact. Ministers from very selective Baptist colleges are least likely to be dispensationalists, followed by those from prestigious state and private universities, smaller Baptist colleges, other state schools, and, finally, small private colleges. Pastors from SBC seminaries are generally not dispensationalists, although this varies by school, but those who attend the growing contingent of independent seminaries are overwhelmingly so (Turner and Guth, 1988).

Of course, social background and education interact in many ways. Those of higher social status are likely to receive better educations. Thus the effects of social class on religious orientation are often mediated by education. Such is the case here: controlling for educational attainment virtually eliminates the influence of social class on millennial views. For example, working-class ministers with schooling equivalent to those from middle-class homes do not differ in millennial orientation. Other background traits

Table 11.1
Demographics (in percentages)

	DISPEN-SATIONAL	PREMIL-LENNIAL	NONPREMIL-LENNIAL	Gamma
Current Family Income				
To $19,999	40	36	24	.21*
$20,000 to $34,000	38	29	33	
$35,000 to $49,999	30	32	37	
Over $50,000	19	19	62	
Father's Occupation**				
Farmer	34	41	25	.13*
Blue-Collar	32	38	30	
Business and Clerical	22	45	34	
Professional	25	37	38	
Size of Home Community				
Rural Farm or Mill Community	47	30	23	.14*
Small Town	34	29	37	
Small City	32	35	33	
Suburban or Large City	31	26	43	
Social Class of Congregation**				
Working Class, Blue Collar	36	41	23	.23*
Lower-Middle	30	46	24	
Mixed	27	36	37	
Upper-Middle	20	35	45	
Region				
Deep South	43	29	28	.27*
Midwest	39	38	23	
Far West	27	29	44	
Border States	26	30	44	
Northeast	14	14	71	
Secular Education				
High School or Less	69	20	11	.45*
Some College	51	37	12	
College Degree	26	31	43	
Postgraduate	24	27	49	
Seminary Education				
None	58	29	13	.50*
Bible College Only	60	23	17	
Some Seminary	51	30	19	
Seminary Degree	24	31	45	

*Chi square p < .05.
**Date from 1984–85 sample.

also "wash out." Thus the extent, type, and institutional locus of ministerial education is crucial to the existence of millennialist attitudes (compare Noll, 1986: 59).

THEOLOGICAL ORIENTATIONS

Most observers have agreed that dispensationalism fostered theological positions that became central to fundamentalism: insistence on Christian orthodoxy, "heightened supernaturalism," and belief in biblical inerrancy (Noll, 1986: 57–60). As Table 11.2 shows, Baptist dispensationalists certainly stand out on such measures, even in comparison with their traditionally orthodox colleagues.

First, millennial views are strongly related to theological self-identification. Indeed, fully 71 percent of all self-identified Southern Baptist "fundamentalists" are dispensationalists; the rest are traditional premillennialists. Note, however, that dispensationalists are not confined to the fundamentalist camp; in fact, they constitute more than one-third of those choosing the most popular designation, "conservative." Their preference for this label no doubt reflects, in part, the unpopularity of the term "fundamentalist" among many Southern Baptists, who have long associated it with the "uncooperative" movement led by Frank Norris in the 1920s (Thompson, 1982). Traditional premillennialists are also concentrated in the conservative camp, while non-premillennialists are divided between "conservative" and more moderate

Table 11.2
Theological Orientations (in percentages)

	DISPEN-SATIONAL	PREMIL-LENNIAL	NONPREMIL-LENNIAL	Gamma
Theological Self-Identification				
Fundamentalist	71	24	5	.74*
Conservative	36	35	29	
Moderate	7	16	78	
Liberal	0	0	100	
The Scriptures and Christian Doctrine				
Bible Inerrant in All Matters	98	84	40	.76*
Adam and Eve Real Historical Persons**	98	96	70	.77*
Very Sure There is Actual Devil	94	80	48	.73*
Jesus's Resurrection Surely True**	92	91	68	.50*
Very Sure of Virgin Birth**	91	93	59	.59*
Hell is Real Physical Location**	89	81	47	.60*
Plagues on Egypt Supernatural Events	84	76	47	.43*
Jesus Thought Earth Flat (Disagree)	73	65	34	.46*
Jesus Understood All Human Languages	69	52	23	.52*
God Instructs for Everyday Decisions	56	49	28	.37*
Myth/Symbol Not Important in Bible**	43	30	13	.27*
Nature of Salvation				
Jesus Is Surely Only Way to Salvation**	97	95	71	.74*
Once Saved, Always Saved (Str. Agree)	92	86	58	.63*
Atonement Substitutionary (Str. Agree)	82	52	30	.66*
Man Incapable of Good**	71	66	35	.40*
Never Hear Gospel/Go to Hell	68	61	43	.28*
A Child Is Born Guilty of Sin	61	51	25	.40*

*Chi square p < .05. Gammas are for entire table on each item.
**Data from 1984–85 sample.

labels. More intriguing is the theological pilgrimage of each group. Half the dispensationalists say they have become *more* conservative theologically since their youth. Premillennialists have moved in a similar direction, but nonpremillennialists have not changed much or, in some cases, have become more liberal. These patterns are consistent not only with the previously noted impact of education, but with theories that dispensationalism represents not just unreflective adherence to traditional orthodoxy, but a vigorous defense of that orthodoxy against the onslaughts of modernity (Marsden, 1980: 51).

These theological labels are also good measures of specific religious beliefs. Virtually all dispensationalists are biblical inerrantists, as are most premillennialists, but only a minority of the nonpremillennialists. On most doctrines, dispensationalists are both "literalist" and "supernaturalist": believing in the historicity of Adam and Eve, the actual existence of the Devil, the physical resurrection of Jesus, the Virgin Birth, the reality of Hell as a physical location, and a view of Jesus that denies any human limitations. They are also convinced that God instructs Christians on everyday decisions. Not surprisingly, almost half deny that understanding myth and symbol is necessary for interpreting the Bible. Dispensationalists are also convinced that belief in Christ is the only route to salvation, that salvation is once-for-ever, that the substitutionary atonement is the only correct understanding of Jesus' sacrifice, that human beings in their natural state are sinners from birth, and that people who have never heard the Gospel will go to hell. Traditional premillennialists look more like the dispensationalists than the nonpremillennialists who, though fairly traditionalist, are much less adamant in their orthodoxy.

The millennial ideas of each group are even more distinct (Table 11.3). Although virtually all Baptist ministers expect the physical return of Jesus to earth, the two premillennial groups hold the doctrine most firmly. Dispensationalists make belief in the Second Coming essential to the faith, a view less common among premillennialists and held by a minority of nonpremillenialists. Pastors differ sharply on the Rapture, the doctrine that Jesus will return and rescue the faithful from the world, regarded as vital by dispensationalists and many premillennialists, but rejected or relegated to minor status by nonpremillennialists. Thus, like nineteenth-century millenarians, Southern Baptists are enduring another "rupture over the Rapture" (Halsell, 1986: 8).

These millennial beliefs certainly affect ministers' actions. Dispensationalists preach about the Second Coming and stress the horrors confronting the unsaved during the last days. They agree that these exercises have at least two purposes: references to the Second Coming encourage the faithful in godly living and prompt sinners to turn to God. Hence the doctrine has

Table 11.3
Millennialism and the End Times (in percentages)

	DISPEN-SATIONAL	PREMIL-LENNIAL	NONPREMIL-LENNIAL	Gamma
Sure Jesus Will Return to Earth**	96	93	66	.70*
Doctrine of Second Coming Essential	72	63	36	.51*
Sometimes Refer in Sermons to Terrors Facing Unsaved in the "End Times"	83	57	37	.59*
Reference to Second Coming Important				
Encourages Christians in Godly Life	75	59	32	.50*
Encourages Conversions	69	53	27	.45*
Doctrine of the Rapture				
Very Important Doctrine	87	56	14	.82*
True, but Not Essential	13	37	32	
Do Not Believe or Not Sure	0	7	54	
Opinion Concerning Book of Revelation:				
Important Teaching and Prophecy	85	56	13	.81*
Spiritual Teaching More Important	13	36	31	
Mainly Spiritual/Past Events	2	9	54	
Confusing, Shouldn't Be in Bible	0	0	2	
Opinion of Hal Lindsey's The Late Great Planet Earth?				
Like It, Generally Correct	37	14	1	.78*
Like It, but It Has Some Errors	47	46	10	
Undecided or Neutral	12	22	19	
Dislike It	4	18	70	
Is The Creation of Israel a Fulfillment Of Prophecy Concerning the "End Times"?				
Yes and the End Is Near	51	26	4	.72*
Yes but the End May Not Be Near	39	52	23	
Can Not Tell	5	13	25	
Has No Significance for End	5	10	48	
Will The World End in a Nuclear War?				
Certainly or Probably	23	17	2	.33*
Uncertain. Symbols Difficult	44	35	42	
No. Bible Doesn't Tell How	29	43	47	
Bible Doesn't Predict Distruction	4	5	9	

*Chi square p < .05. Gammas are for entire table on each item.
**Data from 1984–85 sample.

the salutary practical effects noted a century ago by D. L. Moody and documented so ably by T. P. Weber (1987). For many ministers, then, the doctrines of the End Times are both vital and useful.

THE COURSE OF HISTORY AND ROLE OF THE CHURCH

What impact do these theological orientations have on social and political attitudes? The debate over the influence of dispensationalists centers not on their arcane theological system, but over its implications for social and political activity. Critics have argued, not always consistently, that dispensationalism encourages a fatalistic view of inevitable destruction from which Christians will be rescued, a paranoia concerning persecution of a faithful remnant by worldly powers, and disinclination or even active aversion to social and political reform.

If the end is already determined, dispensationalists are convinced they can discover that future through interpretation of Biblical "prophecy." As Table 11.3 shows, they regard the book of Revelation not only as important spiritual teaching, but as a blueprint for the future. Nonpremillennialists, on the other hand, either see the spiritual teachings as primary or treat the book as history. Just as notable is the ministers' reaction to Hal Lindsey's best-selling gloss on Daniel and Revelation, *The Late Great Planet Earth* (1970), which outlined a scenario for the End Times that was both vivid and imminent. For Lindsey, Israel's birth in 1948 signaled the approaching end: the European Community would soon emerge as the revived Roman Empire, under the Antichrist. After a false period of alliance with the Jews, he would initiate a coup d'etat and install himself as rule in Jerusalem. Then, all the world powers, including the Arabs, Russians, and Chinese, would converge on Palestine for a series of military encounters, prompting God's intervention and the total destruction of the contending forces at Armageddon, perhaps by nuclear warfare.

With some variations, this was the scenario predicted for 1982 by presidential aspirant Pat Robertson, who more recently admitted that "his sense of impending Armageddon has passed" (Ingwerson, 1988; Morken, 1988). For most dispensationalists, however, Lindsey's predictions still ring true. As Table 11.3 shows, dispensationalists admire his work, premillennialists are more skeptical, and most nonpremillennialists dislike it. A small majority agree that Israel's appearance means the end is near. Whether the final horrors involve a nuclear holocaust, as predicted by Lindsey and others, is not as clear. Even some dispensationalists admit indeterminacy in the form of ultimate destruction.

Thus far, dispensationalists conform to their stereotype. Do they also exhibit the historical pessimism attributed to them by critics? For the most part they do (Table 11.4). To begin with, they share the persecution complex of the "faithful remnant," agreeing that unbelievers try to destroy the Christian's faith, while nonpremillennialists are not so sure. Dispensationalists also think that living a Christian life has become harder in recent years. Finally, a narrow majority agree with the fatalistic assessment that the world is getting worse and nothing can be done about it, although a considerable minority think Christians could change it. Such disagreements may explain the split between dispensationalists who still shun politics and

Table 11.4
The World and the Church (in percentages)

	DISPEN-SATIONAL	PREMIL-LENNIAL	NONPREMIL-LENNIAL	Gamma
Christians in the World				
Unbelievers Try to Destroy Our Faith	61	52	35	.30*
Harder to Be a Christian Today Than It Was Twenty Years Ago	55	48	39	.19*
Direction of the World:				
Worse, and Nothing Can Be Done	52	38	16	.59*
Worse, but Christians Could Change	47	58	45	
Uncertain About Direction	1	4	33	
Getting Better Tho Not Easy to See	0	0	5	
Christians in America				
Religion is Losing Influence	49	43	31	.16*
Status of Christians in America:				
Mistreated Minority	22	13	7	.24*
Mistreated Majority	16	14	9	
Too Few Real Christians To Tell	40	46	54	
A Highly Respected Group	22	26	31	
Social Transformation				
If Enough Are Saved, Social Ills Would Take Care of Themselves**	82	68	49	.37*
Church Should Emphasize Transforming Social Order, Not Individual Reform** (Strongly Disagree)	40	35	21	.15*
Importance of "Church Growth"				
Most Important; Shows Faithfulness	27	8	8	.32*
Important, but Not Always Possible	25	27	20	
Other Things of Equal Importance	36	51	45	
Other Things More Important	12	15	27	
Importance of Social Ministry				
Not Very Important	6	1	2	.44*
Second to Evangelism	61	53	34	
Important: Makes Evangelism Possible	33	43	44	
Important As Evangelism By Itself	1	3	19	
More Important Than Evangelism	0	0	1	

*Chi square p < .05. Gammas are for entire table on each item.
**Data from 1984–85 sample.

those who join the Christian Right. On the other hand, very few non-premillennialists share the fatalism of the dispensationalist majority.

The ministers' assessment of religion in the United States fills out this picture. Dispensationalists are prone to perceive religion losing influence in the United States and Christians as a mistreated group, whether a majority or minority. Nonpremillennialists, on the other hand, are the most likely to think that Christians are highly respected. Note, however, that all groups are inclined to say that the status of believers is hard to determine because so few actually lead a Christian life. To summarize, then, in the words of John Davis, dispensationalism "has some attractiveness for a group of the godly who find themselves as an embattled minority in church and society. It provides a way of understanding—if not rationalizing—why we lost the denominations, why we lost the churches, and why society seems to be so ungodly" (Christianity Today Institute, 1987: 7).

What is the role of the church in this seemingly hopeless mess? One reaction for those who see the world inevitably growing worse and worse is to "go out there, grab as many as they can, and get them saved" (Christianity Today Institute, 1987: 5). Social reform, on the other hand, is not only futile, but diverts energy from missions. Although T. P. Weber (1987: 66) has argued that often the practice of dispensationalists was "better than their principles," they pointedly rejected the social ministry or political reform efforts characteristic of the Social Gospel.

The rise of the Christian Right might seem to herald a budding appreciation for social reform among premillennialists—or even a reversion to postmillennialism (compare Hadden, 1987). Although some on the Right, such as the Reconstructionists, have reverted, there are few prospects that Southern Baptists will. All groups, but especially dispensationalists, agree that social ills can be cured only by massive individual conversions (clearly an unlikely event) and deny that the church should put more emphasis on social transformation in accord with Christ's teachings (Table 11.4). The preference for evangelism over social reform is explicit in other responses. Dispensationalists tend to measure faithfulness to God by church growth, although a plurality says that other things are of equal or greater importance. Social ministry, however, is clearly not among those things. Two-thirds of the dispensationalists say such activities are of secondary importance at best, while a roughly similar group of nonpremillennialists see social ministry either as a prelude to evangelism or as valid in its own right. Ironically, there are no differences in the actual growth of ministers' churches or the size of their social ministries (see Turner and Guth, 1988).

THE POLITICS OF DISPENSATIONALISM

Quite clearly, dispensationalists have a very coherent worldview. Does that religious ideology include a comprehensive political perspective? Scholars disagree on whether dispensational theology has contributed to the rise of the Christian Right or dominates its political outlook. Outside analysts often assign a generous role to dispensationalism (Halsell, 1986; Martin, 1982; Mojtabai, 1986), but evangelical scholars tend to minimize the connection, stressing the diversity of fundamentalist and evangelical politics (T. P. Weber, 1987; Marsden, 1980). Marsden, for example, concedes that dispensationalists in the past leaned toward political conservatism, but had no real interest in politics; while Weber argues that the two movements had some affinities, but lacked a natural theoretical link. Whether the conservatism of dispensationalists (if it exists) is a comprehensive one, or is confined to a few issues, is even less clear.

As a first cut at the political perspectives of the clergy, we use their ideological self-identifications, usually a good summary measure for activists' views. On a seven-point ideological scale, a solid majority of dispensationalists are either extremely or very conservative, with most of the rest somewhat conservative; nonpremillennialists, at the other end, are more often either moderates or liberals. Traditional premillennialists, once more, fall in between. Interestingly, many dispensationalists say they are more conservative than the people in their pews, whereas nonpremillennialists are often more "liberal." Still, most ministers agree with the politics of their flocks—not surprising, given Baptist congregational polity (data not shown).

The dispensationalists' conservatism comes through on contemporary political issues as well. As critics charge, they are hawkish, thinking that the United States needs a strong military, needs to spend more on defense, and should avoid taking strategic arms talks with the Soviets too seriously. Although we doubt that they actually favor militarization because it hastens the Rapture, the data suggest a powerful tendency to distrust the Soviets and approve the arms race. Still, as Weber reminds us, not all dispensationalists are so strongly militaristic.

There is also no surprise in finding dispensationalists to be consistently more conservative than other groups on social issues. They are the strongest proponents of a right-to-life amendment, of "the right to bear arms," of a school prayer amendment, and of tuition tax credits for private schools. They are also, of course, foes of the Equal Rights Amendment and gay rights. Several of these stances, especially on tuition tax credits and school prayer, run against traditional denominational policies. Note, finally, that dispensationalists also think that government is providing too many services, that environmental protection is not a priority (lots of James Watt fans here), and that the federal government is doing enough about poverty, poor housing, and education. Only on the relative merits of fighting inflation and unemployment do they resemble their colleagues.

This comprehensive conservatism is reflected in the pastors' vote for president in 1984. Virtually all dispensationalists and premillennialists voted for Reagan, as did two-thirds of the nonpremillennialists. The president's popularity, then, cut across theological lines, although the group percentages remain in the expected order. Whether the president's popularity and ministers' conservatism have been translated into allegiance to the GOP is less clear. Immediately after the 1984 election there was a surge in Republican self-identification (Guth, 1985–86), paralleling changes among

Table 11.5
Political Orientations (in percentages)

	DISPEN-SATIONAL	PREMIL-LENNIAL	NONPREMIL-LENNIAL	Gamma
Ideology				
Extremely or Very Conservative	56	37	17	.52*
Somewhat Conservative	38	42	38	
Moderate	5	19	32	
Somewhat, Very or Extremely Liberal	1	2	13	
Defense Issues				
The U.S. Needs Strong Military	98	90	72	.58*
Increase Defense Spending**	69	49	27	.51*
SALTIII Not a Top Priority**	50	34	23	.29*
Social Issues				
Favor Right to Life Amendment**	89	85	52	.53*
Oppose Equal Rights Amendment**	89	84	64	.40*
Oppose Equal Rights for Gays**	85	75	53	.43*
Oppose Gun Control**	78	71	42	.40*
Public Prayer in School Beneficial	78	62	30	.55*
Favor School Prayer Amendment**	75	61	26	.52*
Oppose Affirmative Action for Blacks**	61	50	35	.31*
Pro Tax Credits for Christian Schools**	53	38	17	.41*
Economic Issues				
Government Giving Too Many Services**	78	78	50	.39*
Environment Protection Not a Priority**	55	45	31	.24*
Oppose More Federal Social Welfare**	50	47	29	.22*
Inflation, Not Unemployment, Main Foe**	39	43	36	.05
Candidate and Party				
Voted for Reagan, 1984	92	89	67	.53*
Party Identification				
Republican or Lean Republican	62	59	45	.20*
Pure Independent	12	15	10	
Democratic or Lean Democratic	27	26	45	
Christian Right Orientation				
Support Moral Majority**	90	71	31	.71*
Back Robertson for President	16	9	3	.40*

*Chi Square p < .05. Gammas are for entire table on each item.
**Data from 1984–85 sample.

all white southerners. The 1986–87 study shows this movement has slowed, and perhaps even reversed slightly. Nevertheless, pastors still favor the GOP, with dispensationalists in the lead. Only among nonpremillennialists are the ministers' old party ties still alive, with Democrats keeping pace with the Republicans.

The link between the new millenarianism and right-wing politics is incontrovertible by another measure: attitude toward the Christian Right. Virtually all dispensationalists back the Moral Majority, most premillennialists do, but few nonpremillennialists approve Jerry Falwell's lobby. This does not mean, however, that ministers can be mobilized for just any Christian Right cause: few supported Southern Baptist minister Pat Robertson's quest for the presidency. He does best among fellow dispensationalists, but does not mount an impressive showing even there. Although we can only speculate, there are probably at least three reasons for this poor performance. First, the 1984–85 Baptist clergy study showed that only 40 percent approved of a minister running for office. Second, Robertson's charismatic beliefs no doubt hurt his image in the traditionally anticharismatic SBC. Third, some ministers obviously have reservations about either his experience or positions on important issues. Although Robertson made some inroads among Southern Baptist pastors later during his 1988 campaign, these barriers to political mobilization remained (Straus, 1988).

Although Southern Baptist clergy have become quite active politically (Guth, 1988) and, as we have seen, quite conservative, the focus of their activity is not so clear. To determine their political agenda, we asked "What are the two or three most important problems confronting the United States?" As we might expect, given their doctrines on the inevitable decline of civilization, dispensationalists named spiritual and social issues, while nonpremillennialists listed the economic and foreign policy questions that preoccupy most Americans (Table 11.6). A more directed question, asking ministers how often they had addressed specific issues in sermons, public statements, and other political activities, supports this pattern. Most pastors still stress traditional "sin issues," along with abortion, school prayer, and gay rights, but the dispensationalists once more lead the way.

This social traditionalism seems to us the core of the movement: inside or outside the church, dispensationalists are most likely to cling to "old values": they oppose ordination of women, claim that God ordained male superiority in the family, disapprove of divorced and remarried persons entering the ministry, favor blue laws to control activities on the Lord's Day, oppose social drinking and dancing, and dislike living in a socially diverse community (Turner and Guth, 1988: 34). These findings certainly support Weber's (1987: 63) claim that dispensationalism "maintained the traditional cultural taboos of the evangelical movement." Nonpremillennialists, on the other hand, are much more "modern" on such issues, though leaning to the conservative side. They may be more akin to the "coming generation" of evangelicals studied by Hunter (1987: 56–64), who have fewer and weaker moral "taboos."

POLITICAL STYLE: CIVIL RELIGION AND CIVIL LIBERTIES

Their militant traditionalism hints that dispensationalists are unlikely to view with sympathy those who deviate from their moral or political ideals.

Table 11.6
Political Agenda (in percentages)

	DISPEN-SATIONAL	PREMIL-LENNIAL	NONPREMIL-LENNIAL	Gamma
Nation's Most Important Problem**				
Social or Spiritual Issue	61	53	37	.28*
Economic or Public Welfare	28	33	38	
Foreign Policy/International	11	14	26	
Addressed "Very Often" or "Often":**				
Family Issues	94	89	89	.14*
Alcohol and Drug Abuse	94	87	79	.37*
Pornography	90	78	55	.47*
Abortion and Right to Life	85	71	42	.50*
School Prayer	75	50	29	.52*
Hunger and Poverty	71	71	79	-.04
Gay Rights, Homosexuality	70	49	22	.46*
Israel and Middle East	70	18	6	.70*
Gambling Laws	68	52	45	.27*
National Defense, Nuclear Arms	39	22	22	.21*
Women's Issues, ERA, Equal Pay	39	23	23	.20*
Civil Rights	38	36	43	.01
Unemployment, the Economy	29	22	20	.14*
Federal Deficits, Government Spending	19	14	13	.15*
Environmental Problems	16	18	22	-.11*
U.S. Policy in Latin America	9	4	4	.27*

*Chi square p < .05. Gammas are for entire table on each item.
**Data from 1984–85 sample.

Indeed, they invariably regard adherence to traditional moral standards as a mark of the true Christian, using these to maintain the boundary between themselves and "the world" (Ammerman, 1987). Nor is dispensational theology itself conducive to tolerance. As A. J. Mojtabai (1986: 163) argues, the two-sided cosmic struggle in dispensationalism does not encourage coexistence: "If the world is divided between absolute good and absolute evil, between followers of the Lord and Satan, accommodation or negotiation with the enemy becomes unthinkable." Thus we expect dispensationalists to exhibit considerable political intolerance and be especially susceptible to the ethnocentric claims of American civil religion.

We report in Table 11.7 the results of a Sullivan, Piereson, and Marcus (1982) test for political tolerance. First we asked pastors to name the most "dangerous political group in the United States." Quite evidently, dispensationalists and nonpremillennialists have different fears: the former list Communists, Socialists, the ACLU, and that bugaboo of the Christian Right, "secular humanists"; the latter mention the Christian Right itself and far-right groups such as the Ku Klux Klan. When asked whether they would allow members of such groups to engage in lawful, peaceful, and constitutionally guaranteed activities such as making public speeches, holding rallies, running for public office, or teaching in public schools, dispensationalists were much less likely to say "Yes." Indeed, over half consistently opposed exercise of civil liberties by the groups they named. Indeed, dispensationalists not only exclude their foes from the political process, but from heaven as well: a large majority argue that it would be hard to be a true Christian and a political liberal (much less a socialist). Even after controlling for education, which is strongly associated with libertarian views, dispensationalists are more intolerant. Thus civil libertarians are not entirely amiss in their skepticism about the Christian Right's devotion to the Bill of Rights. Hunter's (1984) more sanguine views on the political tolerance of students at elite evangelical colleges should not be applied to all conservative Protestants.

The dispensationalists' social traditionalism is also expressed in adherence to some aspects of American civil religion. Many scholars have remarked upon the tension between early dispensational thought, which denies theological status to any worldly entity—except for Israel—and evangelicals' historic tendency to see a special role for the United States (Moorhead, 1978). In the first version of *The Late Great Planet Earth*, Hal Lindsey was almost apologetic over his failure to find any real place for the United States in the cosmic drama; indeed, the United States was consigned to a bit part, shadowing a revived Roman Empire. Later, however, his revised scenario incorporated an American appearance, but the whole effect seemed very forced (Lindsey, 1980; Weber, 1987; 217–219).

Although our questions here are not very numerous, they do suggest some possibilities (Table 11.7). Dispensationalists are much more inclined to see the United States founded on Christian principles than are the nonpremillennialists; they are also more likely to have the U.S. flag gracing the sanctuary, but the differences here are not so marked. They also concour overwhelmingly that among economic systems, only free enterprise is really compatible with Christianity. This may help explain why many politically

Table 11.7
Political Tolerance and Civil Religion (in percentages)

	DISPEN-SATIONAL	PREMIL-LENNIAL	NONPREMIL-LENNIAL	Gamma
Most Dangerous Political Group in U.S.**				
Communists and Socialists	27	19	14	.36*
American Civil Liberties Union (ACLU)	18	18	8	
Atheists, Secular Humanists	12	10	3	
Gays	11	13	8	
KKK and Nazis	3	7	15	
Christian Right	1	4	25	
Totals				
Left Extremist	43	34	22	
Liberal	47	46	28	
Conservative	2	6	29	
Right Extremist	8	14	22	
Would Allow Members of This Group To:**				
Make Speeches in a Public Place	46	62	73	.34*
Hold Public Rallies	41	58	71	.37*
Run for Public Office	39	57	68	.34*
Teach in Public Schools	15	31	43	.39*
Summary Index				
Strongly Anti-Libertarian	53	36	24	.35*
Mixed	32	33	35	
Strongly Libertarian	15	31	41	
Hard to Be a True Christian and a Political Liberal	63	45	18	.51*
Civil Religious Orientations				
US Founded As a Christian Nation	85	64	38	.53*
Have American Flag In Sanctuary	73	77	62	.17*
Only Capitalism Can Be Christian**	70	55	31	.44*
Government Must Support Religion to Uphold Morality**	43	32	18	.29*
US is God's Chosen Nation	17	11	3	.28*

*Chi square p < .05. Gammas are for entire table on each item.
**Data from 1984–85 sample.

active dispensationalists regard government economic regulation as proof of the approaching end. On two other civil religion indicators the evidence is mixed. Dispensationalists are almost evenly split on whether the government should support religion to uphold morality. Although this is a classic posture of the Christian Right, it runs against the dispensationalists' historic distrust of the state and, especially, religious establishments. Although dispensationalists are more likely than other ministers to see the United States as God's chosen nation, only a small minority hold this position.

DISCUSSION AND CONCLUSIONS

In summary, then, we have discovered much about millennialism in the nation's largest Protestant denomination. We have found that dispensationalists are a sizable minority of the clergy and, along with other premillennialists, constitute a large majority. Their theological beliefs generally conform to portraits by Marsden, Weber, and other scholars, although with minor variations: they are hard-core traditionalists, insisting firmly on the "old time religion."

We have also confirmed that dispensationalists hold, at least verbally, many of the social attitudes attributed to them. They are pessimistic about prospects for temporal reform, about human ability to achieve a better world, and about the ultimate fate of most of humanity. The role of the church, in their view, is really limited: to remain pure and to save a few souls before believers are rescued by the Lord in the Rapture. Finally, dispensationalism is clearly related to political conservatism. Indeed, adherents are not only conservative on social and spiritual issues but, as their critics charge, on most foreign policy and domestic issues as well. This ideology has manifested itself in support for conservative candidates, such as President Reagan, and for the conservative party, the GOP. Indeed, as a predictor of political attitudes, millennial views outperform almost any other theological indicator, including theological self-identification.

Despite these important findings, our study raises far more questions than it answers. Although we would expect to find similar results among ministers in many other conservative Protestant denominations, we also need to assess the influence of these ideas in the mass public. Much collateral evidence suggests that dispensationalism is widespread among Protestants, extending far beyond fundamentalist and evangelical churches. The continuing demand for the Schofield Bible, the sales of Hal Lindsey's books, the popularity of "Last Days" movies among church people, and the frequent use of apocalyptic terminology by those far removed from fundamentalist congregations—all confirm Weber's claim that these ideas are part of popular religious culture.

There are also tantalizing hints that they matter politically. Stockton (1987) showed that fundamentalist and evangelical Christians are likely to see the nation of Israel as fulfillment of biblical prophecy. Smidt (1988c) found that evangelical voters are not only more conservative on social issues, but also favor more defense spending and hard-line foreign policy, especially vis-a-vis the USSR. Sabato (1988: 123) noted that although fundamentalists' political attitudes are not always that different from those of other voters, "their sometimes apocalyptic and pessimistic outlook is readily apparent." Many scholars have found conservative Protestants scoring quite low on political tolerance (Hunter, 1984). Such findings may well reflect the socialization of many laypersons into a dispensational world view.

Of course, laity are seldom as theologically sophisticated as clergy. Social scientists studying eschatological beliefs in the mass public would probably not find self-identification measures productive. Rather, a number of items, each tapping one aspect of popular dispensationalist or premillennialist beliefs, would be required. Although the research costs may seem prohibitive, scholars might discover that "what is believed about the final destiny of the world and of individual persons" may influence social and political attitudes (Benson and Williams, 1986: 13-14). Indeed, the power of millennial orientations to predict other attitudes may lie in their very proximity to the "predoctrinal" or "foundational beliefs" that social scientists are just beginning to study.

A second question raises an even more fundamental issue: what is the nature of the connection between dispensationalism and conservatism? Although it is easy to see how dispensationalism fosters political intolerance, or encourages pessimism about the prospects for social reform, or engenders hostility toward Satanic powers such as the Soviet Union—all of which derive from explicit doctrinal teachings—some other results are harder to explain, including the rise of conservative political *activism*. We suspect that the connection is really functional, rather than logical. Dispensationalism serves as a defense of traditionalism, during a period of considerable social stress, especially for those unable to control their own destinies as the world changes around them. Southern Baptists have experienced fundamental social changes in recent decades: urbanization, industrialization, the rise of education, the civil rights movement, and women's liberation. For many clergy and laity these developments are threatening indeed, especially for those "left behind": the rural, the poorly educated, and blue-collar constituencies within the SBC (compare Barkun, 1974). Dispensationalism both explains the decline of their world and offers imminent escape. The doctrine also serves as a defense of the traditional untrained, "called" clergy of the denomination, against the claims of professional education and the competition of professionally trained ministers.

Millennial visions, however, often take on a social and psychological life on their own. Although the doctrines of the movement may denigrate temporal aspirations, the task of mobilizing the faithful remnant and the achievement of modest interim successes may entice believers into seeking part of the Coming Kingdom in this world. This is especially likely when, as in the contemporary United States, those left behind by modernity are not that far behind, not without social and political resources. Hence the Christian Right's temptation to "Christianize America," a task that dispensational theology regards as futile. Such a vision can energize and empower the dispossessed, sometimes, ironically, undercutting the very basis of the ideology (Walzer, 1965).

ACKNOWLEDGMENTS

The authors would like to acknowledge the contributions of Dana Research Fellows Lea Alexander, Sandra Hack, and Alicia Lehnes on earlier phases of this project. We are also grateful for the financial assistance of the Furman University Committee on Research and Professional Growth and the American Political Science Association.

APPENDIX: DISCRIMINANT CLASSIFICATION OF 1984-1985 SAMPLE

To make use of the richer set of political variables available in the 1984-85 survey, we experimented with a series of discriminant function analyses, using various combinations of identical questions from both surveys. Eventually we arrived at an optimal set of nine common variables that, in the 1986-87 sample, correctly identified known dispensationalists and nonpremillennialists 88.41 percent of the time. The function predicted dispensationalist identification correctly in 90.9 percent of the cases, nonpremillennialist identification in 86.0 percent. Using the Fisher's linear discriminant coefficients, we then calculated predicted dispensationalism scores for all ministers in the 1984-85 sample, classifying those with the highest scores as dispensationalists, roughly in proportion to the numbers in the original sample (30 percent), those with the lowest scores (30 percent) as nonpremillennialists, and the remaining 40 percent in the intermediate category—again, roughly equivalent to the traditional premillennial group plus the unclassified ministers in the 1986-87 sample (40 percent).

We should stress that this operation is exploratory. Still, the hypothetical categories behave remarkably like those produced by direct measure in the 1986-87 survey. We compared results on identical questions (those not ultimately used for the discriminant analysis) and discovered similar results, whether on demographic characteristics, theological views, or political attitudes. Thus we are very confident that the overwhelming majority of those in the 1984-85 sample actually hold the "hypothetical" positions assigned them.

Variable	Standardized Canonical Function Coefficient	Unstandardized Canonical Function Coefficient
Role of Israel	.56246	.85517
SBC President Vote	.31725	.59744
Biblical Inerrancy	.29381	.24605
State of Residence	-.25891	-.14725
Ideological ID	-.23199	-.17388
Women's Ordination	-.13034	-.95136
Secular Education	.11369	.12087
Seminary Education	.11167	.99488
Age	-.09631	-.41860
(Constant)		-2.059054

Fisher's Linear Discriminant Functions

Variable	Dispensationalists	Nonpremillennialists
Role of Israel	3.572206	5.688395
SBC President Vote	.767513	2.245948
Biblical Inerrancy	2.642785	3.251832
State of Residence	.245889	-.118436
Ideological ID	2.392533	1.962264
Women's Ordination	2.960435	2.725013
Secular Education	.669522	.968628
Seminary Education	-.686112	.177579
Age	.670178	.566592
(Constant)	-20.98669	-26.01883

[In the discriminant analysis, the variables are coded in the following directions: Role of Israel (1 = Very Important to 4 = Not Important); SBC President (1 = Fundamentalist to 2 = Moderate); Inerrancy (1 = Strong Inerrantist to 5 = Strongly Non-Inerrantist); State of Residence (1 = Northeast and Midwest to 6 = Deep South); Ideological ID (1 = Extremely Liberal to 7 = Extremely Conservative); Women's Ordination (1 = Strongly Approve to 5 = Strongly Disapprove); Secular Education (1 = Less than High School to 4 = Graduate Work); Seminary Education (1 = None to 4 = Seminary Graduate); Age (20–29 = 1 to 65–90 = 9).]

12
The Dance of Legislation: Church Style

Mary T. Hanna

"Once begin the dance of legislation, and you must struggle through its mazes as best you can to its breathless end. . . ."

Woodrow Wilson, *Congressional Government*

Newsweek (Woodward and Foote, 1983: 26) called the bishops' 1983 letter on nuclear war "by far the most ambitious and daring political statement the bishops have ever produced." Their 1986 economics pastoral was considered an even more controversial document. Hundreds of articles have been written condemning, praising, and analyzing these two pastoral letters and the new radical stance they signal on the part of the bishops. Little attention has been paid to the fact that the bishops adopted an equally radical approach to their writing and passage. The letters challenge much traditional opinion regarding both the U.S. defense and free enterprise economic systems. The process by which they were developed is imbedded in American ideas of representation, consultation and accountability. The letters criticize much congressional legislation, but the bishops writing them patterned their pastoral policy making after Congress's own policy-making process.[1]

The bishops themselves understood this. At hearings before the Joint Economic Committee of Congress in December 1986, Archbishop Rembert Weakland described the economics pastoral as "a very American letter" (U.S. Congress, 1986). He was referring as much to the process by which it had been developed as to its contents. Speaking to reporters in November 1986, Archbishop John May emphasized how American traditions and practices influenced the bishops: "We Americans work in different ways. Take, for example, the process Archbishop Weakland used in developing the economics letter. Bishops in other parts of the world wouldn't under-stand that process, but we're Americans and so we do things that way." If foreign bishops found the process strange, no American political scientist would. To a political scientist familiar with democratic policy making, the method and the philosophy behind it are easily recognizable.

Traditionally pastorals are addressed to their faithful and written by bishops in their role as teachers and pastors. As the U.S. Catholic Church and its bishops became increasingly active politically, pastoral letters took on new dimensions. They were no longer addressed only to Catholics but to all Americans. They were no longer conceived only as moral, ethical, in-trachurch teaching instruments but as contributions to general debate on important societal questions and to the political policy-making process. "Our hope is that we're one part of a debate that leads to a helpful out-come," Rev. J. Bryan Hehir, the bishops' original chief of staff for the economics letter, told the senators and representatives of Congress's Joint Economic Committee.

What the bishops did in a partial way with the nuclear war letter and far more completely with the economics pastoral was to devise a pastoral-writing process that took the pastorals through several drafts over a number of years. The process involved setting up a legislative committee composed of bishops representative of the U.S. church; requesting expert advice from all sides of the particular issue, in and out of the church; floating ideas in the press to provoke response from columnists, leaders in various fields, and the general public; systematically seeking amendment and criticism from organized Catholic groups, priests, nuns, the laity, and their fellow bishops; and finally debating, amending, and voting the pastorals on the floor of their annual national assembly.

THE PROCESS

The bishops probably devised this new formula for several reasons. First, they realized that if they were going to appeal to the general public, they had to do it on a basis of not just theology but rationality. As Jesuit John Langan (1984: 586–587) argued, the economics letter and similar church documents with general societal as well as intra-Catholic aims, have to meet "both the test of conformity with Catholic social teaching as this has been propounded by recent popes and by Vatican II and the tests of plausibility and applicability within the current American context."

I think there was a second reason. At a press conference during the bishops' debate on the economics letter, Archbishop Weakland, who chaired the bishops' committee that wrote the letter, said that bishops could afford to take long-range views of political, social, and economic issues because "we don't have to run for election." Bishops, he implied, don't have to worry about votes. That is only partially correct, however. Bishops aren't elected to office, their own episcopal sees; they are appointed by the pope. Pastoral letters, however, to be validated as official teachings of the church, must be passed by an extraordinary majority, two-thirds, of all the active bishops of the U.S. church acting under the aegis of their formal, country-wide organization, the National Conference of Catholic Bishops (NCCB). When the NCCB began to delve into such controversial issues as trenchant criticisms of our defense policies and our economic system, the bishops charged with preparing the letters may well have felt that they needed a process that would demonstrate widespread collaboration, that would slowly and surely gather support, both to legitimize their undertaking and reassure hesitant colleagues. In much the same way do political legislators undertake innovative policy making.

Political scientists point out that policy making involves a number of steps. First, policy origination: some person or institution must call for a response to some perceived need or problem and then the initiators or other persons or groups must actually introduce a written proposal to Congress. Second, policy formulation: under Congress's system of legislating through specialist committee, the proposal is lengthily reviewed by a particular committee with input in the form of criticism, support, and amendment. This comes formally during hearings through testimony by administration officials, interest group leaders, and experts of various kinds. It also comes informally through constituent letters, newspaper editorials, and such. In response to the deficiencies and arguments pointed out, the committee may go through many drafts in reformulating the bill. This consultation process does several things: it uncovers the bill's deficiencies; permits diverse opinions to be aired; and, hopefully, allows consensus, support, to build for the bill in the country and in Congress. Third, policy debate and vote: the bill is brought to the legislative floor for formal debate, possibly more amendment, and then for a vote (Woll, 1985: 405–453; Ripley, 1985: 123–203).

All of these formal steps are guided by democratic principles accepted in our country as the norms for the licit and proper making of policy. Among the most important are representation—Congress's perceived ability to represent the people in their action; consultation—freedom accorded everyone with an interest or desire to have his or her opinion on the legislation heard; accountability—Congress's perceived responsiveness to the original problem but also to the wishes of the country regarding the kind of response made. These policy-making steps are also guided by the formal and informal rules of the legislating institution, derived in part from the democratic principles described and in part from the need for efficiency.

It would be wrong to assert that the bishops adopted their new pastoral-writing process only for political aims or only from political patterns. They themselves often insist on their moral, even prophetic aims. They point to the collegiality inspired by the Vatican Council and its documents as their model, to the idea that, as a post-conciliar catch-phrase had it, "all people are priests" and therefore must share in the life and decisions of the church. As the bishops moved into action in political areas, however, they did adopt recognizably political organizations, formats, and rules worth examining.

This chapter will not discuss the contents of either the nuclear war or the economics letter except incidentally. Much has been written about both. I will instead analyze the process the bishops devised to write them, concentrating on the economics letter where it is most fully developed. As part of that analysis, I will point to the parallels that can be drawn between the bishops' process and U.S. political policy making.

THE PARTICIPANTS

Every year in November the bishops of the United States assemble in Washington, D.C., for a four-day national meeting. They receive committee reports, vote on proposals, elect new officers and committee members, and decide on further business. The 1980 bishops' meeting proved landmark, for the bishops that year voted to set up committees to consider the questions of both nuclear war and the U.S. economy.

Proposals for new legislation in Congress often grow out of the questions uncovered in writing past legislation. One bill gives rise to proposals for another. The bishops in 1980 debated and passed a pastoral letter on Marxism. The letter, in decrying Marxist political and economic systems, also contained criticisms of our own, especially our failure to tackle the systemic roots of injustice (*Origins*, 1984: 338). During the debate on the Marxism letter, Bishop Peter Rosazza urged that the bishops also undertake a critique of capitalism. A number of his brother bishops seconded the proposal and the assembly then voted to set up an ad hoc committee of bishops to examine Catholic social teaching and the U.S. economy.

The NCCB has a number of standing committees to work on ongoing U.S. church concerns: canonical affairs, for example, vocations, the church in Latin America. Like Congress, however, the NCCB also sets up ad hoc committees to consider and make recommendations on particular issues. The members of such ad hoc committees are appointed by the NCCB's president. Shortly after the November 1980 conference, then president Archbishop John Roach appointed five bishops to the new ad hoc committee on the U.S. economy: Bishops Peter Rosazza, William Weigand, and George Speltz; Archbishops Thomas Donnellan and, as chairman, Rembert Weakland.

Just as Congress tries generally to assure the representativeness of its committees, balancing senior and junior members, easterners and westerners, big city and rural congressmen, so Roach seemed to try to assure that this committee would represent the diversity existent within the hierarchy and within the U.S. church. Committee members represented different layers within the hierarchy: one, Rosazza, was an auxiliary or assistant bishop; two were bishops—that is, men who headed their own dioceses; and two were archbishops, a title reserved for bishops heading the largest, most important dioceses in a country. Two were among the oldest of the active bishops in the church—Speltz at 74 and Donnellan at 72; two, among the youngest—Rosazza was 51 and Weigand, 49. They came from dioceses located in very different parts of the country—St. Cloud, Minnesota; Atlanta, Georgia; Hartford, Connecticut; Salt Lake City, Utah; and Milwaukee, Wisconsin. They were also men of very different backgrounds and experiences, reflecting the variegated nature of U.S. Catholicism.

Rosazza was a graduate of Ivy League Dartmouth College and of St. Sulpice Seminary in Paris, but his roots lay in the Italian-American immigrant communities of the Northeast. He had spent nearly all his life in the large, heterogeneous, often poor and ethnically divided cities of the Atlantic seaboard.

Speltz was the committee's rural specialist. A former president of the National Catholic Rural Life Conference, an organization dating to the 1920s that brings agricultural specialists, religious and farm families together to improve rural life, he had spent 40 years working among the rural people of the Midwest.

Weigand was the committee's westerner, born in Bend, Oregon, educated in that state and Washington, ordained in Boise, Idaho. He had also spent almost ten years as a missionary priest in Colombia. At a press conference after the economics pastoral was passed, he told reporters that he had "always been interested in international concerns."

Donnellan's career followed a pattern more typical of the pre-Vatican Council church than of younger bishops today. His experience was largely managerial. He spent years climbing through the New York Archdiocese's administrative ranks: curate of St. Patrick's Cathedral, then assistant chancellor, vice-chancellor and secretary to Cardinal Spellman, and, finally, archdiocesan chancellor, concerned with financial, personnel, and administrative problems. In 1968 he was appointed Archbishop of Atlanta, Georgia, and so he had first-hand experience with both the aging cities of the North and the new, urban South, with the cycles of economic growth and decay.

The most intriguing member of the committee member was its chairman, Rembert Weakland. Weakland had personally known poverty. His mother was forced to go on welfare when her husband's early death left her with six small children to care for. He grew up to be both a Benedictine priest and a musician, a graduate of the Juilliard School of Music. His fellow Benedictines elected him abbot primate in 1967 and for ten years he served as head of this worldwide order with its 220 monasteries and 10,000 priests and brothers. A prominent "liberal" among bishops, Weakland had sold his predecessor's mansion and appointed women to key positions once he was named archbishop. He has been described as one of a small group of bishops "who have earned their colleagues' respect through past performance or by establishing intellectual or spiritual credentials" (Castelli, 1983: 160).

Congressional committee members may change but their committee staffs are often made up of long-time experts. As soon as the economics committee was formed, the bishops on it began, as do congressional committees, to gather a staff of experts and consultants to aid them. Like Congress, they had a ready-made group of professionals to call upon.

When the NCCB was formed following the Vatican Council, the bishops also set up the United States Catholic Conference as their "operational secretariat." The USCC is the bishops' national bureaucratic arm, staffed with professionals and specialists of various kinds to perform research, administrative, educational, and liaison work for them. One branch of the USCC, the Department of Social Development and World Peace, had had almost 15 years' experience with political, social, and economic issues before the bishops' committee on the U.S. economy was formed.

The bishops drew on this department for their staff. As their permanent chief of staff, they chose Ronald Krietemeyer, director of the USCC's Office of Domestic Social Development and a man with master's degrees in both theology and public policy from the University of Minnesota. Krietemeyer believes he was chosen because his education involved "both economics and ethics." This combination of theology and public policy seemed to be the hallmark the committee used in choosing their outside consultants as well: Jesuit Donald Hollenbach, professor of moral theology from the Weston School of Theology in Cambridge, Massachusetts; John Donahue, professor of biblical studies at the Jesuit School of Theology at Berkeley; Charles Wilber, a Notre Dame economist; and Donald Warwick, professor at Harvard University's Institute for International Development.

To gather expert information and diverse opinions both about religious thinking and traditions regarding economic issues and about the economic problems themselves, the bishops' committee embarked on an extraordinary series of hearings, which eventually stretched over a four-year period and involved 150 expert witnesses. This, again, emulates the process Congress uses in its own policy making to develop information and assure that all sides of an issue are heard.

The bishops began their hearings by talking to two groups of people—ethicists and social scientists, especially economists. They then met with labor union leaders, banking and industrial executives, and representatives from agriculture, farm organization leaders, and state agriculture experts. They interviewed people who led various kinds of private and government social welfare and community action agencies. For the first time in the history of U.S. Catholic pastoral letters, they also sought what Weakland called "ecumenical collaboration," meeting with prominent Jewish and Protestant clergy and lay leaders. Finally, as they turned to what would prove one of the knottiest sections of their letter—Third World economic problems—they met with a group of foreign, mainly Latin American, scholars and with eight Latin American bishops.

The experts they talked to were not only varied in their experience and outlooks but people of recognized accomplishment: Michael Harrington, whose book, *The Other America*, helped spur the Kennedy-Johnson antipoverty program; Alice Rivlin, the first director of the Congressional Budget Office, respected for her expertise and nonpartisanship by both Republicans and Democrats; Robert Bellah, who was about to publish one of the decade's most acclaimed books, *Habits of the Heart*; Sargent Shriver, who directed both the Peace Corps and the Office of Economic Opportunity; John Kenneth Galbraith, Harvard economist and friend to both John F. Kennedy and William F. Buckley; Herbert Stein, chairman of the Council of Economic Advisers for Presidents Nixon and Ford.

The bishops who wrote the pastoral on nuclear war, which occurred almost concurrently with the writing of the economics pastoral, also used the hearings process but much more tentatively. Over a year's time, they heard 36 witnesses. The economics committee developed the hearings system much more fully. When Bishop James Malone was moved in a poetic moment to say the economics letter had involved "the Whole People of God," he was exaggerating, but not by much.

INVOLVING THE PUBLIC

The bishops moved to a second stage in their consultation effort in November 1984. The hearings had been private and no one outside the committee knew the direction the committee was going. The bishops now wanted not just expert advice but general reaction and opinion and so they released the first draft of their proposed pastoral to the press and public. "In 1919," said Krietemeyer (1986), when following World War I Catholic bishops offered proposals for postwar reconstruction, "the bishops paid a media expert to make sure they had professional response to their letter. Ours made a splash in the media immediately and the response was everything we hoped for."

All three of the national newsweeklies featured the draft letter as their cover stories. Newspapers from the *New York Times* to the *Walla Walla Union Bulletin* played the story on their front pages. Magazines as diverse as the *Chronicle of Higher Education* to Britain's *Economist* ran lengthy articles dissecting it. What followed was the kind of national debate, waged through the media, that occurs on important bills as the public and press become aware they are under congressional consideration.

The national debate would go on for two more years as a second and then a third draft were released. Much of the early reaction was negative, especially from Catholic columnists such as James J. Kilpatrick and William F. Buckley, and from the business community. As time went on, however, the drafts and the bishops' explanations were more carefully examined; some changes and clarifications were made in response to questions raised; and arguments deepened and matured. Reaction slowly became more positive. When the letter was finally passed by the NCCB in 1986, response from press and public was almost wholly positive. This is akin to the result Congress, and especially the Senate with its more flexible agenda and debate rules, tries to evoke through stimulating lengthy public consideration of legislative proposals. It is a way both to uncover deficiencies in and disagreements regarding bills and to build consensus for them.

The bishops' committee also devised a systematic way to involve the ordinary American Catholic, in effect their constituents, in the economics pastoral. In November 1984 the first draft of the letter was given to all bishops at their annual meeting. The bishops were asked to take the drafts back to their dioceses and to solicit and report back criticisms and suggestions from local Catholic individuals and groups. Krietemeyer (1986) reported that the bishops "all got response forms and they were asked to convene committees or hold hearings to decide responses. But *they* decided how they would do this. We got 10,000 pages worth after the first draft." After the second draft was written, it, too, was sent back to the dioceses for local comment. "There was an opportunity," said Krietemeyer, "for lay involvement in this letter such as we never had before."

Returning to their dioceses, bishops used a variety of ways to involve local Catholic groups and individuals in this vast consultation process on the proposed letter. Cardinal John O'Connor, who presides over the skyscrapers and ghettos of Manhattan, brought together a committee of Catholic Wall Street executives to discuss the letter and, "to get a spectrum of opinion," also brought neighborhood groups together from the South Bronx, the Lower East Side, and Harlem. In Alabama, Archbishop Oscar Lipscomb held meetings with poor black parishioners in Tuskeegee. In Oregon and Washington state bishops asked parish priests to set up task forces of interested laypeople, nuns, and priests to study the letter.

A participant in one of these local groups described the consultation experience in his parish (Solbach, 1987). "We selected a chairman [an officer in the Army Corps of Engineers] and we drew up a set of discussion guidelines and then every week for months we worked through the letter, section by section." They met in an empty room in a local Catholic school and as they developed questions and comments on the text they wrote them on large squares of paper and pinned them to walls. "By the end, the walls were completely covered." A rural community, they were especially interested in the sections on agriculture and the environment and made a number of suggestions for changes. Toward the end of their work, their bishop came to the parish and met with them. "It was a real satisfaction to be able to explain our ideas to him and to know that he would be taking them back to the committee."

In the congressional bill-writing process, bills are amended in response to questions and criticisms voiced by constituents, experts, interest groups, and other political leaders. The bishops' committee amended the various drafts of their letter as a result of the general public discussion voiced through the press and their diocesan consultations with their Catholic constituents. In an article published just before the 1986 bishops' meeting that would finally approve the letter, Archbishop Weakland outlined the changes his committee had made in response to suggestions and criticisms. They had added, he wrote, more on the family, especially family breakdown and its ties to the economic structure and the feminization of poverty; more on educational failures and their ties to poverty; a more lengthy treatment of Third World debt, and a more extended historical tie-in between the biblical and ethical sections (Weakland, 1986). Changes evoked through the public and parish consultations were also alluded to during the floor debate on the letter at the November 1986 meeting. Bishop Thomas Costello remarked that most of the amendments proposed by a Center of Concern meeting in his diocese had been accepted by the committee. Lipscomb asked for an amendment on remedial education, which he said had been proposed by his Tuskeegee parishioners. Weakland urged rejection of the amendment, but only because his committee had already so greatly strengthened the education section of the pastoral as a result of responses from this parish and other groups.

Congressmen and senators debate and vote on bills in their own elegant chambers. Catholic bishops do this in the much more mundane setting of a ballroom in a Washington, D.C., Hilton Hotel. The setting is different but anyone who has observed the Senate or House in action immediately recognizes that the procedures are the same. Religious revelation today does not come in a burst of prophecy, but through rules, argument, rebuttal, and vote.

Over the years the bishops have devised rules to govern debate and voting, even enlisting a parliamentarian to help keep them on track. On the first day of the November 1986 national bishops' meeting, Archbishop Weakland outlined the rules as they would apply to the economics pastoral. At the beginning of the debate, a half hour would be set aside for bishops who wished to comment on the document as a whole. Then the bishops would work their way through 71 amendments submitted before the deadline imposed. One minute would be allotted to the amendment's author so that he might explain his reasoning; one minute to the committee chair, Weakland, so that he might explain the committee's recommendation of acceptance or rejection; then one minute each to anyone wishing to speak for or against the amendment. The bishops would then vote on the amendment. When all amendments had been acted upon, the bishops would vote by secret ballot on the pastoral as a whole. As is true for all pastoral letters, a two-thirds vote of the bishops would be necessary for passage.

The debate itself showed that many of the formal and informal norms that govern the Congress in debate and voting are also present among the bishops when they undertake the same activities. Bishops followed their own formal rules for debate and voting, perhaps even more faithfully than our partisan and increasingly fractious Congress now does. The informal norms of deference, courtesy, and the "rules of the game," practiced by Congress, were also in play.

The debate began on Wednesday afternoon, November 12. Adoption of the pastoral, *Economic Justice for All: Catholic Social Teaching and the U.S. Economy*, was moved by Weakland and seconded. In the time set aside for general discussion of the letter as a whole, an opponent and a supporter rose to speak. Archbishop Philip Hannan, an elderly cleric who takes a feisty role in all of the bishops' assemblies and who had opposed the nuclear war letter, suggested sharp changes in tone and substance in this one, too. Cardinal Joseph Bernardin rose to support it and, especially, to refute arguments brought against it by a group of wealthy, prominent Catholic laymen, among them Michael Novak, William Simon (President Ford's Treasury secretary), and former Secretary of State Alexander Haig.

Then, at the request of NCCB president Bishop James Malone, Archbishop Weakland took the podium to guide the bishops through discussion of the individual amendments. The other committee members sat at his side, ready to confer with him when necessary. Slowly the nearly 300 bishops, seated behind rows of tables ranged down the length of the ballroom, worked their way through the amendments, all printed out for them on color-coded bundles of paper. The debate went on for three hours that afternoon and for most of the following morning.

Congressmen traditionally defer to one another's expertise. Arguments and amendments may be made to bills but there is general recognition that the committee members who developed the bill are the real "specialists" regarding it and that the time and thought they have put into it should be deferred to by their colleagues. The bishops obviously shared this deference norm. The deference they felt for the five years of work and experience the committee had invested in the letter showed in the fact that only one amendment was passed over the committee's objections. Bishop John McRaith, a man who had entrusted important positions in his diocese to women and worked closely with them, argued forcefully that sexism was a moral sin akin to racism and that this must be acknowledged and denounced in the letter. The amendment passed by voice vote. At another point in the debate, a bishop argued that the letter must draw a clear distinction between the legal and moral responsibilities managers have toward their stockholders because "many people in the United States assume anything 'legal' is O.K." Weakland conferred whisperingly with his committee colleagues and then announced that the committee had originally rejected this amendment, 0–5, but now, hearing the bishop's reasons for offering it, they had changed their minds and urged its adoption. This amendment, too, was passed by voice vote.

The few bishops who seemed to be opposing the letter rose again and again to argue amendments—Archbishop Lipscomb, six times. Bishop Robert Banks offered three amendments, one of which would have stressed that on the letter's policy recommendations "there has been and continues to be much debate even among ourselves." In Congress, the so-called rules of the game require giving opponents a careful, thorough hearing, even an extra measure of time and attention. The bishops who opposed the letter, few though they seemed to be in number, received the same kind of careful, courteous attention. Weakland painstakingly explained his committee's consideration of their arguments and detailed its reasons for urging their rejection.

The same sort of courteous statement, sometimes approaching grandiloquence, which Congress uses to grease the wheels of the legislative process and help maintain order and affability in what could easily become an acrimonious undertaking, was evident in the bishops' debate as well. At one point, Bishop McRaith, in a graceful speech from the floor, expressed warm "appreciation to the committee for how good the letter is." Weakland, at another point, thanked his brother bishops for the confidence they had shown in him as chairman, saying that in permitting his work on the letter they had provided him "truly a moment of grace and growth."

When the vote finally came, 225 bishops voted for the pastoral, 9 against it. The pastoral on Catholic social teaching and the U.S. economy was now an official document of the U.S. Catholic church. The bishops on the floor broke into prolonged applause that turned into a standing ovation. The long process was over.

CONCLUSION

The process, for all it owes to American principles and congressional practice, has now become the accepted method for developing church pastorals. In April 1988 Bishop Joseph Imesh released the first draft of the NCCB's proposed pastoral on the role of women in the church and society. The accompanying documentation showed that his committee was following many of the procedures used to prepare the economics letter. The committee had put together a staff and consultants, made up mainly of women Ph.Ds. In March and August 1985 it had held a series of hearings with representatives of 24 national Catholic women's groups. It had also held consultation with women in 100 dioceses, and on 60 college campuses and 45 military bases. In his April letter to the USCC Administrative Board, Bishop Imesh asked for approval to distribute the draft to all American dioceses for criticism and comments by local Catholic lay and religious. At the same time, he released it to the national media for public response (*Origins*, 1988: 759-760).

This new Catholic process for developing church teachings and proclamations is not to everyone's liking. Protestant theologian Richard Neuhaus reacted to the pastoral and process by saying: "This would be something truly new in human history: prophecy by consenses, or a consensus in support of the prophetic (Lawler, 1986: 23).

The bishops themselves, however, take quite a different view. They believe that this new legislative process fulfills the Vatican Council-inspired impetus to involve all Catholics in their church and its actions and to more closely relate church and world and that it gains them greater legitimacy by being congruent with long-accepted and honored U.S. democratic values and practices. In his presidential address to the November 1986 bishops' assembly, Bishop Malone echoed the statements made by many of the American bishops:

Together as a national hierarchy, we have found a new and collegial method of teaching. For centuries, hierarchies have been publishing pastoral letters, but for the first time the people of God have been involved in their formation in a more intense manner. For the first time, the Church has taught not simply through a finished product, but through the process that led to the finished document. . . . Too often pastoral letters in the past taught little, not because they said nothing but because few were listening. We have found a method in which our collegial teaching engages and gathers into community all sectors of the church and many of these outside the Church, men and women of good will who are as concerned as we about nuclear war and economic injustice (*Origins*, 1986: 395).

NOTE

1. In 1986 I was invited as an observer to attend the annual meeting of the National Conference of Catholic Bishops, held in Washington, D.C., November 10–13. This was the meeting at which the bishops' pastoral letter, *Economic Justice for All: Catholic Social Teaching and the U.S. Economy*, was debated and passed. Much of the information in this chapter comes from my experiences at that meeting. I was able to interview key participants in the writing of the pastoral and to attend the press conferences, held after each morning and afternoon session, at which the bishops involved in the sessions made statements and answered reporters' questions. I was also present throughout the bishops' floor debate and the vote on the letter. Press conference quotations in this chapter are from the press conferences I attended. Quotations from the floor debate are also from notes I took as an observer at that debate. Somewhat abbreviated versions of the floor debate can also be obtained from the United States Catholic Conference, Washington, D.C.: NCCB General Meeting, November 12, 1986, Afternoon Session; NCCB General Meeting, November 13, 1986, Morning Session.

13
God and the GOP: Religion among Republican Activists

James L. Guth and John C. Green

One aspect of American exceptionalism that has long puzzled scholars is the absence of confessional political parties. Although partisan alignments in the West have varied with national historical experience (D. Martin, 1978), a division between religious and secular groups has been one important basis of party cleavages. As Suzanne Berger (1982: 1) argued in *Religion in West European Politics*, the dominant pattern there "has been a tight association between religion and the Right, as demonstrated in an extensive scholarly literature on local, national, and cross-national settings, with analysis of data from historical, electoral, opinion survey, and case studies, all converging on the same general conclusions."

Ironically, at the very time observers see this tie unravelling in Europe, harbingers of similar alignments have appeared in the United States. Although U.S. parties have always had distinct ethnocultural roots (Kleppner, 1985), the absence of a state church, denominational pluralism, and almost universal religious attachments among Americans precluded struggles between religious and secular forces for control of the state. More recently, however, the kind of conflicts characteristic of social and political modernization in Europe have begun to appear here, as secular elites in political and cultural institutions have battled the forces of "order and tradition" over the role of religion in public life, prayer in schools, control of educational institutions and curricula, sexual morality, and "family issues."

In the 1980s Republicans ardently wooed the religious with traditionalist appeals, apparently with considerable success. The New York Times/CBS Poll found that 81 percent of white "born-again" Christians voted for Reagan in 1984 (Clymer, 1984), accelerating a long-term shift of theologically conservative Protestants (especially younger ones) toward the

Republicans (Kellstedt, 1986; Smidt, 1987). Many conservative Protestant clergy, such as Southern Baptists, have also joined the GOP (Guth, 1985–86). The same trend appears among activists: Republican state convention delegates (Baker, Steed, and Moreland, 1986), national convention delegates (Kirkpatrick, 1976), and party donors (Guth and Green, 1986) are all more observant than their Democratic rivals. Activists in the GOP's allied interest groups and social movements are even more religious than the Republicans. All this led Thomas Edsall (1985: 8) to contend that "the muscle of the Christian right in the GOP is roughly parallel to the power of the AFL-CIO" within the Democratic party.

This movement of the religious into the GOP raises the specter of internal feuds, as "social issue" conservatives battle old-style "business" Republicans or new "Yuppie" libertarians. Whether such divisions threaten the GOP's future is debatable. In Europe, the Christian Democrats have often attracted both religious and business classes; in the United States such alliances should be facilitated by the documented religiosity of American business leaders (Pollock et al., 1981). Still, scholars have detected a secularist trend among upper-middle-class Americans, especially "New Class" professionals, which has also affected "cosmopolitan" elements of the business community (Roof and McKinney, 1987: 115).

In this chapter, we address the role of religion in the GOP by analyzing a vital group of activists: major financial donors. The data are drawn from a mail survey of a stratified random sample of 3,200 contributors to state and national Republican committees and to multicandidate Political Action Committees (PACs) sponsored by six presidential hopefuls: Baker, Bush, Dole, DuPont, Kemp, and Robertson. To represent the full range of Christian Right activists, we also included donors to Jerry Falwell's "I Love America PAC." The survey elicited 1,148 returns (a response rate of 40 percent after excluding 305 contributors who had died or could not be reached at their listed address).[1] The questionnaire is 10 pages long, contains 426 items, and is designed to distinguish among varieties of GOP activists. We used Federal Election Commission data for the 1985–86 election cycle to weight the sample so as to approximate the distribution of contributors in the Republican financial community.[2]

In the pages that follow we hope to answer these questions: (1) How religious is the GOP's financial elite? (2) What social and demographic differences underlie religious divisions? (3) Do the religious have a distinct agenda or ideological perspective? (4) Do religious Republicans have a characteristic political style? (5) How does religion influence GOP factionalism? (6) How well are the religious integrated into the party? (7) Finally, how will religious divisions influence the GOP's future?

HOW RELIGIOUS IS THE GOP?

The more we try to measure "religion," the more elusive it becomes. Scholars agree that religion is multidimensional, but they argue about the number and nature of dimensions. A recent study, for example, found no fewer than seven distinct dimensions (Hilty, Morgan, and Burns, 1984). Other analysts contend, however, that one dimension, usually orthodoxy, or perhaps salience, is central and predicts most religious attitudes and behaviors (Lindsay, Sirotnik, and Heeren, 1986). Still others suggest that we focus less on such dimensions, based on traditional doctrinal and behavioral measures, and develop instead more powerful religious indicators, such as self-identification (Wilcox, 1986; Smidt, 1986a; Beatty and Walter, 1987) or, perhaps, "predoctrinal" or "foundational" beliefs (Benson and Williams, 1986; Leege and Welch, 1986).

In this chapter, we rely primarily on traditional items that tap important religious dimensions: denomination, representing both group membership and, for many analysts, theological orthodoxy (Lopatto, 1985); frequency of church attendance (ritual dimension); importance of religion (salience dimension); church membership and activism (organizational dimension); and Biblical literalism and belief in life after death (belief or orthodoxy dimension). We also use questions on civil religion, the political influence of religious publications and leaders, and proximity to prominent religious groups. In that our prime concern is to detect religious cleavages within the GOP, these measures are appropriate. To assess the infiltration of the GOP by various theological movements (i.e., fundamentalists, evangelicals, or born-again Christians), we will also utilize a battery of self-identification items.

We have shown elsewhere that Republican contributors are, on the whole, considerably more religious than Democratic donors (Guth and Green, 1986). This strong religiosity appears once again here (Table 13.1). A solid majority claim that religion is of great importance; a similar number believe in life after death. Fully 70 percent are church members; 40 percent go to church at least once a week, with another 20 percent attending at least once a month. In these respects, Republican donors closely mirror the religious behavior and attitudes of the American public—one of the most observant in the Western world (compare Gallup, 1984: 32, 54, 56).

On two other items, however, the GOP differs from the mass public, albeit in predictable ways. On the nature of the Bible, most Republican donors regard it as inspired by God, but not to be taken literally. Compared to the mass public, fewer Republicans choose a literal description (14 versus 37 percent) and somewhat more opt for a "book of fables" (24 versus 11

Table 13.1
Measures of Religiosity (in percentages)

Importance of Religion		Believe in Life After Death	
(1) Extremely	33	(1) Yes	46
(2)	16	(2)	9
(3)	12	(3)	7
(4) Somewhat	21	(4) Unsure	19
(5)	6	(5)	1
(6)	4	(6)	2
(7) Not at All	9	(7) No	16

Church Membership		Church Attendance	
Active Member	39	Every Week +	9
Member	31	Once a Week	31
Not a Member	30	Twice a Month	12
		Once a Month	7
View of the Bible		Few Times/Year	18
Literal	14	Once a Year	4
Inspired	61	Seldom/Never	20
Fables	24		

Denomination*		Self-identification**		Only this ID
Charismatic	1	Charismatic	3	46
Fundamentalist	4	Fundamentalist	14	14
Evangelical	10	Evangelical	8	16
Cons. Mainline	18	Born Again	9	9
Mainline	17	Conservative	38	66
Catholic	12	Mainline	29	70
Lib. Mainline	29	Liberal	7	76
Jewish	2	Other Religious	3	78
Liberal	1	Humanist, Other	3	60
None	6	Agnostic/Atheist	6	86

*Examples of denominations included: Charismatic = Assemblies of God, all Pentecostal bodies; Fundamentalist = All independent Baptists, Conservative Baptist, General Association of Regular Baptists, independent Bible churches; Evangelical = American and Southern Baptist, Christian Reformed Church, Christian Church, various evangelical Presbyterian bodies; Conservative Mainline = All Lutherans, Presbyterian Church (USA) and predecessors; Reformed Church in America; Mainline = Methodists, Disciples of Christ; Catholic = All Roman Catholic and Orthodox; Liberal Mainline = Episcopal Church, United Church of Christ; Jewish = All Jewish; Liberal = Unitarian-Universalist, Quaker, Ethical Culture.

**Multiple self-identifications possible; next column contains percentage choosing only that particular self-identification.

percent). The GOP figures, however, parallel those for Americans of comparable socioeconomic status (compare Gallup, 1982: 74). Denominational preferences also reflect the high status of contributors: only one-third come from evangelical or conservative mainline churches. A majority are from mainline denominations such as the United Methodist Church or from liberal mainline groups, such as the Episcopal Church or United Church of Christ. Thus Republican donors are quite traditionalist, but are usually found in churches often seen as theologically and politically "liberal."

The religious self-identification measures prove most intriguing. Few respondents have any difficulty answering or feel the need to write in alternatives; apparently the terms are familiar and meaningful. As Table 13.1 shows, the most frequently chosen identities are "conservative Christian" (38 percent) and "mainline Christian" (29 percent). Labels usually associated with evangelicalism are selected by many fewer, with "fundamentalist Christian" more popular than "evangelical," "born-again," or "charismatic." Note, however, that each is often chosen in conjunction with one or more others, suggesting considerable overlap in meaning. "Charismatic Christian" is a partial exception, as the only identification of almost half of those choosing it.

Despite the many possible combinations of self-identification, we discovered that these items are summarized well by a nine-point scale, ranging from secular choices (atheist, agnostic) to the most conservative (fundamentalist, charismatic) and centered on "mainline Christian" (=five), with "conservative Christian" (=six) and "liberal Christian" (=four) on either side. The rest of the scale is determined by the number of conservative or liberal choices, rather than specific labels (e.g., a score of seven representing two conservative labels, eight representing three, and nine representing four). This scale predicted other religious and political variables better than any single identification item. Although the meaning of these labels requires more analysis, we suggest that multiple identities, whether on the traditionalist or secularist end, represent a mixture of intensity, sophistication, and interest.

To reduce all these measures to more manageable ones, we performed a factor analysis, with varimax rotation. Contrary to our expectations of two or more dimensions, all religious items load on a single factor with an eigenvalue of 3.9. The salience question (importance of religion) has the highest loading (.84), followed by church attendance (.76), belief in life after death (.69), and religious self-identification (.68). View of the Bible (.66), church membership (.63), and a Stark-Glock (1970) denominational orthodoxy scale (.56) also load quite strongly. This factor explains 56 percent of the total variance. Thus items often thought to represent distinct aspects of religiosity (salience, theological orthodoxy, denominational preference, organizational activism) are all part of a single dimension here, suggesting a high level of "religious constraint" among these well-educated, affluent activists. Those for whom religion is salient also attend church regularly, hold orthodox views, take "conservative" labels, and, increasingly, belong to traditionalist denominations (Roof and McKinney, 1987: 103). To borrow from Tamney and Johnson (1987: 13–14), they constitute "conservative Christianity."

To analyze whether this traditional religiosity influences GOP factionalism, we divided the range of factor scores into four equal parts, producing four religious groups: "Religious" (21 percent of the sample, n = 242), "Conventional" (43 percent, n = 493), "Nominal" (23 percent, n = 264) and "Secular" (13 percent, n = 149) Republicans. A brief description will give the reader some idea of their nature. Among the Religious Republicans, 88 percent say religion is extremely important, 91 percent attend church at least once a week, and 47 percent are Biblical literalists. Most are in evangelical or conservative mainline denominations. Conventional donors are less zealous, but still committed to the church: 32 percent say that religion is extremely important, 45 percent go to church every week, and most see the Bible as "inspired" (only 8 percent are literalists). They are concentrated in mainline Protestant and Catholic churches. The Nominal accord religion little importance, avoid church services, and split evenly on whether the Bible is "inspired" or "a book of fables." Most belong to (or at least "prefer") liberal Protestant or Jewish traditions. Finally, as their name implies, the Secular are low on all religious indicators.

We should note here that the explicitly Christian Right donors make up less than 10 percent of the Religious in the 1985–86 weighted sample. Thus, besides contributors to Pat Robertson and Jerry Falwell, the GOP financial corps has a much larger Religious component, committed to other GOP candidates or committees. For now we shall ignore such differences, returning later to a comparison of the Christian Right and other Christian Republicans.

RELIGIOSITY AND DEMOGRAPHIC TRAITS

A constant theme of the literature on conservative religion is that it is "sociologically distant from the institutional structures and processes of modernity" (Hunter, 1983a: 60). For example, in the United States, conservative Protestants are more numerous in the South and rural areas, and among those with more modest educations, less prestigious occupations, and lower incomes. They are also more likely to be women and older than other religious identifiers and secularists. Indeed, these traits may increasingly characterize the faithful in mainline Protestant and Catholic traditions as well. If so, European-style differences between "modernized" secular and "traditional" religious populations may be developing here (D. Martin, 1978; Roof and McKinney, 1987).

Speculation on the impact of religious traditionalists on the GOP has also centered on their social traits, purportedly different from those of old Republican elites (Shafer, 1985; Freeman, 1986). According to this theory, "cultural politics" threatens GOP unity by introducing social diversity, with traditionalists confronting more modern, secular activists. Does this sociological gap exist? In Table 13.2, we compare the demography of

Table 13.2
Religiosity and Demography (in percentages)

	RELIGIOUS	CONVEN.	NOMINAL	SECULAR	Gamma
Region of Residence					
Northeast	15	22	30	36	-.20*
West	22	22	26	22	
Midwest	23	23	17	17	
South	41	33	26	26	
Size of Place					
Rural, Small Town	33	28	18	20	-.15*
Small City	19	28	20	24	
Large City	20	9	20	14	
Major Metro Area	28	35	42	43	
Length of Residence					
More than 10 years	90	86	81	69	-.30*
Gender					
Female	19	17	12	13	-.15*
Age					
Under 50 years	18	26	32	28	-.08*
50 to 65 years	45	35	37	37	
Over 65 years	37	39	32	36	
Marital Status					
Never Married	6	8	12	17	-.31*
Divorced/Remarried	10	16	22	28	
Always Married	83	77	66	55	
Education					
High School or less	16	7	7	4	.15*
Some College/Trade	25	20	17	18	
College Graduate	24	31	31	28	
Postgraduate Training	36	43	45	50	
Occupation					
Professional	31	36	39	36	-.10*
Management	31	35	36	42	
Small Business	22	19	18	18	
Other	16	10	7	4	
Income					
To $50,000 a year	23	16	12	12	.23*
To $100,000 a year	25	25	19	17	
To $500,000 a year	47	48	53	43	
Over $500,000 a year	5	11	16	28	

*Chi Square p < .05.

religious groups and find many of the expected differences. The geographic influence is evident: Religious Republicans come disproportionately from the South or Midwest, while the Secular are more concentrated in the East. A majority of the Religious are from rural areas and small cities, while the Secular live in major metropolitan areas. The Religious are not only older but more "localist": 90 percent have lived in their current state for ten years or more, compared to only 69 percent of the Secular (compare Roof, 1978: 72–73). Women are also more numerous among the Religious, as are donors from "traditional" families—that is, those married only once to their current spouse. While most contributors have high status, the Religious have somewhat lower levels of education, occupational prestige, and income. Note, on the other hand, the elevated status of Secular donors, consistent with Roof and McKinney's (1987: 115) recent claim that well-to-do Americans are the secularist vanguard.

Clearly, then, the GOP's religious division is in part a social one. The background, life experiences, and status of the Religious and the Secular differ. Whether the glass is half full or half empty is another question: the status resources of the Religious are still impressive, however they may compare with those of other Republicans. In these respects, the Religious are not too far from "modernity." Their appearance in contemporary politics may reflect the oft-noted upward mobility of religious traditionalists in recent years (Roof and McKinney, 1987: 109–115). In fact, Religious Republicans are those most likely to report that they are "much better off" financially than their parents.

Although upward mobility may have put many Religious activists in the GOP's financial elite, their numbers are augmented from another source. Though almost two-thirds of the donors have stayed within the same denominational families since childhood, some have not: 14 percent have left mainline churches for more sectarian groups, while 25 percent have moved to higher status, more liberal churches. The former are extremely religious and politically conservative; the latter are much less religious and markedly more liberal, especially on social issues. Thus Republican activists, like other believers, are regrouping around "clusters" of compatible theological, social, and political attitudes (Roof and McKinney, 1987: 69). Although rooted in demography, the GOP's religious cleavages are buttressed by a "theological realignment" among high-status activists.

RELIGIOSITY AND ISSUE CLEAVAGES

Scholars and journalists often claim that the religious have a very different agenda and very different opinions than old-style GOP activists. As the carriers of cultural traditionalism, they are more concerned with, and more conservative on, social issues. Conversely, the most secular are the core advocates of economic conservatism. Neither group, the theory goes, shares the other's priorities or preferences: the religious, given their modest status, are seldom whole-hearted economic conservatives, and the cosmopolitan secularists scoff at traditional values (Shafer, 1985).

Do Religious and Secular Republicans have different agendas? To find out, we used two different salience measures. First, we asked respondents to list the two or three most important problems confronting the country. Surprisingly, the Religious are only slightly less likely to name an economic issue (67 percent) than Conventional (75 percent), Nominal (71 percent), and Secular (76 percent) Republicans. Indeed, only 16 percent of the Religious mentioned a social issue first. When asked how much issues influence their vote, however, the Religious are much more prone to say that social and foreign policy concerns are very important. For example, 50 percent of the Religious claim that a candidate's stance on school prayer "greatly" affects their vote, a much larger proportion than the Conventional, Nominal, or Secular donors (21, 16, and 13 percent). Similar patterns appear on other social and—to a lesser extent—foreign policy issues. Even on economic issues, however, the Religious are slightly more likely to claim an influence on their vote (Guth and Green, 1987a: 20).

The Religious also have fairly distinct opinions. As Table 13.3 shows, the differences Smidt (1987) found between evangelicals and nonevangelicals among voters are, if anything, intensified among activists. Not surprisingly, the Christian Right's "pro-family" agenda stands out: the Religious are most willing to regulate private sex between consenting adults, allow more local regulation of pornography, severely restrict abortion, enforce marijuana laws, oppose public provision of birth control information, and allow school prayer. They are also much more inclined to pass laws guaranteeing the rights of Christian schools, gun owners, housewives, and the traditional nuclear family—but not gays. Still, on most social issues, a majority of all Republican donors take conservative positions, which vary mostly by intensity. On foreign policy, the Religious are less distinctive: more hawkish on defense spending, protectionist on trade, and in favor of the Strategic Defense Initiative, aid to the contras, and U.S. withdrawal from the United Nations. Contrary to expectations, however, they are notably less enamoured of Israel and no more likely to reject strategic arms talks with the USSR, or to differ on U.S. policy toward South Africa.

Although most GOP donors are economic conservatives, the Religious are sometimes more "moderate," worrying more about unemployment than inflation, favoring a graduated income tax over a "flat" tax, and backing government aid to small business—attitudes that no doubt reflect their more precarious economic status as small businessmen, farmers, and

Table 13.3

Religiosity and Issues (in percentages)

Most Conservative Response
(on seven-point scale)

Social Issues	RELIGIOUS	CONVEN.	NOMINAL	SECULAR	Gamma
Regulate Adult Sex	31	6	2	3	.56*
Restrict Pornography	82	60	49	32	.44*
Restrict Abortion	61	29	25	14	.44*
Drug Enforcement	81	64	54	35	.41*
Oppose Birth Control	25	12	8	10	.29*
Support School Prayer	79	71	66	54	.22*
More Rights For:					
Christian Schools	46	25	23	5	.40*
Gun Owners	35	27	23	13	.21*
Housewives	29	25	22	7	.11*
"Traditional Family"	27	27	30	12	.10*
Foreign Policy Issues					
Increased Defense Funds	36	23	21	17	.25*
Pro Trade Restrictions	46	32	32	18	.18*
Support "Star Wars"	65	48	44	42	.17*
Support for Israel	51	62	67	68	-.16*
Support Contra Aid	28	17	18	24	.10*
Withdraw from UN	31	16	14	18	.10*
Economic Issues					
Inflation vs. Unemploy.	20	24	18	37	-.17*
Budget Amendment	33	38	22	24	.15*
Favor "Flat" Income Tax	33	29	40	43	-.15*
Line-item Veto	62	57	58	48	.13*
Favor Small Business Aid	50	38	37	27	.13*
Favor Gold Standard	25	15	24	13	.10*
Conservative ID	31	16	15	13	.19*

*Chi Square p < .05. Gammas are for entire table on each item.

marginal professionals. However, they are also more likely to favor a constitutional amendment to require a balanced budget and to support a presidential line-item veto. On domestic issues such as social security, welfare, the environment, civil rights, and regulation, however, they are hard to pick out from other Republicans (data not shown). The Religious, then, differ primarily in their adamant social conservatism and bellicose defense and foreign policy postures, but look much like other Republicans on economics. Still, the cumulative effect is evident: the Religious say they are "extremely conservative" more often (31 percent) than do the Conventional (16 percent), Nominal (15 percent), or Secular (13 percent).

RELIGIOSITY AND POLITICAL STYLE

To this point, we have confirmed some speculation about the Religious: their demographic traits and policy preferences set them apart. But much popular and scholarly commentary suggests that the crucial difference is political style: the Christian Right is characterized by belief in civil religion, amateur motivations, purist political norms, and anti-libertarian perspectives. Moreover, these assertions are not without foundation. First, there are dramatic differences in the way Republicans link their faith with political life. As Table 13.4 shows, the Religious are much more likely to assert that God has blessed the United States above all other nations. And God works through His People: 40 percent said their religious views were "extremely important" in deciding how to vote. A somewhat smaller group insisted that churches and clergy could appropriately lobby Congress and endorse candidates. Thus, for the Religious, theological perspectives and church organizations play an explicit and important role in their political world view.

The ideological fervor of the Religious suggests the portrait of the classic political "amateur" (J. Q. Wilson, 1962; Polsby and Wildavsky, 1984). Indeed, the Religious are somewhat more likely to cite purposive incentives, such as a sense of civic duty or a desire to pursue important issues, but they are also high on the supposedly professional trait of working to help their party win elections. Still, in modern U.S. politics, such incentives are characteristic of most activists (Green and Guth, 1986). The Religious do take "purist" stances more often: that only one philosophy can be correct, that political compromise represents betrayal, and that losing an election is preferable to compromising principles. They are also somewhat more prone to see politics as conflictual rather than a matter of consensus around key values. Finally, they are less tolerant of political expression, seeing self-gratification as too widespread in society and thinking that "people who get in trouble for their political views have only themselves to blame." They are also less willing to accept civil liberties for political groups they think are "dangerous." As we show elsewhere, GOP donors are less likely than Democrats to allow such groups to exercise basic constitutional rights (Guth and Green, 1984), but among Republicans, the Religious are most reluctant.

Therefore, much of the notice generated by the Religious can be attributed to their special political style. While their social traits and policy preferences do distinguish them from fellow Republicans, other factors reinforce these differences: greater ideological rigor, less tolerance for opposing perspectives, and, above all, a conviction that religious ideas and institutions have direct political application. In combination, these may well produce a degree of self-conscious factional identity.

Table 13.4
Religiosity and Political Style (in percentages)

Most Extreme Response

	RELIGIOUS	CONVEN.	NOMINAL	SECULAR	Gamma
Civil Religion					
Religion Affects Vote	40	8	2	1	.64*
God Blessed America	75	26	14	2	.57*
Churches in Politics	25	7	9	12	.22*
Amateur Motivations					
Civic Duty	64	48	44	37	.21*
Back Good Candidates	74	63	61	58	.16*
To Help Win Elections	49	38	35	27	.16*
Pursue Important Issues	67	54	56	49	.13*
Purist Attitudes					
One Philosophy Correct	19	6	3	6	.26*
Compromise is Betrayal	25	16	7	6	.18*
Lose Versus Compromise	38	26	26	19	.10*
Basically Politics Is					
Conflict	20	12	8	11	.26*
Compromise	24	27	41	34	.18*
Consensus	53	60	54	54	.01
Antilibertarian Values					
Today there is too					
much self-gratification	42	23	23	20	.13*
Trouble due to political					
views is one's own fault	34	20	16	24	.12*
Members of "Dangerous"					
Groups Should Be Allowed To					
Teach in Public School	15	17	20	22	-.24*
Run for President	39	45	52	53	-.18*
Speak in Public Place	45	52	59	57	-.17*

*Chi Square p < .05. Gammas are for entire table on each item.
Civil religion, political purism and anti-libertarian values are measured on seven-point scales, amateurism on a five-point scale.

RELIGIOSITY AND INTERNAL PARTY ALIGNMENTS

Obviously, religiosity is an important element in Republican politics, influencing the priorities, issue preferences, and political style of activists and, presumably, internal alliances. In fact, the leadership preferences of the Religious differ from other groups, but in an unexpected way. Neither the Religious nor the Conventional differ from other Republicans in their affection for mainstream figures such as George Bush, Howard Baker, Bob Dole, or Gerald Ford, but the Religious do "feel closer" to conservative notables. As Table 13.5 indicates, however, they view Jack Kemp, Jesse

Helms, Strom Thurmond, Ed Meese—and even James Watt—more favorably than Christian Rightist Pat Robertson, who is warmly regarded by only one-quarter of the Religious. This combination of support for both mainstream Republicans and ideological conservatives is also reflected in contributors' political history. When a conservative is a possible winner of the GOP nomination, such as Goldwater in 1964 or Reagan in 1976 and 1980, he does better with the Religious than among the Conventional, Nominal, or Secular groups. In 1952 and 1968, however, the Religious preferred front-running moderates: Eisenhower over Taft and Nixon over Reagan. This suggests a very considerable degree of both ideological conservatism and party regularity (data not shown).

Table 13.5
Religiosity and Political Alliances (in percentages)

	RELIGIOUS	CONVEN.	NOMINAL	SECULAR	Gamma
Feel Close To					
Pat Robertson	28	8	3	1	.43*
Jesse Helms	52	30	28	17	.30*
Ed Meese	44	31	28	11	.26*
James Watt	35	19	21	13	.19*
Strom Thurmond	50	45	29	27	.18*
Jack Kemp	69	51	54	53	.16*
Feel Close To					
Moral Majority	35	14	11	5	.40*
Right to Life	44	22	17	9	.37*
American Legion	50	54	45	26	.27*
Natl Rifle Association	53	37	24	24	.24*
Natl Catholic Conference	8	13	5	2	.18*
Natl Council of Churches	18	20	17	16	.17*
John Birch Society	16	5	7	10	.17*
American Jewish Comm.	13	8	7	11	.13*
Belong To					
Right to Life Groups	17	5	7	1	.43*
"Pro Family" Groups	18	12	8	2	.35*
Gun Clubs	22	14	10	9	.28*
Farm Organizations	13	14	6	6	.27*
Veterans Groups	38	33	14	16	.20*
PTA or School Groups	38	19	16	16	.19*
Conservative Groups	24	19	15	13	.17*
Political News From					
Religious Publications	38	10	2	0	.78*
Christian Broadcasting	36	11	3	1	.73*
Clergy	32	11	4	1	.68*
Single Issue Magazines	16	14	10	5	.24*
Direct Mail	60	47	37	37	.18*

*Chi Square p < .05. Gammas are for entire table on each item.

The Religious donors' organizational preferences show a similar mixture of mainstream affiliations and ideological commitment. While they feel just as close as other Republicans to business and professional lobbies, such as the U.S. Chamber of Commerce, National Association of Manufacturers, and American Medical Association, they are much closer to right-wing groups. However, just as Pat Robertson trails other conservatives, so the Moral Majority draws less support than the Right to Life movement, American Legion, or National Rifle Association. Once again, although religiosity does incline activists toward a more favorable assessment of Christian Right organizations and leaders, the Christian Right attracts at best only one-third of the Religious, illustrating both the limited inroads of extant Christian Right groups and the much greater potential of "Christian conservatism" (Guth and Green, 1987b).

These "national" preferences are clearly rooted in both the demography of the Religious and their local organizational commitments. They are more likely than the Secular to belong to "pro-family," anti-abortion, and conservative organizations. Beyond their obvious church involvements, they are more frequently found in the characteristic associations of rural and small town United States: farmers' organizations, veterans' groups, gun clubs, and PTAs. They are also slightly more likely to join civic, service, or cultural associations, but the differences are modest. Overall, Religious donors are more deeply embedded in the organizational life of their communities than are their Secular counterparts.

The information sources used by the Religious also differ somewhat. All Republicans depend equally on TV and newspapers for political information, but the Religious are more likely to seek insight from their own media: Christian broadcasting, religious publications, the clergy, and single-issue newsletters. Thus the political activity of some religious activists is mobilized, coordinated, and directed more frequently by outside, specialized religious sources. Still, note that only a minority of Religious donors say they get a "lot" or "some" information from religious sources. Beyond TV and newspapers, only direct mail is used by a majority of the Religious (and many other Republicans).

The picture of Religious activists' attachments is quite clear: they prefer the GOP's conservative wing and conservative movement organizations seeking to influence party policy. These attachments are hardly "insurgent," however; they are grounded in networks extending back into contributors' home communities, including not only churches and affiliated groups, but other traditionalist associations as well. Thus the religious right has strong roots in the social and political environments of many U.S. communities.

RELIGIOSITY AND PARTISANSHIP

The mixture of both "insurgent" and "establishment" traits among religious donors brings into clear relief two contrasting theories on their role in the GOP. That the Religious support conservative movement leaders and organizations and themselves possess amateur traits suggests that they are new to the GOP, less attached to the party, and marginal to its activities (Freeman, 1986). Their organizational commitments and political history, however, are consistent with a different view: that religiosity reinforces other commitments. Presumably, then, the Religious ought to be strongly tied to the party and its policies (Lipset and Schneider, 1987: 105; Pollock et al., 1981: ch. 2).

To make a long story short, the Religious are more integrated within the party than are the Secular. As Table 13.6 shows, they are more often "strong" Republicans, at both the national and state level, more approving of party leaders' work, and more supportive of the party's platform on virtually all issues. This advantage extends to participation as well: the Religious exceed the Secular in virtually every type of party activity, although in a few areas, such as fund raising and contributing, the advantage is small. Indeed, the "establishment" character of the Religious is especially evident if we analyze contributors by type of committee: the closer to the grass roots, the more the Religious dominate. For example, fully 70 percent of state party contributors fall into the Religious and Conventional groups, compared to 60 percent of national committee donors. The presidential donors look much like the national committee Republicans: Kemp has 63 percent, Dole 61 percent, and Bush 56 percent. This advantage of the Religious in local and state parties is compatible with evidence on other activists, such as state convention delegates (Baker, Steed, and Moreland, 1986). Thus the Religious are at the core of both GOP local establishments and of the ideological movements that have transformed the national party.

THE CHRISTIAN RIGHT AND CHRISTIAN REPUBLICANS

This mixture of establishment and insurgent traits may in part result from confounding data on the Christian Right and the other 90 percent of the Religious—whom we might call Christian Republicans. As we argued in an earlier analysis of Pat Robertson's contributors, the Christian Right is much more characterized by insurgent traits (Green and Guth, 1988). As the future of GOP religious activism may ride on the Christian Right's ability to mobilize Christian Republicans, a comparison of these two groups is in order.

Table 13.6
Religiosity, Partisanship, and Activism (in percentages)

Most Extreme Response

	RELIGIOUS	CONVEN.	NOMINAL	SECULAR	Gamma
Strong Natl Republican	82	68	66	61	.23*
Strong Local Republican	73	58	47	52	.23*
Strongly Approve Of					
President Reagan	75	62	56	42	.29*
Natl Republican Party	24	23	14	14	.23*
State Republican Party	21	20	12	6	.20*
House Republican Leaders	29	23	14	14	.18*
Local Republican Party	17	16	8	2	.17*
Senate Republicans	46	28	28	21	.15*
Strongly Approve of GOP Positions On					
School Prayer	50	21	14	13	.39*
Abortion	51	25	23	18	.30*
Drug Enforcement	66	52	43	37	.28*
Pornography	57	23	21	16	.20*
Civil Rights	50	25	25	16	.14*
Arms Control	59	29	26	21	.30*
Defense Spending	59	38	30	25	.29*
Contra Aid	59	40	36	33	.26*
USSR Policy	59	36	30	31	.25*
Trade Restrictions	46	23	26	22	.24*
Interest Rates	55	41	31	22	.23*
Unemployment	57	37	34	34	.21*
Budget Deficits	43	26	18	18	.20*
Inflation	65	55	47	49	.19*
Tax Rates	53	38	33	35	.18*
In 1984 or Previously					
Served GOP Natl Comm.	12	7	8	2	.26*
Served GOP State Comm.	33	31	17	5	.24*
Served GOP Delegate	22	23	15	9	.23*
Campaigned door-to-door	55	47	42	38	.22*
Vote GOP Primary/Caucus	37	34	24	18	.21*
Worked in Cong Campaign	49	44	42	18	.21*
Worked in State Campaign	48	51	40	25	.17*
Worked in Pres Campaign	50	41	40	37	.16*
Worked in Local Campaign	46	44	40	24	.15*
Served GOP Local Comm.	24	22	24	13	.13*
Attended Political Rally	46	46	40	37	.12*
Lobbied Public Official	36	36	28	27	.12*

*Chi Square p < .05. Gammas are for entire table on each item.

Christian Rightists are a distinct subset of the Religious Republicans. They are slightly more religious on the factor score, but that results largely from their residence in the most theologically conservative denominations (to which they are often converts). The Christian Republicans are concentrated in both "evangelical" and conservative mainline denominations, while the remaining GOP donors are found mostly in mainline and liberal mainline churches. The demographics of the Christian Right and Christian Republicans are also distinctive: both are equally likely to live in the South, but Christian Right activists are less numerous in the Midwest and more likely to reside in the Northeast or West. They are more often from rural areas and small towns, are younger, more female, more often divorced, and more downscale in education, occupation, and income than the Christian Republicans.

Christian Right donors have more insurgent features than Christian Republicans: they are much more often recent entrants into politics and converts from independent or Democratic identification. On each of these points, Christian Republicans look like their less-religious colleagues. As we might expect, Christian Right donors feel closer to right-wing leaders and organizations than do Christian Republicans and are much higher on purism, civil religion, and anti-civil liberties attitudes. Still, Christian Republicans score above other Republicans on these traits. Thus many Christian Rightists are insurgents, but find already on the scene established Christian Republicans who may at least be recognized as religious kin—and the largest part of the family.

On contemporary political issues, the Christian Right and Christian Republicans differ in two ways: first, the Christian Right is usually more conservative, and second, it has a different agenda. The Christian Right's conservative margin is most evident on social questions, smaller on foreign policy, and almost invisible on economics. The Christian Republicans, in turn, are more conservative than other GOP donors on social issues but quite similar on economics and foreign policy. Ideological self-identification summarizes these differences: 42 percent of Christian Right donors are "extremely conservative," compared to 30 percent of Christian Republicans and only 17 percent of all other Republicans. Where Christian Rightists differ most, however, is in their agenda: a majority (55 percent) name a social problem as most important, compared to 15 percent of Christian Republicans and 11 percent of all other GOP donors. This trend appears on "issue voting" as well. Thus Christian Republicans share the Christian Right's social conservatism—but only to a degree.

The Christian Right's position in the GOP is quite different, moreover, from that of Christian Republicans. Christian Republicans include more "Strong" identifiers (87 percent), than do other Republicans (65 percent) or

the Christian Right (54 percent), with a similar pattern in state party identification. While Christian Right donors match Christian Republicans' approval of President Reagan (75 percent "excellent"), they are far less
friendly toward other GOP leaders. Ironically, here they resemble Secular
Republicans; it is Christian Republicans who are the bulwark of support for
party leaders across the board. This is also reflected in performance of party
duties: although the Christian Right is quite active in many ways, Christian
Republicans are far more likely to have held party office.

These comparisons underscore both the strengths and weaknesses of
the Christian Right in the GOP. Identifiable Christian Right activists are a
minority, even among the Religious, but they have a chance to activate a
much larger group of Christian Republicans who share many of their
views—but not necessarily their priorities. Christian Republicans are much
more entrenched in the party and its local establishments—the core of non-
metropolitan Republicanism. They also share enough of the Christian
Right's political style to empathize, if not sympathize, with the effort to
turn the United States back to God's values, even in the face of Secularist
opposition.

DISCUSSION AND CONCLUSIONS

Our findings answer some questions and raise others. Among activists,
the GOP is already a "religious" party, about as religious as the U.S. public
and considerably more so than the Democratic party. Although our data
suggest some increase in secularism, based on movement to more liberal
churches, there is a striking, if smaller, countercurrent to traditionalist
bodies. Moreover, the great majority of Republicans have remained in their
childhood religious homes. Despite the GOP's overall religious tone,
religion is also a source of conflict, creating fissures over social issues,
fostering differing alliances, and encouraging divergent political styles.
Although the Religious have many features of political insurgents, they
possess establishment traits as well: they are well-off financially, ensconced
in community organizations, and well-integrated into the GOP itself, at
least if the history of their activism is any guide. In sum, they resemble both
the "new" Christian Right and the "old" Republican establishment.

The Christian Right's fate within the GOP will hinge on its ability to
mobilize the Christian Republicans—and perhaps some of the Conventional
as well. These groups differ little on most important economic issues, and
despite Pat Robertson's failure to transcend his sectarian base, social traditionalism may yet provide common ground for such an alliance. Simple
resistance to modernity will not suffice; even Christian Republicans are
unlikely to push for creationism statutes. However, reasonable and

moderate emphasis on conservative social values will meet the approval of most Republicans, whatever their religious views. Much of this appeal derives from the "family and community" orientation of local establishments everywhere. Although Abramson and Inglehart (1987) may see an inevitable and linear decline in such "materialist" values, even in the most "optimistic" scenario many traditionalists will remain in the United States for a long time to come. Indeed, traditional values may even develop a new demographic base in a post-industrial world. In any case, as the "party of order and tradition," the GOP will probably not become a religious party, but may well become the party of more of the religious.

ACKNOWLEDGMENTS

The authors would like to acknowledge the financial assistance of the Furman University Research and Professional Growth Committee and the American Political Science Association. We would also like to thank our Dana Research Fellow, Sharon B. Smith, for her invaluable assistance.

NOTES

1. We are now in the process of compiling extensive biographical data on nonrespondents from other sources, in part to check on the possibility of response bias. Preliminary analysis indicates no serious bias on variables identifiable from Federal Election Commission lists, including sex, region, and size of contribution. Major metropolitan areas, however, are slightly underrepresented.

2. We chose to use the 1985–86 election cycle reports to weight the data for two reasons: first, the sample was drawn from contributors during that period and, second, nonpresidential year donors probably reflect more accurately the GOP's permanent activist corps. The results change only slightly if preliminary 1987–88 figures, which include the millions raised by Pat Robertson, are used. The main effect is to increase slightly the size of the Religion faction, described below, and to bolster the Christian Right to about 40 percent of that faction, instead of the estimate of 10 percent based on the earlier period. Details on weighting are available on request from the authors.

14
Politics and the Evangelical Press: 1960-85

James D. Fairbanks

INTRODUCTION

Little attention was paid to the political beliefs and activities of evangelical Christians prior to the 1980 elections. The conventional view regarding evangelical Christians conveyed in much of the literature was that of a people who deliberately turned away from the pressing issues facing society, leaving political concerns to "the world while they focused their attention on the world to come" (Neuhaus and Cromartie, 1987: vii). Morality regulations were thought to be the only policy issues in which they had an interest. The highly visible efforts of television evangelists and conservative activists to mobilize evangelicals on behalf of Ronald Reagan's presidential campaign brought about a reconsideration of this conventional view and heightened appreciation of the significance of evangelical Christians as a voting bloc. The term "Evangelical Right" entered the political lexicon and journalists and political scientists began to see revolutionary changes occurring in U.S. political life because of the emergence of these heretofore apolitical Christians.[1] How much change there has actually been in the political behavior of evangelicals is not altogether clear since many of the recent studies have no historical points of comparison.

Much of the effort to understand the nature of evangelical political involvement has focused on the television ministries of such men as Jerry Falwell and Pat Robertson. Researchers' preoccupation with the "televangelists" is understandable since leaders of no other movement have ever had access to such a sophisticated communications network before. With 1,370 radio stations, 221 religious television stations, three Christian networks broadcasting 24 hours a day, 414 organizations producing religious television programs, and 596 organizations producing religious radio programs, "change oriented evangelicalism" has a communications structure that is unprecedented in U.S. political history (Hadden and Shupe, 1988: 292). While the size and technology of these media empires is impressive, the men who control them should not automatically be assumed to be the most representative or influential of evangelical leaders. There is great diversity among the television ministries and the indiscriminate use of terms like Evangelical Right often confuses more than it clarifies. Ministers such as Jerry Falwell and Pat Robertson have been among the most active of those trying to mobilize Christians on behalf of conservative causes but, unlike evangelists such as Billy Graham, they lack close ties with mainstream evangelical institutions. Nevertheless, because of his high visibility, Falwell's many pronouncements on topics ranging from relations with Taiwan to military spending to abortion came to be treated as identifying the evangelical positions that both media and scholarly publications then sought to analyze. In the early 1980s, Jerry Falwell was generally recognized as the stereotypical evangelical political leader, both in terms of the positions he espoused and his separatist background. Studies might acknowledge the existence of a small evangelical left represented by such journals as *Sojourners* and organizations such as Evangelicals for Social Action, which did not accept the Moral Majority's political agenda, but they generally have just ignored evangelical spokesman other than Falwell and his fellow television evangelists.

THE "MAINSTREAM" OF AMERICAN EVANGELICALISM

In his autobiography, Falwell tells how he once took a strong position against religious leaders speaking out on political issues but that his Damascus Road experience after the Supreme Court's abortion ruling made him realize the Christian's responsibility to fight for basic morality in his society (Falwell, 1987: 338). Falwell's renunciation of political involvement was not unusual for someone coming from a separatist, fundamentalist, Southern background but it was not typical of evangelicals in general. Distinctions between fundamentalists and evangelicals are difficult to explain in summary fashion but they should be considered in political analyses.[2] Those conservative Protestants who began to use the evangelical label in the 1940s did so to distinguish themselves from fundamentalists like Carl McIntire and his followers in the American Council of Christian churches (ACCC). The ACCC was a separatist organization in its refusal to associate with churches affiliated with the Federal Council of Churches (FCC) but not in the sense of withdrawing from the political arena. The political goals of the fundamentalists in ACCC were clear: "patriotic adherence to the ideals of the Republican party and nineteenth century laissez-faire capitalism and also a repudiation of Communism—found, they believed, in the New Deal, the American Civil Liberties Union, the Democratic party, atheism, evolutionism, modernism, the Federal Council of Churches and the Social Gospel" (Hunter, 1987b: 43). McIntire's energetic efforts on behalf of right-wing political causes continued into the 1960s though he never enjoyed the recognition or had the impact of the later televangelists (Reichley, 1985a: 313).

In 1942 a larger group of evangelicals who, like McIntire, were distressed over the apostasy of the FCC but also uncomfortable with the absolutist tendencies and negativism of the ACCC formed the National Association of Evangelicals (NAE). While the membership of those denominations holding membership in the NAE constitutes only a small percentage of those Christians who adhere to the basic beliefs of Evangelical Christianity (see Fowler, 1985: 93–94), it is the organization of the evangelical "establishment" and provides the movement's institutional voice. Though in the organization's early years it avoided direct political lobbying, in part to disassociate itself from the highly politicized course McIntire had charted for the ACCC, the NAE has never endorsed the type of separatism characteristic of some of the more extreme fundamentalist groups. Billy Graham, the television evangelist with the strongest ties to the NAE, has consistently addressed political issues throughout his career. In recent years, the NAE has established a Washington lobbying presence but continues to avoid close identification with what Billy Graham calls the "hard right" (Reichley 1985a: 329).

Another reflection of the two strands of conservative Protestantism represented by the ACCC and the NAE has been their respective attitude toward intellectual inquiry. Those associated with NAE-linked denominations and seminaries repudiated the anti-intellectualism characteristic of McIntire and his followers "in favor of a scholastic attitude dedicated to preserving the essentials of Evangelical orthodoxy on thoroughly rational grounds" (Hunter, 1987b: 48). Many evangelical scholars have also shown increasing sensitivity to the social implications of the gospel and a willingness to work with others in the larger Christian community. In contrast, by the end of the 1950s, the term "fundamentalism" had come to be applied primarily to strict separatists, mostly dispensationalists, who were unhappy with the compromises of the new "evangelical" coalition represented by Billy Graham. Fundamentalists were also adamant in condemning pentecostal evangelicalism, while the former fundamentalist new-evangelicals, despite some reservations, saw pentecostals as allies in their permanent task of leading people to Christ (Marsden, 1987: 64).

There is no one authoritative voice to speak for evangelicals but there is a network of denominations, ministries, seminaries, colleges, and publications that is generally recognized as constituting the mainstream of the U.S. evangelical movement. Because of the NAE and its affiliated organizations, and because of the prominence of Billy Graham, there have been, since the 1950s, something like "card-carrying" evangelicals, people with "a sense of belonging to a complicated fellowship and infrastructure of trans-denominational organizations for evangelism, missions, social services, publications and education" (Marsden, 1987: 64). Three publications that have helped to create and sustain this sense of community among evangelicals are *Christianity Today*, *Christian Herald*, and *Eternity Magazine*. This remainder of this chapter will provide a systematic review of the political content of these magazines over a 25-year period. It is intended to suggest the various ways "mainstream" evangelicals have viewed politics and to show the extent to which the evangelical press simply reinforces the political messages of the televangelists and the extent to which it communicates an alternative message.

CHRISTIANITY TODAY

The publication having the clearest identification with this evangelical mainstream and the greatest influence in it is *Christianity Today*. In 1956, the year of its creation, *Christianity Today* was called by *Newsweek* a "fairly high brow evangelical fortnightly" and it has consistently aimed its reporting at the educated leadership of the church. It is, as one of the magazine's critics put it, "the clear voice of the new Evangelicalism," (Oliver 1975: 26). Its readership surveys show that half of its 185,000 subscribers are pastors, associate pastors, or workers in church agencies, while most of the remainder are lay leaders. *Magazines for Libraries* describes it as a "conservative protestant church journal of faith and opinion with a strong biblical favor, covering theological, social and political issue" (Katz and Katz, 1986: 214).

Christianity Today was founded by a group of evangelical leaders including Billy Graham, Graham's father-in-law L. Nelson Bell, and theologian Carl F. H. Henry. Henry, the first editor, was widely known for his efforts to prod conservative Christians toward greater social and political involvement. Henry's 1947 book, *The Uneasy Conscience of Modern Fundamentalism*, had indicted evangelicals for their preoccupation with "individual sin rather than social evil" and Henry was clear in his intentions to use the new magazine to get evangelical Christians more actively engaged in the great social movements of their day (Hadden and Swann, 1981: 153). The magazine was founded in part for the express purpose of relating evangelicalism to the crucial issues facing contemporary society (Flake, 1984: 166). The publication's statement of purpose makes this clear:

We intend to proclaim Christ's Gospel with passion and to apply the ethical teachings of the Bible to the contemporary social crisis. We will resolutely declare what we believe God's revelation and its implications are in such problem areas as war, youth, race, relations, poverty, the environment, lawlessness, over-population, drugs, and pornography. [10/9/70]

On many contemporary issues, *Christianity Today* opened its pages to writers of sharply differing positions. While the magazine has published articles by many political moderates as well as by evangelicals on the left of the political spectrum who are highly critical of the church's complacency in the fight for economic and racial justice, its overall reputation is that of conservatism. Streiker and Strober (1972: 114) charged sixteen years ago that despite its stated commitment to such problems as race, class struggle, and national imperialism, very little appears in its pages that would "disturb the most conservative defenders of wealth and privilege." They commended *Christianity Today* for calling attention to pressing issues that evangelicals might otherwise have ignored but complained that its articles often leave the impression that personal salvation by itself can somehow solve all of the social, political, and ecological problems in the United States.

In a April 7, 1978, interview with liberal theologian Harvey Cox, then editor Kenneth Kantzer admitted that *Christianity Today* has "at times spoken in ways inconsistent with its own prophetic and biblical commitment." Kantzer also acknowledged that Biblical instruction regarding a Christian's obligation to the poor and disfranchised was unequivocal and indicated he would welcome contributions from those who would encourage the church to be more politically and socially active.

Some studies have suggested that over the years *Christianity Today's* has developed a greater interest in exploring the social implications of the Gospel. James Hunter reviewed the contents of *Christianity Today* along with that of three other evangelical journals and found evidence of a heightened awareness and concern about the changing cultural milieu in which evangelicals have found themselves. On moral issues he found less harsh condemnation and greater sympathy for the anguish of the parties involved (Hunter, 1987a: 61). A content analysis by Wuthnow (1983: 172) comparing articles in *Christianity Today* during 1969–70 with those appearing in 1979–80 found that articles in the latter period encouraged political involvement while the earlier ones had been largely critical of it. Wuthnow also found that the percentage of articles devoted to political themes had nearly tripled (5.5 to 15.4 percent) over the ten-year period.

CHRISTIAN HERALD

Christian Herald is an evangelical family magazine that began publication in 1878. Its masthead states that its goal is to publish those truths that will help make ordinary people into extraordinary people and their world more compassionately Christlike. Begun as a U.S. edition of a British Evangelical weekly of the same name, *Christian Herald* was purchased by New York businessman Louis Klopsch two years later. DeWitt Talmage, "a rip-roaring, crusading Brooklyn minister[,] was its first editor." The magazine actively backed a variety of social reforms in the nineteenth century. During the depression, it was rescued from bankruptcy by department store magnate J. C. Penney, who wrote a regular column for the *Herald* in addition to providing financial support. *Magazines for Libraries* describes *Christian Herald* as "conservative and evangelical in its point of view" and notes that it has won the Evangelical Press Association's "Award of Excellence" three out of the last four years. Its current circulation is approximately 200,000.

The individual most responsible for shaping the magazine's character in the twentieth century was Dariel A. Poling, who served as its editor from 1925 to 1965. Poling was a New York clergyman but his "muscular Christianity" took him into a number of political activities including a race for the Ohio governorship on the Prohibition ticket in 1912. He remained closely identified with the Prohibition cause throughout his life. He was also known for his internationalist views, reflected in his best-selling book *A Preacher Looks at War* and his leadership in the crusade against "immoral and unchristian pacifism" prior to U.S. entry into World War II. While he was editor, *Christian Herald* described itself as a magazine dedicated to the promotion of evangelical Christianity, church unity, religious and racial understanding, world peace, the solving of the liquor problem, the service of the needy, cooperation with all who seek a more Christian World."

Christian Herald Ministries, the publisher of *Christian Herald*, operates several social service programs in New York City, and stories about the disadvantaged people they serve are featured regularly in the magazine. These social services include a mission on the Bowery in New York City, a children's house, and numerous foreign mission programs. While rarely calling for the expansion of government programs, the magazine does continually remind its readers of the Christian's responsibility to aid the poor and abandoned. A September 1980 editorial on government spending urged readers to remember that successful curtailment of government's growth will depend on how much the church is able to do for the disadvantaged.

Religion's role in politics was discussed frequently in editorials in the early 1960s, often in the context of issues raised by Kennedy's Catholicism. A

July 1962 editorial voiced the opinion that the church should not work directly in politics but should "change men and send them into society as Christian missionaries and into politics to help change the government." President Nixon's ties to the evangelical community were examined in a January 1973 article entitled "Politics and Evangelical Power." The *Herald* seldom ventures into highly controversial areas though it does occasionally run the opposing views of men like Reinhold Niebuhr and Carl F. H. Henry on a topic like government welfare programs (January 1962). In addition to expressing conventional evangelical views on such topics as personal morality, respect for the law, and the threat of communism, the magazine has consistently urged support for minority rights, compassion for the poor, and attention to the problem of world hunger.

While using many of the same writers as *Christianity Today*, *Christian Herald* does not strive for the same level of intellectual appeal in its features. Articles seldom cover theological questions and they tend to address political topics through human interest stories or guest features by well-known public officials. The topic of presidential religion was treated, for example, in such articles as "When President Ford Visited Our Church" and "Jimmy Carter's Sunday School Class." In many ways, *Christian Herald* appears to be striving to be the evangelical counterpart to the *Readers Digest*. Articles by J. Edgar Hoover with such titles as "Let's Fight Communism Sanely" and "Bad Men Cannot be Good Citizens" were frequently featured in the 1960s, but columns by liberal Democratic Senator Maurine Neuberger and Republican moderate Mark Hatfield were also run. Other celebrities whose contributions have appeared in *Christian Herald* have included Senator Robert Kerr, columnist Carl Rowan, General Douglas MacArthur, General Chiang Kai-shek, Congressman Walter Judd, Julie Nixon Eisenhower, Senator Harold Hughes, Senator George McGovern, Surgeon General C. Everett Koop, and LaBelle Lance.

ETERNITY MAGAZINE

Another winner of Evangelical Press Association awards is *Eternity Magazine*, a monthly periodical "for committed Christians, applying all of God's word to all of life." The magazine's origins go back to 1931 when Donald Gray Barnhouse, an influential radio preacher of the 1920s and 1930s, started publishing a magazine called *Revelation* for his radio listeners. In 1950 Barnhouse made significant format changes in the magazine and renamed it *Eternity*. Several smaller religious publications have merged with it over the years. *Eternity's* circulation is only around 40,000 but it regularly features articles by the nation's leading evangelicals and targets an educated readership.

Eternity was Barnhouse's creation and continued to reflect his ideas even after his death in 1960. Like Henry and Poling, Barnhouse was never part of the separatist fundamentalist tradition and regularly used the pages of his magazine to examine the problems confronting contemporary U.S. society. He maintained close ties with mainline Protestant denominations and often exhibited sympathy with their social concerns. In September 1960 a lengthy editorial in *Eternity* was devoted to investigating conservative charges of communism in the National Council of Churches. Barnhouse wrote that

the real issue is not communism in the churches, for the N.C.C. and its member denominations are clearly opposed to communism. The real issue is theological conflict over the doctrine of the church. It is one thing, however, to disagree on a theological issue but quite another to cloak that issue in the robes of patriotism and then, to the tune of the "Star Spangled Banner" and "Stand Up for Jesus," proceed to indict one's opponents for what amounts to treason."

In reviewing this controversy, the more liberal Protestant weekly *Christian Century* (December 7, 1960) described Barnhouse as a man who while conservative in his theology had shown himself honorable in controversy, exhibiting the highest Christian integrity in his responsible and honest handling of the truth.

Ten years after Barnhouse's death, political sophistication and social concern continued to be an *Eternity* trademark. In the September 1970 issue, the editors posed the hypothetical question of "Does *Eternity* always have to talk about problems?" They then went on to explain the magazine's basic purpose. "Like the Apostle, we are living in a world that is engulfed with problems. *Eternity's* task is not only to report on those problems but also to shed biblical light on them as well. Like Paul, we know God's Word is the only place to turn for adequate answers." The specific problems addressed in that particular issue included campus unrest, sex and the new morality, racial prejudice, Northern Ireland, women's liberation.

While generally striking a more prophetic stance than the other two periodicals, *Eternity* still publishes many of the same authors who also appear in *Christian Herald* and *Christianity Today*. Billy Graham, Francis Schaeffer, C. Everett Koop, Charles Colson, Tom Skinner, Carl F. H. Henry, Keith Miller, Mark Hatfield, and other evangelical celebrities are regular contributors. In addition to these "mainstream" evangelicals, *Eternity* has, particularly during the turmoil of the 1970s, opened its pages to writers such as Jim Wallis of *Sojourner Magazine*, Ron Sider, author of *Rich Christians in an Age of Hunger*, and other Evangelical social activists. Articles such as "Is God Still a Republican?" (November 1976), "How Radical Must You Be to Be A Christian" (September 1972), and "Was Jesus A Revolutionary—A Bold Charge But Perhaps Truer than We Realize" (February 1972) suggest the magazine's willingness to question conservative orthodoxy.

A 25-YEAR SURVEY OF POLITICAL COMMENTARY IN THE EVANGELICAL PRESS

This section offers a more systematic analysis of the amount and type of coverage given political topics in *Christianity Today*, *Christian Herald*, and *Eternity* between 1960 and 1985. By examining and classifying every editorial and feature article according to its political content, it is possible to see if there have been significant changes in the general concern shown political and social issues generally, as well as changes in the coverage of specific topics.[3] Editorials on broad topics such as the decline of the West or the nation's religious heritage were counted as political as well as those on more specific issues. After political stories were identified, they were classified into one of the following 11 subject categories: basic democratic values, communist ideology and the cold war, foreign affairs and defense policy, economy and domestic welfare, law and order, church and state, civil rights and race relations, U.S. political process, Christian's civic duty, morality and life-style issues, and other. In this analysis, stories were classified only on their subject matter, not on the point of view expressed.

Table 14.1 shows the number of politically related stories appearing in each of the three periodicals over the 25-year period. Comparisons over time are complicated by changes in format. Because all three publications reduced the total number of stories run per issue between 1960 and 1985, the table shows the percentage of stories that were political in nature as well as the actual number of stories that appeared. *Christianity Today* was the only publication to publish columns clearly designated as editorials for the whole time of the study. In the 1960s, *Christian Herald* ran several pages of editorials each issue but then replaced its editorials with a "News and Commentary" section. Editorial commentary appearing here has been included in the Table 14.1 data. In the 1980s, an "Editor's Notes" feature appeared that sometimes stated an editorial position and other times merely previewed the articles in that issue. *Eternity* also began the period with a clearly designated editorial section but dropped editorials completely in 1974. An "Editor's Ink" section was begun in the 1980s but it too often did little more than preview articles.

Table 14.1 also demonstrates that all three of the evangelical periodicals were giving significant coverage to political topics long before the New Right's efforts to mobilize evangelicals got under way. For *Christianity Today*, there appears to have been an increase in the amount of its editorial space devoted to political topics, though the actual number of political editorials in the 1980s is rather small compared to earlier periods. These differences are mainly due to the journal's decision to run fewer but more substantive editorials than they had in the past. For example, a spring 1969 issue ran a total of 13 editorials, 7 of which (riots, Ireland, Charles de Gaulle, Richard Nixon, Abe Fortas, poverty, and American values) were

Table 14.1
Political Stories Appearing in Three Leading Evangelical Periodicals, 1960–85*

Time Period	Christianity Today (Editorials Only)	Christian Herald (Editorial Comment)	Eternity (Articles Only)
1961-65	279 (38%)	115 (72%)	118 (23%)
1966-70	355 (36%)	115 (34%)	107 (22%)
1971-75	430 (44%)	30 (48%)	135 (30%)
1976-80	155 (39%)	8 (24%)	93 (23%)
1981-85	73 (55%)	7 (17%)	92 (30%)

*Percentages are based on the total number of editorials published in each periodical for the time period indicated.

classified as political. In 1985 no issue ran more than two editorials and the majority ran only one, but when political topics like liberation theology or South Africa were covered, they were covered in much more depth than topics had been in the earlier decades.

The dramatic drop in political commentary found in *Christian Herald* is not just an artifact of format changes but reflects a change in orientation. Under Daniel Poling's editorship, the magazine was willing to voice its opinion on a wide range of political topics. The *Herald's* editorials in 1960 covered such topics as the danger of labor unions, Catholic political power, recognition of Communist China, birth control, the United Nations, pornography, juvenile delinquency, civil rights, television regulations, peace movements, and the presidential election. By the 1980s it was giving much more emphasis to family features. An editorial in 1985 still proclaimed that "we at *Christian Herald* take very seriously our role as an instrument of the hands of God to bring about change," but the magazine had become far more cautious about tackling political controversy than it had been earlier. Political editorials that year were on such general topics as the Christian's civic responsibility and the need to operate society according to the moral law of God.

Feature articles rather than editorials were used to measure *Eternity*'s degree of involvement with political issues over the years because of the infrequency with which *Eternity* ran formal editorials. *Eternity* has been consistently less predictable in its political coverage than either *Christianity Today* or *Christian Herald*. Even in the 1960s, *Eternity* was running articles that raised questions about the John Birch Society, the church's responsibility to the city, and whether or not an anti-communist foreign policy was Christian. Its effort to provide a forum for Christians from across the political spectrum is reflected in the "Why I am a Political Liberal" and "Why I am a Political Conservative" features run in the October 1985 issue. In the 1980s *Eternity* continued to demonstrate its independence from Moral Majority-type conservatism. Topics covered by feature articles in 1985 included nuclear weapons, animal research, teenage suicide, crowded prisons, the sanctuary movement, the "unholy" alliance between private and public sectors, and Judeo-Christian values and social justice.

A summary of the political content found in leading evangelical periodicals is given in Table 14.2. The data do not support the claim that only in recent years have evangelical political interests expanded beyond the topics of anti-communism and issues of personal morality. *Christian Herald* did give slightly more emphasis to moral issues in the 1960s than it has recently, reflecting in part Editor Poling's strong ties with the prohibition movement. For both *Christianity Today* and *Eternity*, however, more attention has been devoted to moral issues (abortion and pornography have been the most common topics) in the 1980s than in the 1960s. The relative amount of political commentary devoted to racial problems decreased for all three publications between the two periods. The larger number of stories appearing in the first period reflects the prominence of the civil rights issue in the 1960s, but it also shows that these journals were actively involved in the civil rights debate. The larger number of law and order stories in the 1970s similarly shows that the three publications were closely following the major domestic issue of that decade.

In regard to coverage of the economy and domestic welfare programs, *Christianity Today* is giving less attention than in the past while *Eternity* is giving more. In *Christianity Today*'s case, the change represents a declining tendency to run conservative stories on the evils of big labor and big government, while the change at *Eternity* represents the magazine's increased openness to the views of evangelical social activists. All three journals ran stories on environmental issues in the early 1970s, stories included in the "Other" category in Table 14.2.

The attention given communism declined in all three journals though other foreign affairs topics (including defense questions) continued through all three periods to attract more attention than any other topic in both *Christian Herald* and *Eternity*. *Christianity Today* editorials on foreign affairs declined in number as did editorials warning of the dangers of communism and of the imminent collapse of Western culture.

All three journals closely tracked the rise of Moral Majority-type groups in the late 1970s and commented regularly on the issues they raised, though

Table 14.2
Distribution of Political Stories by Topic*

Topical Category	Christianity Today (Editorials Only)			Christian Herald (Articles Only)			Eternity (Articles Only)		
	1961-65	1971-75	1981-85	1961-65	1971-75	1981-85	1961-65	1971-75	1981-85
Democratic Values	15% (42)	10% (44)	10% (7)	10% (16)	8% (9)	9% (8)	7% (8)	7% (10)	8% (7)
Communism Cold War	9% (26)	7% (30)	0% (0)	5% (8)	0% (0)	4% (3)	14% (16)	0% (0)	3% (3)
Foreign Affairs	19% (54)	18% (78)	10% (7)	23% (37)	14% (16)	24% (20)	18% (21)	13% (18)	21% (19)
Economy & Welfare	13% (35)	8% (36)	5% (4)	9% (15)	19% (22)	13% (11)	7% (8)	13% (18)	15% (14)
Law & Order	4% (11)	13% (57)	4% (3)	8% (13)	9% (11)	5% (4)	3% (3)	10% (13)	8% (7)
Church & State	9% (24)	7% (31)	21% (15)	6% (10)	9% (10)	11% (9)	14% (16)	4% (6)	7% (6)
Civil Rights & Race	14% (39)	5% (22)	5% (4)	14% (23)	8% (9)	5% (4)	11% (13)	11% (15)	5% (5)
Am. Politics- General	3% (7)	4% (18)	3% (2)	4% (7)	3% (3)	4% (3)	4% (5)	9% (12)	3% (3)
Christian's Civic Duty	8% (22)	6% (26)	19% (14)	7% (11)	13% (15)	8% (7)	9% (11)	12% (16)	11% (10)
Morality and Life-Style	5% (13)	13% (56)	22% (16)	10% (16)	9% (10)	8% (7)	6% (7)	13% (18)	14% (13)
Other	2% (6)	7% (31)	1% (1)	4% (6)	9% (11)	10% (9)	9% (10)	7% (9)	5% (5)
Column Totals**	101% (279)	98% (430)	100% (73)	100% (162)	101% (116)	101% (85)	102% (118)	99% (135)	100% (92)

*Percentages indicate the percent of political editorials or articles appearing in each periodical on each topic during the time indicated. The actual number of editorials or articles published on each topic is shown in parentheses.

**Percentage sums do not always equal 100 because of rounding.

Christianity Today was the only periodical to increase significantly the number of stories run attempting to analyze the Christian's civic responsibilities. Many of its editorials contained warnings against the type of political activities the Religious Right was often accused of promoting. For example, a December 12, 1980, editorial cautioned "politically conservative evangelicals against taking too much credit for the outcome of the election . . . as a minority in a pluralistic society, conservative evangelicals must neither expect or encourage Mr. Reagan to adopt a dogmatic, uncompromising stand on all positions of deep concern to them."

CONCLUDING OBSERVATIONS

This survey of leading evangelical periodicals does not support the view that post-war evangelicalism remained outside the political arena—a withdrawal broken only by participation in sporadic rear-guard actions through fringe movements and extremist crusades. Throughout the period studied, these journals have been engaged with the issues of the day and while their politics have generally been moderate to conservative, they have been well within the mainstream of U.S. politics. The frequency with which national political figures have written for these periodicals suggests that at least since 1960, mainstream evangelicals have had good lines of communication with the political establishment. The pages of *Christianity Today* and *Christian Herald* do not suggest a fringe movement alienated from society's mainstream and incapacitated by a sense of powerlessness.

Several writers have noted that the sudden attention paid evangelical political activities in the late 1970s was more the product of selective perception by the secular media than a sign that a massive religious change had taken place (Hadden and Shupe, 1988: 118). This analysis supports that view. Evangelicals were talking (or at least writing) about political issues throughout the 1960–85 era, but as Table 14.3 shows, the secular press did not deem the positions they were taking as newsworthy until the Jerry Falwell era. Within the pages of these three journals, leading evangelicals were taking stands on civil rights bills, war policies in Vietnam, the Watergate scandals, and a myriad of other issues, but these efforts to shape opinion among the evangelical rank and file were never subject to either journalistic or scholarly inquiry.

That the political commentary appearing in magazines like *Christianity Today*, *Christian Herald*, and *Eternity* has generally been ignored by the secular media does not mean that it is without influence among the "card carrying" evangelicals described earlier in this chapter. The often-expressed fear of the early 1980s that millions of recently mobilized evangelicals stood ready to follow the beck and call of television evangelists in a right-wing

Table 14.3
Citations of Articles on Religion and Politics in Major U.S. News Magazines, 1961-85*

Time Period	Total Number of Religion and Politics Citations	Percent of Cited Articles Which Featured Evangelical Activities
1961-65	17	0% (0)
1966-70	14	0% (0)
1971-75	7	14% (1)
1976-80	20	50% (10)
1981-85	49	43% (21)

*Citations were tabulated for *Newsweek*, *Time*, and *U.S. News and World Report*. The citations used appeared under one or more of the following headings in the *Readers Guide to Periodical Literature*: Church and State, Church and Politics, Religion and Politics, and Evangelicalism and Politics.

political crusade rested on a number of faulty assumptions, but one of relevance to this study was the assumption that a few television evangelists controlled the only national communications network serving the evangelical community (see, e.g., Conway and Siegelman, 1982). The periodicals examined in this chapter constitute an important and well-established part of the infrastructure of mainstream evangelicalism. As this chapter has shown, sometimes these journals have supported the political positions taken by television evangelists (who are themselves a diverse group), but other times they have not. Clearly, the pages of *Christianity Today* and *Eternity* suggest an evangelical political orientation that is significantly different than that suggested by Moral Majority pronouncements.

This 25-year review suggests several patterns that some of the literature on the religious right has overlooked. The most interesting trends are those involving the increasing attention paid morality issues and the decreasing attention given to economic and welfare issues for the conventional wisdom is that evangelicals were only interested in a few narrow moral issues prior to the 1970s but since that time they have strongly committed themselves to supporting the economic and defense policies of the secular right. The dramatic political reorientation of evangelicals described in some of the literature finds little support in this study. All three magazines were more predictably conservative in their political orientations than they were in the mid-1980s. The political evolvement that was discernible in this study of reading evangelical periodicals suggests that the evangelical establishment was actually reassessing some of its conservative commitments at the very time others were proclaiming a new alliance between evangelicals and the secular right. This reassessment has resulted in few major changes in these magazines' basic political orientation, however, and the overall picture to emerge from this study is one of continuity rather than discontinuity.

NOTES

1. Supporters and critics of the movement made equally extravagant claims about its potential to make radical changes in U.S. political life. See, for example, Falwell (1980) and Conway and Siegelman (1982).

2. For a discussion of these differences, see Marsden (1987) and Fowler (1985).

3. All stories were classified by the author or his assistant. If an article fit in more than one of the categories, it was placed in the most specific. The *Christian Herald* and *Christianity Today* classifications were made on the basis of an examination of both title and text. The majority of the *Eternity* stories were classified on the basis of the title and of the synopsis given on the Table of Contents page.

15
Faith and Access: Religious Constituencies and the Washington Elites

Allen D. Hertzke

While the literature on religious interest groups is growing (Fowler, 1985; Reichley, 1985a; Weber, 1982a, 1982b; Wald, 1987; Hertzke, 1988; Moen, 1986; Zwier, 1987), most of it focuses on the activities of the groups seeking influence, with incidental attention paid to those being lobbied. Mary Hanna's (1982) discussion of the link between key senators and the Religious Right is one of the few clear exceptions. Lack of attention to this side of the lobbying matrix leaves us with an incomplete picture of the role of religion in U.S. politics. To what extent do Washington political elites provide access to diverse religious leaders and interest groups? What facilitates this access or inhibits it? What do these patterns of access tell us about the relationship between constituencies and political leaders?

Following research on national religious lobbies (Hertzke, 1988), I sought preliminary answers to these questions in order to better understand the broader impact of religious faith and mobilization on national politics. This exploration is based primarily on interviews with Washington elites conducted in June 1987, supplemented by earlier interviews with religious lobbyists and congressional staff members conducted in December 1984 and March 1985. The interviews with Washington elites included 7 members of Congress, 20 congressional aides, 4 White House officials, and 3 top officials of national party organizations. The time span provides a modest measure of change and continuity.

FAITH AND ACCESS: THE CONGRESS

One religious lobbyist claimed that elite access was remarkably easy to get; all it takes, he said, is "chutzpah." Yet the pattern of access that emerges from this analysis suggests that it may not be so easy, at least for some religious groups. The ability to mobilize constituents, of course, is important, as is access to information useful to policy makers. Often overlooked, however, is the ideological lens through which elites view the religious groups. The findings of the Benson and Williams (1986) study should alert us to the possibility, nay probability, that congressional members and other Washington elites bring to their work highly integrated religious world views that color their interaction with religious leaders. Indeed, my interview research suggests that elites' religious values or world views are a vital, and at times dominant, factor in determining the extent of access they provide to religious constituencies.

The responses of congressional members to the Religious Right—which seemed to be based more on the ideological and religious predilections of members than the nature of their constituencies—are a graphic illustration of this. For example, of the seven members interviewed, five are from Bible belt states with substantial evangelical and fundamentalist constituencies. Yet the extent to which they provide access to the Religious Right is dramatically divergent. Indeed, two of the most radically different responses to the Religious Right come from congressional members in districts with very similar constituencies. One, a conservative evangelical Republican (first elected in 1986), is extremely sympathetic with the aims of the Religious Right (I will call him Mr. Presbyterian). Prior to running for Congress this member, as a city mayor, did not hide his light under a bushel: "We had Young Life meetings at the mayor's office. We were singing 'What a friend we have in Jesus.' The ACLU said 'don't.' We didn't stop." When asked what issue tugged on his conscience, he responded without hesitation: "Abortion." Moreover, he asserted that the Moral Majority is misunderstood, that all it is trying to do is counter the vocal minority that has blocked what the majority of Americans want—school prayer, for instance. His language is filled with evangelical imagery that gives meaning to his setbacks:

My opponent spent $700,000 in the primary, used everything, my business failures. . . . So we named our campaign the "Romans 3 Verse 5 Campaign," which is about suffering as character building. God had a plan. . . . Look at me, a year ago I was bankrupt, lost everything. Now I am a member of Congress.

Mr. Presbyterian has a natural affinity with the fundamentalist lobbies. He will fight for school prayer and against abortion. He views much welfare spending as a "ripoff," opposes gun control, and supports the Reagan fight against communism. Clearly, he provides access to the Religious Right, not primarily because of his constituency, but rather because of his own religious and political values.

The liberal Democrat, Mr. Episcopalian, represents a similar Bible belt district, but had nothing but contempt for the fundamentalists. To him the phenomenon of the Religious Right was a sole result of the televangelists. When asked about the rise of the Religious Right, he pointed dramatically to his TV screen: "There are a lot of lonely and desperate people out there, and Jim and Tammy Faye are more interesting than their local minister." Indeed Mr. Episcopalian had a colorful way of referring to the Religious Right: "And then we have prayer and abortion and all that *crap*." Speaking of his district he said, "I have the right-to-God-damn-lifers. But this is the way it is around here. If I win by 7 percent of the vote, then I try to deal with them; if I win by 30 percent, I'll tell them to f___ off."

For this member the Religious Right was a potential strategic problem, particularly when his district, not surprisingly, became a key target for electoral mobilization:

The Baptists are big in my district. Reagan is popular. The initial push of the Religious Right came in '82 and '84, and they were a force. We keep a tab on it. For example, we monitor the voter registration filings in the district on Monday and Thursday; those are mobilized by the Religious Right—after Sunday church and Wednesday prayer. We would see big jumps on those days for a while, but haven't seen recently.

I asked what he did after these voter registration drives: "We take it head on, go there, to those precincts."

The point is that in spite of mobilized fundamentalists in his own district and the electoral threat they implied, this member still provided no access to the Religious Right. Indeed, Mr. Episcopalian, a self-described, "open-minded" person, appeared to screen out any sympathetic reading of the constituencies of the Religious Right. The contrast between him and Mr. Presbyterian could not be a more forceful illustration of the power of the ideological lens through which constituencies are viewed. As Fenno observes in *Homestyle* (1978), what a member sees in the district is a function of the filter through which interpretations are made.

Even when the member does not begin with such a strong prejudice, he may give up trying to gain a particular group's support, thus discounting its district constituency. As one moderate Democrat (a Lutheran) from a Bible belt state noted, "Conservatives wrote me off, I just couldn't meet their litmus test. I'm pro-choice on abortion, for example." He casually mentioned that "during election cycles they would leaflet churches with their lies and slander." But the impact of such tactics is blunted by his strong image (which he said was not phony) of being a family man rooted in traditional values. Still, this member is clearly uncomfortable with pietistic religion: "I have a hard time applying the person of Christ to modern governmental problems.'' He criticized a colleague who held prayer meetings with his staff. Thus a cultural gulf clearly impedes the access of fundamentalist lobbies to this member.

Another member, a moderate Republican Congregationalist, also discounted religious constituencies:

I manage to be on the wrong side of both the left and right. I am opposed to unilateral disarmament in the high tech area, but I supported ERA and I can't support opposition to abortions under any circumstances. On abortion the votes have been extreme. One amendment, under one interpretation, would have banned first aid for a rape victim, because of the possibility of interrupting embryo development. I couldn't support that.

Mr. Congregationalist apparently felt secure enough electorally to dismiss lobby efforts contrary to his own views.

The point is that a congressional member may give up trying to get a group's support, particularly if the ideological price seems too high, leaving the Washington lobbies with little leverage. Moreover, while the electoral threat implied in lobbying may be influential, it may backfire if it is tried and fails. For example, a newly elected member of Congress, a moderate Democrat from the South (we will call him Mr. Baptist), faced a Republican opponent who circulated a "Dear Christian" letter to ministers making a case against the Democrat. The letter, according to Mr. Baptist, probably helped him more than it hurt, in part because he himself is a Southern Baptist and an active church member, but also because "It probably helped me with the some of the young (yuppie) Republicans." Moreover, Mr. Baptist was keenly aware of the divisions within conservative Protestantism and the difficulties of mobilizing them: "The fundamentalists in my district are not monolithic, a small minority gave Falwell a positive rating . . . fundamentalists are not easily mobilized, are oriented toward individual salvation." What won the election for him, he suggested, was a combination of a favorable TV image and Democratic voting habits in his district. In this case the religious-based attacks on him appeared to have given him a greater sense of security than if they had not happened.

Liberal lobbies face a similarly mixed access based upon ideological predilections of the elites. One example is a tale of two devout Episcopalians: one a liberal House Democrat (whom we have already termed Mr. Episcopalian), the other a conservative Republican congressman (we will call him Mr. Right Episcopalian). The liberal House member expressed enthusiasm for the Washington Office of the Episcopal Church, one of the most liberal of the mainline lobbies in Washington. He viewed the Episcopalians, along with the Catholics, as being the "best" on concern for the poor. When confronted with the accusation by the Prayer Book Society, a conservative group within the Episcopal Church, that the national lobby "was opposed to the convictions of a majority of Episcopalians," the House member sent back an unusually pointed letter defending the Episcopal lobby and its director:

The Reverend William Weiler is truly a man of God present for all of us here. . . . The resolution's statement that the activities of the [lobby] Office are "neither accurate nor honest" is an entirely inaccurate and dishonest portrayal of what the Office actually does for us. . . . The ministry of the Washington Office, which I wholeheartedly support, needs to be non-partisan, and it is indeed just that.

Clearly there is access here, a relationship between a church lobby and a member of Congress. What cements this bond is a shared religious vision; both the lobby director and the member would be classed as "people-concerned" religionists (Benson and Williams, 1986). The member, for example, spoke of his faith as requiring compassion for the oppressed, for the "hungry, poor, downtrodden, women, minorities." In other words he spoke the language of the "peace and justice" groups as emphatically as they do.

The views of the conservative Republican Episcopalian, on the other hand, correspond more closely to the Prayer Book Society. He criticized the mainline religious lobbies, accused them of selective morality. More significantly, he noted that even when the liberal lobbies do mobilize in his district, particularly on foreign policy, he discounts them: "I often get letters from the same ten people mobilized by the liberal lobbies." This member, in contrast to the Episcopal Democrat, stressed communism and abortion as issues that tug on his conscience. Thus Mr. Right Episcopalian filters out the information provided by the liberal lobbies, and discounts even those in his district that they mobilize. He welcomes the support of the fundamentalists and evangelicals. Intriguingly, he did not feel that this inhibited him from gaining support from traditional Democratic voters in his district, specifically blacks, 70 percent of whom he claimed voted for him in the last election. Indeed, with support like that in a heavily Republican district anyway, he can afford to screen out the lobbying efforts of the liberal churches.

Our final congressional member is a self-described, "lapsed" Catholic Senator from a rural state. On the one hand he felt his religious upbringing (nine years in parochial schools) influenced his sense of values. On the other hand, his "profound difference with this pope" has led to a disenchantment with the church. He is pro-choice on abortion, and it does not appear that the U.S. Catholic Conference lobby in Washington has any access whatsoever with him. What is intriguing, however, is that the great diversity within the Catholic Church allows him to remain linked in other respects. He lauded the efforts of Catholic Rural Life in analyzing the impact of the farm crisis on the rural United States, and he even made a $1,000 donation to an order of sisters in his state (American nuns, after all, tend to be far more liberal than the Catholic hierarchy). So while he provides little access to, say, the Catholic Bishops, his ideological predilections and continued contact with liberal Catholic groups provide access there.

These examples of congressional members and their attitudes remind us that they are not empty vessels responding solely to "pressures" from constituents or lobbyists. Rather, they bring to their work their own religious world views and political ideologies, screen out conflicting images, and discount constituents that do not fit their political agenda. Groups seeking access, consequently, must be highly strategic and discerning so as not to waste time and effort, must find ways to appeal to the world views of particular members, in short, must accept and work around the perceptual and ideological impediments of those they seek to influence. This is no mean task, especially because religious lobbyists also operate within strongly formulated frames of reference that sometimes blind them to targets of opportunity, as we will see.

RELIGION AND ACCESS: THE WHITE HOUSE

While groups have always sought to influence the president and his staff, formal liaison between the White House and domestic constituencies is a relatively new phenomenon. President Carter formalized these links through the appointment of Midge Costanza as director of Public Liaison and the designation of staff members to work with specific groups, such as blacks, Hispanics, women, environmentalists, and so forth. The Reagan innovation was to assign specified religious constituencies to the staff of the Public Liaison Office. If the Congress presents a highly pluralistic universe of ideologies, experiences, and perceptions among the 535 members, the White House, even with all the celebrated infighting, provides a relatively unified ideological prism, established by the president, through which these religious groups are assessed. Thus access to the White House, with a few exceptions, is largely a function of this screening mechanism.

The Reagan White House has designated three persons—a Protestant, a Catholic, and a Jew—with the task of establishing and maintaining contacts with religious constituencies, a specialization that itself is revealing. While the Protestant office is nominally open to liaison with all Protestants, it was designed to serve the conservative evangelical and fundamentalist constituents that rallied to the president in 1980 and 1984, and its two coordinators, past and present, are evangelicals sympathetic to the Religious Right. However, if the Protestant office is characterized by this form of outreach, the other two offices are similar in that they provide access for those outside the liberal establishment. Thus the person responsible for liaison with Catholics is a right-to-life Catholic and the Jew is a neo-conservative. Operating through the ideological lens of the president, White House liaison provides a special haven for the disparate strands of intellectual attack on liberal politics. Indeed, what is fascinating about these White House staffers is the extent to which participation in the war of ideas is a very real part of their perceived job, as the following discussion amplifies.

Conservative Protestants and the White House

The public liaison officer for Protestants in the White House is an evangelical Baptist with Capitol Hill experience. She noted that the special relationship between Reagan and conservative Protestants was the reason for the office in the first place: "Carter was an evangelical, yet many evangelicals identified with someone who sounded like an evangelical—Reagan. He spoke to those concerns, family, abortion, prayer, and now, AIDS." Her job is to establish outreach to evangelicals and fundamentalists, and involves briefings for religious groups with White House officials, meetings with the president, travel to conventions, and extensive mailings (such as sending out the State of the Union address in advance to the National Religious Broadcasters). As she described it, this develops into an established routine:

For example, the Association of Christian Schools International calls and asks for a briefing. We will set it up. There are a formalized set of expectations. . . . The briefing format will include three speakers, one whose topic is directly related to the group, and two others on other topics, such as welfare reform or SDI.

To a great extent this conservative Baptist views her role as providing access to, and soliciting support from, constituencies previously left out of the process. This involves outreach to those groups wihin the so-called mainline denominations that disagree with the liberal thrust of the national offices. For example, she stressed work with NOEL (National Organization of Episcopalians for Life), Presbyterians for Life, Lutherans for Life, and Good News (conservative Methodist group). But her work also involves advocacy for these constituencies within the conservative camp, which she described as intellectually divided:

People have equated conservative religious people with the New Right, but there is a distinction to be made. . . . The problem is that a lot of conservatives tend to be libertarians [who] will not help on abortion, FCC regulation of porn, and this causes friction. . . . I've been in Washington and you can tell which are the libertarian organizations. They tend to have their token cultural conservative.

To her the evangelicals bring to politics "a justification for why we should hold onto values. They have a well reasoned approach." To exclude cultural traditionalists is "to take the heart and soul out of the conservative movement." This tension is very real, as David Stockman's (1986: 65) sarcastic statements about the "sour matrons of Phyllis Schlafly" attest. Evidently this tension is felt in the White House: "Some on the President's staff don't want to have anything to do with them [the Christian fundamentalists]."

Clearly there is a genuine access to the White House for evangelicals and fundamentalists. The liaison office schedules the President for regular events, such as the annual convention to the National Religious Broadcasters and the Right To Life observance of the anniversary of *Roe v. Wade*. At one of the White House briefings I attended there was an almost reverential atmosphere, with those in the audience asking questions about Reagan's health and so forth. But there is, according to the liaison officer, a two-way communication. Part of her job is to communicate what "her people" are not happy with.

The intense loyalty of conservative evangelicals and fundamentalists to Ronald Reagan was stressed repeatedly; indeed, this was the major contrast between the congressional and White House environments in 1987. Even conservative sympathizers in Congress acknowledge that the overt influence of the Religious Right has waned there, a process accelerated by scandals in the world of televangelism. However, at least some in the White House see a very different reality, a continuing source of support in hard times. As the liaison officer noted:

The major development is growth of pentecostals, Assemblies of God. Everybody thinks Jim and Tammy Bakker are what it's all about, but they don't see the larger development underneath. I represented the president recently at a meeting in Louisiana. There were 9,500 women from the United Pentecostal Church. When they announced that I was representing the president, they gave me a standing ovation. They are ardent supporters of the president.

It is this intensity of commitment, in her view, that provides an important political resource. While acknowledging that the Moral Majority "intensity" varies, she felt that the commitment was still there, especially among the charismatics:

There is a major renewal movement going on. This particular branch—speaking in tongues, gifts of healing—they are more ardently involved, do not give up. One pastor from the Apostolic Pentecostals called up. Wanted to support the President on something. He had personally called 100 people, who were then supposed to activate phone trees. I was astounded. I have never seen this on the Hill.

Of course, this special relationship creates an almost impenetrable barrier between the White House and liberal mainline Protestant groups, whose access is virtually nil. Oddly, this appears in part a choice of the groups themselves. White House officials have attempted sporadically to reach out to these groups. The previous liaison official for Protestants made a point of addressing the annual meeting of IMPACT in 1984, and the current official seemed open to contact: "I'll do a briefing for anybody, but I guess on some things we are so far apart that they don't try. The administration is aligned in a particular way and the mainstream groups are solidly entrenched . . . I have never had them come to me." While she acknowledged that she gets "sidetracked" in attempts to reach out to the liberal Protestants, this official did mention an extremely influential briefing with the Religious Alliance Against Pornography, which included representatives of the National Council of Churches. She expressed hope that the welfare reform issue could offer an opportunity to build bridges with the liberal Protestants. But the ongoing lack of contact she attributed largely to the groups themselves: "The mainline groups don't want access. I've tried to get names of those genuinely interested. But they are so entrenched that many of them don't want to be perceived as cozy with the White House." Whether this assessment is entirely accurate, it suggests the intriguing possibility that for some religious groups gaining access may involve painful trade-offs, and thus is to be avoided.

Jews and the White House

If mainline Protestants are ambivalent about seeking access to the president and his staff, the Jewish groups, which have also been critical of the administration, have not allowed this to inhibit them. Indeed, the pattern of extensive elite access enjoyed by Jews in the Congress is found in the White House, in part because of the strategic importance of Israel in foreign policy calculations, but also because of assertiveness of the Jewish leaders.

This access has evidently paid off. The White House liaison to Jews observed that the Jewish groups were extremely successful on Soviet Jewry: "They brought the entire Congress around, and made this administration, which was sympathetic, move it higher on the agenda." But their success, he argued, is a function of resonance with the broader American public:

You have to remember that effective political involvement depends upon being on the right side of the issue. If the issue is perceived as wrong from the American viewpoint, then you can't succeed. Israel is a case. Most Americans are receptive to the idea of supporting the only democracy in the Middle East. The Jewish community is active across the board on this.

Like his evangelical counterpart, this Jewish White House official spends his time organizing briefings for groups of Jewish leaders and speaking at various functions. While there are issues of agreement between Jewish organizations and the president—Israel and Soviet Jewry—on a number of issues there is wide disagreement, but this does not stop dialogue. The White House official engages the Jewish community on intellectual terms, hoping to get Jews to view some issues in a different light. Echoing the evangelical liaison officer, he cited tension with libertarian themes:

On church-state questions and social issues Jews are pretty united—abortion, gay rights, ERA. I don't try to persuade them on these issues. What I do is articulate an alternative viewpoint, a different way of looking at the issue than they think about. For example, I gave a speech Monday night on the Silberman book [Charles Silberman, *A Certain People: American Jews and Their Lives Today* (New York: Summit Books, 1988)]. Silberman argues that Jews tolerate a wide variety of behavior because societies that are tolerant of the unorthodox are more tolerant of Jews. But I noted that there must be limits, if you take that to its logical conclusion then we should tolerate drug abuse, cock fighting, polygamy.

Or, shrewdly, he reassures the Jewish community:

Another example: prayer in schools. I don't deal with the substance of the issue, but instead try to dismiss the threat. Look, I say, what may happen if it passes won't be so bad. We can live with it. Also, it isn't going anywhere.

Of course, the Reagan embrace of the fundamentalist right has been unsettling to Jewish leaders, a fact that the official acknowledged: "The impact of fundamentalists? It hurts us—the administration—with Jews. If Pat Robertson had a viable chance, it would frighten them to death." The problem, as he discussed it, is a lack of understanding of conservative Protestants: "Jews aren't aware of the diversity in the evangelical camp. NAE [National Association of Evangelicals] is so important, but Jews don't know the difference between the TV evangelists and NAE." Amazingly, this Jew saw conservative Protestants in a benign light:

The influence of religion rises and falls. For a while the secularization was ascendent, now we are seeing reversal. Evangelicals have moved this country; the country is moving toward the center on their concerns. There is a new consensus on teaching values, not values clarification; no one is defending the textbooks. Change is obviously in the works. But when change happens, the war will be over. Most of the evangelical people are rather reasonable. They don't want the Christianization of America.

He lauded the work of the Anti-Defamation League, which conducted the study that found no significant anti-Semitism among Christian fundamentalists. What this official is trying to do is no mean feat: in carrying the Reagan message to an often hostile Jewish constituency, he is simultaneously attempting to build bridges between Jews and evangelicals.

Such a task seems daunting, but history provides other examples of the transformation of images. Indeed, the process by which new relationships are forged in the religious United States is something we should ponder deeply. How does it happen, for example, that historically "anti-papist" fundamentalists now find friends among some Roman Catholics? Because of common alienation from the abortion culture, secular schools, and new class liberalism. Thus it is perhaps not so unlikely that conservative Protestants, who are strongly supportive of Israel and critical of the Soviet Union, may convince Jews that they are natural allies against a growing liberal Protestant consensus, say, in favor of "justice for the Palestinians." The intellectual origins of a potentially broader rapprochement of Jews and conservative Protestants became evident in the interview. When asked about his own background, the White House official replied simply, but cogently, "I identify with the Institute for Religion and Democracy . . . I started out as a democratic socialist, but moved away from that. I'm a pretty typical neo-conservative—Irving Kristol is coming to my son's Bar Mitzvah."

Catholics and the White House

The Catholic liaison official viewed his role as building bridges with various Roman Catholic constituencies, from the Knights of Columbus to the Catholic Health Association, but obviously some groups are more supportive of the Reagan administration than others. The National Conference of Catholic Bishops, for example, has challenged the administration on nuclear arms, Central America, and the economy, but the official remarked that "we try to be as cordial as possible." The NCCB, he noted, was sporadically effective: "They do generate publicity on nuclear weapons and economy, but don't mobilize. Some effectiveness on pro-life, but still not as high [a priority] as it should be. On Central America, by blurring the issue they are effective—ask Obano [dissident Nicaraguan archbishop]." The key difference he had with the Catholic Conference, not surprisingly, had to do with priorities and emphases: "What would affect Catholics more than anything else? Parental choice in education! A high priority item [with the Catholic Conference], but not as high with them as it should be. Few things would have such an impact on Catholic families." One task of the White House office, then, is to encourage the Catholic hierarchy to move certain items resonant with the administration—pro-life, aid to parochial schools—higher on the NCCB agenda, and to blunt criticism of non-resonant items, such as Central American policy and nuclear strategy.

Like his Jewish counterpart this Catholic White House official is sympathetic with the evangelical constituency: "Putting aside the objective merits of the case, it's easy to see how the IRS and FCC were perceived as intruding upon the evangelical churches. For the first time a real intrusion into the real life of the churches . . . a perceived threat." However, there is far more than an academic understanding of the feelings of evangelicals, a deeply shared sense of threat from secular culture. Indeed, this official is far more pessimistic (some might say paranoid) about the ability of U.S. society to accommodate his concerns than either the Jew or the evangelical Baptist:

Secularization will continue. The real question is whether secular society will tolerate that sub-culture which is antithetical to its basis. . . . You have two basic world views—a theistic and a non-theistic one. . . . Neither side is content to co-exist with the other. It's not enough that abortions be established as a private right. No, the pro-choice group has to have federal funding for abortions, and then wants to force private institutions to override religious beliefs and make abortions available. The secular mentality is ascending. Christian schooling is another example. The secular mentality can't tolerate even a small deviation. Ninety percent of schooling is public, and ninety percent of the private schooling is Catholic. So the fundamentalist system is very small, but will not be tolerated. Fundamentalist parents have been thrown in jail for teaching without a certificate.

This official felt that orthodox Catholics, like Christian fundamentalists, would increasingly be threatened by secular advances:

For Catholics, Grove City [Supreme Court decision limiting enforcement of Civil Rights Acts] and abortion are illuminating. Senator Weicker said that under his understanding of the [pending] Civil Rights Restoration Act, Catholic hospitals would have to perform abortions. Then you have the $100,000 a day fine imposed by a judge for the New York Archdiocese to turn over its records to a pro-abortion group. The more this kind of thing happens the more Catholics will perceive a threat. . . . You now have some Catholics who may not feel that America is the greatest—who question the Murray-Kennedy synthesis [belief that Catholics must accommodate religious pluralism].

It is clear from the above why this official would feel more in common with Christian fundamentalists than with liberal Protestants, whom he equated with the non-theistic orientation:

There is no tension at the mainline level. They share the secularized world view, which is basically a relativist view of morality and truth, versus an objective and absolute one. For the liberal church people the moral position is the freedom to decide, versus the substantive outcome. What is moral to them is the locus of decision, not the outcome. So it is easy for them to accommodate the secular world. Yet absolute moral norms is the historical position of Christianity. For the orthodox there is not as much wiggle room with secular society.

The image of the future that emerged from this Catholic political actor and thinker is one in which the orthodox, those with less "wiggle room" in secular society—Orthodox Jews, Christian evangelicals and fundamentalists, conservative Roman Catholics—would become more marginalized and subject to attack. Ronald Reagan, in a sense, is an interruption in an otherwise inexorable process: "How do you maintain a vital Christian community in light of a multi-billion-dollar porn industry, a multi-billion-dollar entertainment industry which contradicts Christian values—heavy metal, drug culture." Moreover, this marginalization of the orthodox is disastrous for society:

I argue that European and American culture has lived off the moral capital of Christian culture—but it is [just about] used up. Look at non-treatment of handicapped newborn. A Christian society would say no to that. Every human being is created by God, has a certain dignity . . . to apply a cost-benefit analysis is a non-Christian way of looking at problems.

White House Summary

Operating through the ideological prism of the president, White House religious liaison has provided access to the disparate voices of objection to the secular and libertarian drift of U.S. society. That this could coalesce around the election of a once-divorced, astrologically influenced Hollywood actor is yet another marvel of U.S. politics. Also fascinating is the tension this effort reveals between religious traditionalists and libertarian conservatives (whose interests often mesh better with secular understandings of reality than orthodox religious ones). The major question that remains is this: what happens after Ronald Reagan? To what extent will the next president provide similar channels of access? If such access is muted, will orthodox religious constituencies view the United States increasingly in terms painted by the pessimistic Catholic official? The electoral environment will, of course, provide the answer.

FAITH AND ACCESS: THE ELECTORAL CONNECTION

Access to power through the electoral process is, perhaps, the ultimate quest, particularly in light of the findings presented here. Both in the Congress and in the White House, the ideological lenses of political elites profoundly shape who is welcomed and who must beat down the door. Influencing the outcomes of elections or otherwise putting those elected on notice that constituencies are monitoring them are means of seizing access.

Few religious groups, however, make the electoral attempt, and for good reason. At the congressional level incumbents are deeply entrenched, and mounting a credible challenge requires plenty of money and a large, aroused district constituency. Even the Christian Right, concentrating formidable resources into congressional races, has met with only modest success (Green, Guth, and Hill, 1988).

At the more volatile presidential level, where party leaders do not control the delegate selection process as they once did, "outsiders" such as Pat Robertson and Jesse Jackson can gain convention delegates and leverage through broad, often church-based, constituency mobilization. It is not surprising, consequently, that acute tensions surfaced over the candidacy of Pat Robertson, who sought to mobilize "ardent pentecostals" and other conservative Christians in an attempt to block the nomination of George Bush. As a result, the normally staid Republican party experienced everything from delegate challenges to name-calling to outright fisticuffs. In Michigan, Peter Secchia, the state committeeman and a Bush supporter, described the Robertson camp as looking "like the bar scene from Star Wars" (Edsall, 1987). Not to be outdone in hyperbole, William DePass, a county GOP official in South Carolina, characterized the Robertson forces there as similar to "a Nazi meeting" (Edsall, 1987). The Robertson campaign reacted in turn. Marc Nuttle, Robertson's campaign director, referred to the "gestapo tactics" of Bush party supporters in Hawaii, who postponed (only temporarily it turned out) the caucuses in the face of a certain Robertson takeover. Of course, Robertson himself implied that the Bush campaign somehow orchestrated Jimmy Swaggart's downfall to hurt his candidacy.

This internecine conflict has some Republican party officials worried. The director of one national campaign committee expressed concern that the battle between the old Republican establishment and the Christian Right was erupting into open "warfare." As he put it:

I am concerned that this is getting out of hand. One presidential campaign has made it a business of beating on the Christian Right whenever it can, especially in Michigan, where the state committeeman did it. You throw grenades at the new right and they will fight back—stupid. And the problem at RNC [Republican National Committee] is that Fahrenkopf [Executive Director of the RNC] and Jarmin [Director of Christian Voice] have been feuding, and making it public.

Clearly the attempt by Robertson and his followers to gain access and influence in the Republican party has threatened some party officials. Ironically, the demise of Robertson's 1988 candidacy stemmed less from this highly visible party conflict than from his own inability to mobilize beyond his relatively narrow pentecostal constituency. Still, the impact of the Robertson candidacy must not be underestimated. Not only did the Robertson newcomers win delegate slots in a number of caucus states, but they also seized control of party offices in a number of primary states where caucuses were used to select local party leaders. Thus, even though the Bush campaign secured his nomination, Christian conservatives mobilized by Pat Robertson moved to entrench themselves in the party machinery, no doubt for future battles. Pat Robertson may remain a viable lighting rod for those orthodox Christians who have much to gain and, indeed, much current access to lose in the 1988 presidential campaign and beyond.

SUMMARY: FAITH AND ACCESS TO POWER

Phenomenologically speaking, the congressman who referred to the "right-to-God-damn-lifers" inhabits a different world from the Catholic official in the White House, for whom abortion is the symbol of the mortal clash between secularism and religion—and herein lies the key to understanding the checkered access enjoyed by lobby groups. The contrasting world views of Washington elites profoundly shape the access they provide to religious leaders and constituencies, a finding that may have implications for our understanding generally of the relationship between political leaders and lobby interests. The wild card in this analysis, of course, will be the new occupant of the White House. A Democratic victory will clearly blunt the access currently enjoyed by conservative Christians and may change the fortunes of the liberal Christians as well, many of whom have never adapted to the Reagan years.

The clearest exception to this pattern is the wide access enjoyed by Jewish groups, access that seemed independent of the ideological predilections of the Washington elites. In response to a question about which religious groups are effective, answers varied widely, as I have shown, largely on the basis of how sympathetic the person was to the group. But there was almost universal agreement on the efficacy of the Jewish groups. Indeed, the seven members of Congress agreed on only one thing: each cited the Jewish groups (without prodding) as among the influential constituencies. This access, as we have seen, extends to the White House, which, through staff allocations, has assigned equal weight to the Jewish constituency as to Roman Catholics and evangelical Protestants. Jews may be an anomaly in part because of their ethnic and religious link to strategic U.S. foreign policy concerns. Equally important, apparently, is the quality of their leadership and the educated and politicized nature of their constituents. Simply put, they are good lobbyists, demand access, and they get it.

This exception suggests that excellent lobbying, under the right circumstances, can overcome the filtering biases of Washington elites. For many groups, however, the lobbying matrix—the complex web of mutual screening and filtering—inhibits access. The reason, perhaps, may lie in the kernel of truth contained in the statement of the White House official that some groups really "don't want access." Or to put it another way, the price of access is too high, the dissonance too great, of making the strategic trade-offs. That this tension exists in the United Methodist Building and not in the Religious Action Center indicates, perhaps, that Jewish comfort with this world is more conducive to practical politics than a Christian tradition far more ambivalent about the City of Man.

Bibliography

Abramson, Paul R. 1983. *Political Attitudes in America*. San Francisco: W. H. Freeman.

Abramson, Paul R., John H. Aldrich, and David W. Rohde. 1986. *Change and Continuity in the 1984 Elections*. Washington, D.C.: Congressional Quarterly Press.

Abramson, Paul R. and Ronald Inglehart. 1987. Generational Replacement and the Future of Post-Materialist Values. *Journal of Politics* 49:231–241.

Adams, James L. 1970. *The Growing Church Lobby in Washington*. Grand Rapids, MI: William B. Eerdmans.

Adrian, Charles R. and Charles Press. 1968. Decision Costs in Coalition Formation. *American Political Science Review* 68:556–563.

Altemeyer, Bob. 1981. *Right-wing Authoritarianism*. Winnipeg: University of Manitoba Press.

Ammerman, Nancy. 1982. Operationalizing Evangelicalism: An Amendment. *Sociological Analysis* 43(2):170–172.

_____ . 1987. *Bible Believers: Fundamentalists in the Modern World*. New Brunswick, N.J.: Rutgers University Press.

Axelrod, Robert. 1970. Where the Votes Come From: An Analysis of Electoral Coalitions, 1952–68. *American Political Science Review* 66:11–20.

_____ . 1974. Communication. *American Political Science Review* 68:717–720.

_____ . 1978. Communication. *American Political Science Review* 72:622–624, 1010–1011.

_____ . 1982. Communication. *American Political Science Review* 76:393–396.

_____ . 1986. Presidential Election Coalitions In 1984. *American Political Science Review*, 80:281–284.

Baker, Tod A., Robert P. Steed, and Laurence W. Moreland. 1986. The Emergence of the Religious Right and the Development of the Two-Party System in the South. Paper presented at the annual meeting of the American Political Science Association, Washington, D.C.

Barkun, Michael. 1974. *Disaster and the Millennium*. New Haven, Conn.: Yale. University Press.

Barnhart, Joe Edward. 1986. *The Southern Baptist Holy War*, Austin: Texas Monthly Press.

Beatty, Kathleen and Oliver Walter. 1982. Religious Belief and Practice: New Forces in American Politics? Paper presented at the annual meeting of the American Political Science Association, Denver.

_____ . 1983. The Religious Right and Electoral Change. Presented at the annual meeting of the Midwest Political Science Association, Chicago.

_____ . 1984. Religious Preference and Practice: Reevaluating Their Impact on Political Tolerance. *Public Opinion Quarterly* 48:318–329.

_____ . 1987. Fundamentalists, Evangelicals and Politics. *American Politics Quarterly* 15:43–59.

Beck, Paul A. 1977. Partisan Dealignment in the Postwar South. *American Political Science Review* 71:477–496.

_____ . 1988. Incomplete Realignment: The Reagan Legacy for Parties and Elections. In Charles O. Jones (Ed.), *The Reagan Legacy*. Chatham, N.J.: Chatham House, 145–171.

Bellah, Robert N., Richard Masdsen, William M. Sullivan, Ann Swidler, and Steven M. Tipton. 1985. *Habits of the Heart: Individualism and Commitment in American Life*. Berkeley: University of California Press.

Benedetti, J. K. and M. B. Brown. 1978. Strategies for the Selection of Log-Linear Models. *Biometrics* 34:680–686.

Benson, John M. 1981. The Polls: A Rebirth of Religion: *Public Opinion Quarterly* 54:576–585.

Benson, Peter and Dorothy Williams. 1986. *Religion on Capital Hill: Myths and Realities*. New York: Oxford University Press.

Berger, Suzanne, ed. 1982. *Religion in West European Politics*. London: Frank Cass.

Berry, Jeffrey M. 1977. *Lobbying for the People*. Princeton, N.J.: Princeton University Press.

_____ . 1984. *The Interest Group Society*. Boston: Little, Brown.

Black, Earl and Merle Black, 1987. *Politics and Society in the South*. Cambridge, Mass: Harvard University Press.

Broad, William J., 1981. Creationists Limit Scope of Evolution Case. *Science* 211: 1331–1332.

Bromley, David G. and Anson D. Shupe. 1984. *New Christian Politics*. Macon, Ga.: Mercer University Press.

Brown, L. B. 1962. A Study of Religious Belief. *British Journal of Psychology* 53: 259–272.

Brown, Steven R. 1980. *Political Subjectivity: Applications of Q-Methodology in Political Science*. New Haven, Conn.: Yale University Press.

Brown, Walter R. 1981. Evidence that Implies a Young Earth and Solar System. *Evidence for Creation Series*. Naperville, Ill.: Institute for Creation Research Midwest Center.

Browne, Eric C. 1973. *Coalition Theories: A Logical and Empirical Critique*. Beverly Hills: Sage Professional Papers in Comparative Politics.

Browne, Eric C. and Mark N. Franklin. 1986. New Directions in Coalition Research. *Legislative Studies Quarterly* 11:469–482.

Bruce, Les, Jr. 1977. *On The Origin of Language*. San Diego: ICR Impact Series.

Buell, Emmett, Jr. and Lee Sigelman. 1985. An Army that Meets Every Sunday? Popular Support for the Moral Majority in 1980. *Social Science Quarterly* 66:426–434.

Burton, Ronald, Stephen Johnson, and Joseph Tamney. Forthcoming. Education and Fundamentalism. *Review of Religious Research*.

Campbell, Angus, Philip E. Converse, Warren E. Miller, and Donald Stokes. 1960. *The American Voter*. New York: Wiley.

Campbell, Donald T. and Donald W. Fiske. 1950. Convergent and Discriminant Validation by the Multitrait-Multimethod Matrix. *Psychological Bulletin* 56:81–104.

Castelli, Jim. 1983. *The Bishops and the Bomb: Waging Peace in a Nuclear Age*. Garden City, N.Y.: Doubleday.

Chalfant, Paul H., Robert E. Beckley, and C. Eddie Palmer. 1981. *Religion in Contemporary Society*. Sherman Oaks, Calif.: Alfred Publishing Co.

Cherny, Robert W. 1981. *Populism, Progressivism, and the Transformation of Nebraska Politics 1885–1915*. Lincoln: University of Nebraska.

Christianity Today. 1984. Critics Fear that Reagan is Swayed by Those Who Believe in a 'Nuclear Armageddon'. *Christianity Today* 28 (18):48–51.

Christianity Today Institute. 1987. Our Future Hope: Eschatology and Its Role in the Church. *Christianity Today* 31 (2):1–13.

Cleghorn, J. Stephen. 1986. Respect for Life: Research Notes on Cardinal Bernardin's Seamless Garment. *Review of Religious Research* 28:192–142.

Clymer, Adam. 1984. Religion and Politics Mix Poorly for the Democrats. *New York Times*, November 25.

Cochran, Clarke, Jerry Perkins, and Murray Havens. 1988. Public Policy and the Emergence of Religious Politics. *Polity* 19:596–612.

Conover, Pamela Johnston and Stanley Feldman. 1981. The Origins and Meaning of Liberal/Conservative Self-Identifications. *American Journal of Political Science* 25:617–645.

Converse, Philip E. 1964. The Nature of Belief Systems in Mass Publics. In David Apter (Ed.), *Ideology and Discontent*. New York: The Free Press, 206–261.

———. 1966. Religion and Politics: The 1960 Election. In Angus Cambell et al., *Elections and the Political Order*. New York: Wiley, 964–1024.

———. 1968. Some Priority Variables in Comparative Electoral Research. Occasional paper No. 3. Glasgow: Survey Research Center, University of Strathclyde.

Conway, Flo and Jim Siegelman. 1982. *Holy Terror*. Garden City, N.Y.: Doubleday.

Cooper, Mary. 1983. Religious Community Public Policy Advocacy in Washington. (Internal working papers.)

Costain, Anne N. 1980. The Struggle for a National Women's Lobby: Organizing a Diffuse Interest. *Western Political Quarterly* 33:476–491.

Curran, Charles E. 1985. *Directions in Catholic Social Ethics*. Notre Dame, Ind.: University of Notre Dame.

Dionne, E. J., Jr. 1981. Catholics and the Democrats: Estrangement but not Desertion. In S. M. Lipset (Ed.), *Party Coalition in the 1980s*. San Francisco: Institute for Contemporary Studies.

Duggan, Ervin S. 1986. The Church in the Political Thicket. *Public Opinion* 9:9–14.

Ebersole, Luke Eugene. 1951. *Church Lobbying in the Nation's Capital*. New York: Macmillan.

Edsall, Thomas. 1985. Pulpit Power: Converting the GOP. *Washington Post National Weekly Edition*, July 8.

_____ . 1987. Will Feuds Sink the GOP? *Washington Post Weekly Edition*, June 15, p. 29.

Edwards v. Aquillard, 1987 (Slip Opinion; Case No. 85–1513).

Eldredge, Niles, 1982. *The Monkey Business: A Scientist Looks at Creationism*. New York: Washington Square Press.

Epperson v. Arkansas, 1968. 393 US 97.

Erbe, Brigitte Mach. 1977. On The Politics of School Busing. *Public Opinion Quarterly* 41:113–117.

Falwell, Jerry. 1980. *Listen America*. New York: Doubleday.

_____ . 1987. *Strength for the Journey*. New York: Simon and Schuster.

Fee, Joan L. and Associates. 1980 *Young Catholics*. New York: Sadlier.

Fenno, Richard Jr. 1978. *Homestyle House Members in Their Districts*. Boston: Little, Brown.

Feinberg, S. E. 1980. *The Analysis of Cross-Classified Categorial Data*, 2nd ed. Cambridge, Mass.: MIT Press.

Filsinger, Erik. 1976. Tolerance of Non-Believers: A Cross-Tabular and Log Linear Analysis of Some Religious Correlates. *Review of Religious Research* 17:232–242.

Flake, Carol. 1984. *Redemptorama: Culture, Politics, and the New Evangelicalism*. Garden City, N.Y.: Anchor Press.

Flalka, John J. 1986a. Conservative Evangelicals' Activism Shakes up Iowa's Traditionally Moderate Republic Party. *The Wall Street Journal* 21:36.

_____ . 1986b. Evangelist Gets Scant Support from GOP in House Campaign. *Wall Street Journal* 21:68.

_____ . 1982. *A New Engagement: Evangelical Political Thought, 1966–1976*. Grand Rapids, Mich.: William B. Eerdman's.

Fowler, Robert Booth. 1985. *Religion and Politics in America*. Metuchen, N.J.: Scarecrow Press.

Frankovic, Kathleen A. 1982. Sex and Politics: New Alignments, Old Issues. *PS* 439–448.

Freeman, Jo. 1986. The Political Culture of Democrats and Republicans. *Political Science Quarterly* 101:327–344.

Fuerst, Paul, 1984. University Student Understanding of Evolutionary Biology's Place in the Creation/Evolution Controversy. *Ohio Journal of Science* 84:218–228.

Futuyma, Douglas J. 1983. *Science on Trial: The Case of Evolution*. New York: Pantheon Books.

Gabbenesch. Howard. 1972. Authoritarianism as a World View. *American Journal of Sociology* 77:857–875.

Galli, Giorgio and Alfonso Prandi. 1971. The Catholic Hierarchy and Christian Democracy in Italy. In Mattei Dogan and Richard Rose (Eds.), *European Politics*. Boston: Little, Brown, 353–359.

Gallup, George, Jr., 1978. *The Unchurched Americans*. Princeton, N.J.: Princeton Religion Research Center.

Gallup, George. 1979. The *Christianity Today*-Gallup Poll: An Overview. *Christianity Today* 23:363–1673.

Gallup, George, 1982. *Religion in America*. Princeton, N.J.: Princeton Religion Research Center.

Gallup, George, J. 1984. *Religion in America*. Princeton, N.J.: Princeton Religion Research Center.

Gallup, G., Jr. and J. Castelli. 1987. *The American Catholic People*. New York: Doubleday.

Gamson, William A. 1961. A Theory of Coalition Formation. *American Sociological Review*. 26:373–382.

Geertz, Clifford, 1973. *The Interpretation of Culture*. New York: Basic Books.

Gibson, James and Kent Tedin. 1986. Political Tolerance and the Rights of Homosexuals: A Contextual Analysis. Presented at the Annual Meeting of the Midwest Political Science Association, Chicago.

Glock, Charles Y. and Rodney Stark. 1965. *Religion and Society in Tension*. Chicago: Rand McNally.

_____. 1966. *Christian Beliefs and Anti-Semitism*. New York: Harper.

Godfrey, Laurie R. (Ed). 1983. *Scientists Confront Creationism*. New York: W. W. Norton.

Goodman, L. A. 1970. The Multivariate Analysis of Qualitative Data: Interaction Among Multiple Classifications. *Journal of the American Statistical Association* 65:226–56.

_____. 1972. A General Model for the Analysis of Surveys. *American Journal of Sociology* 77:1035–1086.

Goodman, Walter. 1984. Political Talk of Doom Fuels Religious Debate. *New York Times*, October 28.

Gorman, James, 1982. Judgment Day for Creationism. *Discover* February 14–18.

Gorsuch, R. L. and C. S. Smith. 1983. Attributions of Responsibility to God: An Interpretation of Religious Beliefs and Outcomes. *Journal for the Scientific Study of Religion* 22:340–352.

Granberg, Donald. 1984. Comments and Letters: On Beatty and Walter. *Public Opinion Quarterly* 48:809–811.

Greeley, Andrew M. 1977. *The American Catholic: A Social Portrait*. New York: Basic Books.

_____. 1978. Catholics and Coalition: Where Should They Go? In S. M. Lipset (Ed.), *Emerging Coalitions in American Politics*. San Francisco: Instituted for Contemporary Studies.

_____. 1981. *The Religious Imagination*. New York: Sadlier.

_____ . 1982. *Religion: A Secular Theory*. New York: Free Press.

_____ . 1984. Religion's Imagery as a Predictor Variable in the General Social Survey. Paper presented to the Society for the Scientific Study of Religion annual meeting. Chicago.

_____ . 1985. *American Catholics Since the Council*. Chicago: The Thomas More Press.

Green, John C. and James L. Guth. 1986. Big Bucks and Petty Cash. In Allan Cigler and Burdett Loomis (Eds.), *Interest Group Politics*, 2nd ed. Washington, D.C.: CQ Press.

_____ . 1988. The Christian Right in the Republican Party: The Case of Pat Robertson's Supporters. *Journal of Politics* 50:150–165.

Green, John C., James L. Guth, and Kevin Hill. 1988. Faith and Election: The Christian Right in House Races, 1978–1986. Paper presented at the Citadel Symposium on Southern Politics, Charleston, S.C.

Gregory W. Edgar. 1957. The Orthodoxy of the Authoritarian Personality. *Journal of Social Psychology* 45:217–232.

Griffith, Ernest S., John Plamenatz, and J. Roland Pennock. 1956. Cultural Prerequisites to a Successfully Functioning Democracy. *American Political Science Review* 50:101–137.

Groennings, Sven, E. W. Kelley, and Michael Leiserson (Eds.). 1970. *The Study of Coalition Behavior: Theoretical Perspectives and Cases from Four Continents*. New York: Holt, Rinehart and Winston.

Guth, James. 1983. The New Christian Right. In Robert Liebman and Robert Wuthnow (Eds.), *The New Christian Right*. New York: Aldine.

_____ . 1985–86. Political Converts: Partisan Realignment Among Southern Baptist Ministers. *Election Politics* 3 (1):2–6.

_____ . 1988. Southern Baptists and the New Right. In Charles W. Dunn (Ed.), *Religion in American Politics*. Washington, D.C.: CQ Press.

Guth, James L. and John C. Green. 1984. Political Activists and Civil Liberties: The Case of Party and PAC Contributors. Papers presented at the annual meeting of the Midwest Political Science Association, Chicago.

_____ . 1986. Faith and Politics: Religion and Ideology among Political Contributors. *American Politics Quarterly* 14:186–200.

_____ . 1987a. God and the GOP: Varieties of Religiosity Among Republic Contributors. Paper presented at the annual meeting of the American Political Science Association, Chicago.

_____ . 1987b. The Moralizing Minority: Christian Right Support Among Political Contributors. *Social Science Quarterly* 67:598–610.

Hadden, Jeffrey K. 1987. Religious Broadcasting and the New Christian Right. *Journal for the Scientific Study of Religion* 26:1–24.

Hadden, Jeffry K. and Anson Shupe. 1988. *Televangelism: Power & Politics on God's Frontier*. New York: Henry Holt.

Hadden, Jeffrey K. and Charles E. Swann. 1981. *Prime Time Preachers*. Reading, Mass.: Addison-Wesley.

Hall, Donald R. 1969. *Cooperative Lobbying: The Power of Pressure*. Tucson: University of Arizona Press.

Halsell, Grace. 1986. *Prophecy and Politics: Militant Evangelists on the Road to Nuclear War*. Westport, Conn.: Lawrence Hill.

Handberg, Roger, 1983. Creationism, Conservatism and Ideology: Fringe Issues in American Politics. Paper presented at the Annual Meeting of the Southwest Political Science Association, Houston.

Hanna, Mary T. 1979. *Catholics and American Politics*. Cambridge, Mass.: Harvard University Press, Denver.

_____ . 1982. Religious Interest Groups and the Congress. Paper, American Political Science Association.

Harrold, Francis B. and Raymond A. Eve, 1986. Noah's Ark and Ancient Astronauts: Pseudoscientific Beliefs About the Past Among a Sample of College Students. *The Skeptical Inquirer* 11 (1):61–75.

Hauss, Charles S. and L. Sandy Maisel. 1986. Extremist Delegates: Myth and Reality. In Ronald B. Rapoport et al. (Eds.), *The Life of the Parties*. Lexington: University Press of Kentucky.

Helmert, Alan. 1956. *Religion and the American Mind: From the Great Awakening to the Revolution*. Cambridge, Mass.: Harvard University Press.

Hertzke, Allen D. 1988. *Representing God in Washington: The Role of Religious Lobbies in the American Polity*. Knoxville: The University of Tennessee.

Hilty, Dale M., Rick L. Morgan, and Joan E. Burns. 1984. Dimensions of Religious Involvement. *Journal for the Scientific Study of Religion* 23:252–263.

Himmelfarb, Gertrude. 1988. Manners into Morals: What the Victorians Knew. *American Scholar* 57:223–232.

Hinckley, Barbara. 1981. *Coalitions and Politics*. New York: Harcourt Brace Jovanovich.

Hoffman, T. J. 1985. Contemporary Political Attitudes of American Catholics. Presented at the Annual Meeting of the American Political Science Association, Washington, D.C.

Hoge, Dean R. and Ernesto De Zulueta. 1985. Salience as a Condition for Various Social Consequences of Religious Commitment. *Journal for the Scientific Study of Religion* 24:21–37.

Hoover, A. J. 1981. *The Case for Teaching Creation*. Joplin, Mo.: College Press Publishing Company.

Horn, Richard D. 1987. Church-State Issues in the Twenties and Thirties. In John F. Wilson, (ed.), *Church and State in America*. Westport, Conn.: Greenwood Press, 185–224.

Hout, M. and A. M. Greeley. 1987. The Center Doesn't Hold: Church Attendance in the United States, 1940–1984. *American Sociological Review* 52:325–45.

Hrebenar, Ronald J. and Ruth K. Scott. 1982. *Interest Group Politics in America*. Englewood Cliffs, N.J.: Prentice-Hall.

Huitema, Bradley. 1980. *The Analysis of Covariance and Alternatives*. New York: Wiley.

Hunter, James D. 1981. Operationalizing Evangelicalism: A Review, Critique & Proposal. *Sociological Analysis* 42:363–372.

_____ . 1983a. *American Evangelicalism: Conservative Religion and the Quandary of Modernity*. New Brunswick, N.J.: Rutgers University Press.

———. 1983b. The Liberal Reaction. In Robert C. Liebman and Robert Wuthnow (Eds.), *The New Christian Right*. New York: Aldine, 150–167.

———. 1984. Religion and Political Civility: The Coming Generation of American Evangelicals. *Journal for the Scientific Study of Religion* 23:364–380.

———. 1987a. *Evangelicalism: The Coming Generation*. Chicago: University of Chicago Press.

———. 1987b. The Evangelical Worldview Since 1890. In Richard John Neuhaus and Michael Cromartie (Eds.), *Piety and Politics*. Washington, D.C.: Ethics and Public Policy Center.

Hyer, Marjorie. 1986. Bishops Approve Letter On Economic Justice. *Washington Post*, November 14, A1, A18.

Ingwerson, Marshall. 1988. Pat Robertson. *Christian Science Monitor*, January 16.

Jelen, Ted. 1981. Christian Fundamentalism and Political Tolerance. Presented at the annual meeting of the Southwest Social Science Association. Dallas.

———. 1985. Images of God as Predictors of Attitudes on Social Issues among Fundamentalists and Non-Fundamentalists. Presented at the annual meeting of the Society for the Scientific Study of Religion, Savannah, Ga.

———. 1987. The Effects of Religious Separatism on White Protestants in the 1984 Presidential Election. *Sociological Analysis* 48 (1):30–45.

Johnson, Haynes. 1986. The Ambassador for Christ Race. *Washington Post National Weekly Edition*, October 13, p. 24.

Johnson, Ronald L. and E. Edward Peeples, 1987. The Role of Scientific Understanding in College Student Acceptance of Evolution. *American Biology Teacher* 49 (2): 93–96.

Johnson, Stephen D. 1986. The Role of the Black Church in Black Civil Rights Movements. In Stephen D. Johnson and Joseph B. Tamney (Eds.), *The Political Role of Religion in the United States*. Boulder, Colo.: Westview Press, 307–324.

Johnson, Stephen D. and Joseph B. Tamney. The Christian Right and the 1980 Presidential Election. *Journal for the Scientific Study of Religion* 21:123–131.

——— (Eds.). 1986. *The Political Role of Religion in the United States*. Boulder, Colo.: Westview Press.

Johnson, Stepen D., Joseph B. Tamney, and Sandor Halebsky. 1986. Christianity Social Traditionalism, and Economic Conservatism. *Sociological Focus* 19:299–314.

Katz, William and Linda S. Katz. 1968. *Magazines for Libraries*. New York: R. R. Bowker.

Keller, Bill. 1982. Coalitions and Associations Transform Strategy, Methods of Lobbying in Washington. *Congressional Quarterly Weekly Report* 40:119–123.

Kellstedt, Lyman A. 1984. Religion and Politics: The Measurement of Evangelicalism. Paper presented at the annual meeting of the American Political Science Association, Washington, D.C.

———. 1986. Evangelicals and Political Realignment. Paper presented at the annual meeting of the American Political Science Association, Washington, D.C.

———. 1988. The Falwell Issue Agenda: Sources of Support among White Protestant Evangelicals. In M. Lynn and D. Moberg (Eds.), *An Annual in the Sociology of Religion*. New York: JAI Press.

Kellstedt, Lyman A. and Corwin Smidt. 1988. Discriminating Fundamentalist from Non-Fundamentalist Evangelicals: A Multi-Dimensional Analysis. Unpublished Paper.

Kelley, Dean. 1977. *Why Conservative Churches Are Growing*. New York: Harper.

Kennedy, Eugene. 1984. America's Activist Bishops. *New York Times Magazine*, August 12, 14–18, 24–30.

Kennedy, Moorhead. 1985. *The Ayatollah in the Cathedral*. New York: Hill and Wang.

Kenski, H. 1988. The Catholic Voter in American Elections. *Election Politics* 5: 16–23.

Kenski, H. and W. Lockwood. 1987. The Political Partisanship of American Catholics: 1952–1986. Unpublished paper.

———. 1988. Re-Imagining American Catholicism: The American Bishops and the Seamless Garment. In I. H. Shafer (Ed.), *The Incarnate Imagination: Essays in Theology, the Arts, and Social Sciences in Honor of Andrew Greeley: A Festschrift*. Bowling Green, Oh.: Popular Press.

King, Morton B. and Richard A. Hunt. 1972. *Measuring Religious Dimensions: Studies in Congregational Involvement*. Dallas: Southern Methodist University Press.

Kirkpatrick, Jeane J. 1976. *The New Presidential Elite*. New York: Russell Sage Foundation.

Kitcher, Philip, 1983. *Abusing Science: The Case Against Creationism*. Cambridge, Mass.: The MIT Press.

Klecka, William. 1980. *Discriminant Analysis*. Beverly Hills: Sage.

Kleppner, Paul. 1985. *The Third Party System, 1853–1892*. Chapel Hill: University of North Carolina Press.

Knight, Kathleen. 1984. The Dimensionality of Partisan and Ideological Affect: The Influence of Positivity. *American Politics Quarterly* 12:305–334.

Knoke, D. 1974. Religious Involvement and Political Behavior: A Log-linear Analysis of White Americans, 1952–1968. *The Sociological Quarterly* 15:51–56.

———. 1976. *Change and Continuity in American Politics: The Social Basis of Political Parties*. Baltimore: John Hopkins University Press.

Kofahl, Robert E., 1980. *The Handy Dandy Evolution Refuter*. San Diego: Beta Books.

Krietemeyer, Ronald. 1986. Interview with Mary T. Hanna. Washington, D.C., November 12.

Krueger, David A. 1986. Capitalism, Christianity, and Economic Ethics: An Illustrative Survey of Twentieth Century Protestant Social Ethics. In Bruce Grelle and David A. Krueger (Eds.), *Christianity and Capitalism*. Chicago: Center for the Scientific Study of Religion, 25–45.

Ladd, Evertt Carll. 1985a. *The American Polity*, 1st ed. New York: W. W. Norton.

———. 1985b. The Election of 1984. *The Ladd Report #1*. New York: W. W. Norton.

————. 1986. Alignment and Realignment: Where Are All the Voters Going? *The Ladd Report*: New York: W. W. Norton.

Lamis, Alexander P. 1984. *The Two-Party South*. New York: Oxford University Press.

Langan, John. 1984. The Bishops and the Bottom Line. *Commonweal* 111:586–587.

Larson, Robert W. 1986. *Populism in the Mountain West*. Las Cruces: University of New Mexico.

Lasch, Christopher. 1978. *The Culture of Narcissism*. New York: W. W. Norton.

Lawler, Philip. 1986. *How the Bishops Decide: An American Catholic Case Study*. Washington, D.C.: Ethics and Public Policy Center.

Leege, David C. and Michael R. Welch. 1986. The Roots of Political Alignment: Examining the Relationship Between Religion and Politics Among Catholic Parishioners. Paper presented at the annual meeting of the American Political Science Association, Washington, D.C.

————. 1989. Religious Roots of Political Orientations: Variations Among American Catholic Parishioners. *The Journal of Politics* (forthcoming).

Leibman, Robert. 1983. Mobilizing the Moral Majority. In Robert Leibman and Robert Wuthnow (Eds.), *The New Christian Right*. New York: Aldine.

Leibman, Robert and Robert Wuthnow. 1983. *The New Christian Right*. Hawthorne, N.Y.: Aldine.

Lenski, Gerhard. 1963. *The Religious Factor: A Sociological Study of Religion's Impact on Politics, Economics, and Family Life*. Garden City, N.Y.: Doubleday.

Lewin, Roger. 1982a. Creationism on the Defensive in Arkansas. *Science* 215:33–34.

————. 1982b. Where is the Science in Creation Science? *Science* 215:142–146.

————. 1982c. Judge's Ruling Hits Hard at Creationism. *Science* 215:381–384.

————. 1987. Creationism Case Argued Before Supreme Court. *Science* 235:22–23.

Lindsay, Donald B., Barbara W. Sirotnik, and John Heeren. 1986. Measuring Christian Orthodoxy. *Journal for the Scientific Study of Religion* 25:328–338.

Lindsey, Hal. 1970. *The Late Great Planet Earth*. New York: Bantam.

————. 1980. *The 1980s: Countdown to Armageddon*. King of Prussia, Pa.: Westgate Press.

Lipset, S. M. and Stein Rokkan. 1967. *Party Systems and Voter Alignments*. New York: Free Press.

Lipset, Seymour Martin and Earl Raab. 1981. The Election and the Evangelicals. *Commentary* 71 (3):25–31.

Lipset, Seymour Martin and William Schneider. 1987. *The Confidence Gap: Business, Labor and Government in the Public Mind*. Baltimore: John Hopkins University Press.

Loomis, Burdett A. 1986. Coalitions of Interests: Building Bridges in the Balkanized State. In Allen J. Cigler and Burdett A. Loomis (Eds.), *Interest Group Politics*. Washington, D.C.: Congressional Quarterly Press.

Lopatto, Paul. 1985. *Religion and the Presidential Election*. New York: Praeger.

Lynd, Robert S. and Helen Merrell Lynd. 1929. *Middletown*. New York: Harcourt, Brace & World.

Maranell, Gary. 1967. An Examination of Some Religious and Political Attitude Correlates of Bigotry. *Social Forces* 454:367–372.

Marsden, George M. 1980. *Fundamentalism and American Culture: The Shaping of Twentieth-Century Evangelicalism, 1870–1925.* Oxford: Oxford University Press.

_____. 1987. The Evangelical Denomination. In Richard John Neuhaus and Michael Cromartie (Eds.), *Piety and Politics.* Washington, D.C.: Ethics and Public Policy Center.

Martin, David. 1978. *A General Theory of Secularization.* New York: Harper.

Martin, J. G. and F. R. Westie. 1959. The Tolerant Personality. *American Sociological Review* 24:521–528..

Martin, William. 1982. Waiting for the End. *The Atlantic Monthly,* 249:31–37.

Massa, Mark S. 1987. Social Justice in an Industrial Society. In John F. Wilson (Ed.), *Church and State in America.* Westport, Conn.: Greenwood, 67–106.

McEvoy, James. 1971. *Radicals or Conservatives: The Contemporary American Right.* Chicago: Rand McNally.

McKim, Donald. 1985. *What Christians Believe About the Bible.* Nashville: Thomas Nelson.

McNamara, Patrick H. 1985. The New Christian Right's View of the Family and Its Social Science Critics. *Journal of Marriage and the Family* 47:449–458.

McWilliams, Peter W. 1980. *Popular Religion in America.* Englewood Cliffs, N.J.: Prentice-Hall.

Mead, Sidney, 1973. The Sanctification of a Particular Culture's Values as Ultimate. In Thomas F. O'Dea and Janet K. O'Dea (Eds.), *Readings on the Sociology of Religion.* Englewood Cliffs, N.J.: Prentice-Hall, 181–191.

Menendez, Albert. 1977. *Religion at the Polls.* Philadelphia: Westminster Press.

Milbrath, Lester W. 1963. *The Washington Lobbyists.* Chicago: Rand McNally.

Mill, John Stuart. 1975. *On Liberty.* London: Oxford University Press.

Miller, Arthur. 1978. Partisanship Reinstated: A Comparison of the 1972 and 1976 U.S. Presidential Elections. *British Journal of Politics* 48:129–152.

Miller, Arthur H. and Martin Wattenburg. 1984. Politics from the Pulpit: Religiosity and the 1980 Elections. *Public Opinion Quarterly* 8:301–317.

Miller, W. E., A. H. Miller, and E. J. Schneider. 1980. *American National Election Studies Data Sourcebook, 1952–1978.* Cambridge, Mass.: Harvard University Press.

Moen, Matthew C. 1986. The New Christian Right and the Legislative Agenda: The Politics of Agenda Setting in the 97th and 98th Congress. Ph.D. Dissertation, University of Oklahoma.

Mojtabai, A. J. 1986. *Blessed Assurance: At Home with the Bomb in Amarillo, Texas.* Boston: Houghton Mifflin.

Moorhead, James H. 1978. *American Apocalypse: Yankee Protestants and the Civil War, 1860–1869.* New Haven, Conn.: Yale University Press.

Morken, Hubert. 1988. *Pat Robertson: Where He Stands.* Old Tappan, N.J.: Fleming H. Revell.

Morris, Henry M., 1968. *The Bible and Modern Science.* Chicago: Moody Press.

_____. 1970. *Biblical Cosmology and Modern Science.* Nutley, N.J.: Craig Press.

_____ . 1972. *The Remarkable Birth of Planet Earth*. San Diego: Creation Life Publishers.

_____ . 1973a. The Universality of the Flood (Parts I and II). In Kelly L. Seagraves (Ed.), *And God Created* (4). San Diego: Creation-Science Research Center.

_____ . 1973b Evidences for a Young Earth. In Kelly L. Seagraves (Ed.), *And God Created* (3). San Diego: Creation-Science Research Center.

_____ . 1975. *The Troubled Waters of Evolution*. San Diego: Creation Life Publishers.

National Conference of Catholic Bishops. 1983. *The Challenge of Peace: God's Promise and Our Response*. Washington, D.C.: U.S. Catholic Conference.

_____ . 1986. *Economic Justice For All*. Washington, D.C.: National Conference of Catholic Bishops.

NBC News. 1984. *NBC News Decision '84*. New York: NBC News.

_____ . 1986. *NBC News Decision '86*. New York: NBC News.

Nelkin, Dorothy, 1976. The Science Textbook Controversies. *Scientific American* 234:33–39.

_____ . 1978. *Science Textbook Controversies and the Politics of Equal Time*. Cambridge, Mass.: MIT Press.

_____ . 1982. *The Creation Controversy* New York: W. W. Norton.

Neuhaus, Richard John. 1984. *The Naked Public Square: Religion and Democracy in America*. Grand Rapids, Mich.: William B. Eerdmans.

Neuhaus, Richard John and Michael Cromartie. 1987. *Piety and Politics*. Washington, D.C.: Ethics and Public Policy Center.

Nie, Norman, Sidney Verba, and John R. Petrocik. 1976. *The Changing American Voter*. Cambridge, Mass.: Harvard University Press.

Niebuhr, Reinhold. 1972. *The Children of Light and the Children of Darkness*. New York: Scribner's.

Noll, Mark. 1986. *Between Faith and Scholarship: Evangelicals, Scholarship and the Bible in America*. New York: Harper.

Norpoth, H. 1987. Under Way and Here to Stay: Party-Alignment in the 1980s? *Public Opinion Quarterly* 51:376–391.

Nunn, Clyde, Harry Crocket, Jr., and Allen Williams, Jr. *Tolerance for Nonconformity*. San Francisco: Jossey-Bass.

Numbers, Ronald L. 1982. Creationism in Twentieth Century America. *Science* 218:538–544.

Oliver, John. 1975. The Word in Print. *Post American* 26–30.

Olmstead, Clifton E. 1970. Social Religion in Urban America. In Philip E. Hammond and Benton Johnson (Eds.), *American Mosaic*. New York: Random House, 139–148.

O'Neil, Daniel J. 1970. *Church Lobbying in a Western State: A Case Study on Abortion Legislation*. Tucson: University of Arizona Press.

Origins. 1984. Washington, D.C.: National Conference of Catholic Bishops Documentary Service: 338–383.

Origins. 1986. Washington, D.C.: National Conference of Catholic Bishops Documentary Service: 393–398.

Origins. 1988. Washington, D.C.: National Conference of Catholic Bishops Documentary Service: 758–788.

Ornstein, Norman J. and Shirley Edler. 1978. *Interest Groups, Lobbying and Policymaking*. Washington, D.C.: Congressional Quarterly Press.

Palmer, Bruce. 1980. *Man Over Money: The Southern Populist Critique of American Capitalism*. Chapel Hill: University of North Carolina.

Palmer, Park J. 1981. *The Company of Strangers*. New York: Crossroad.

Patel, Kent, Denny Pilant, and Gary Rose. 1982. Born-Again Christians in the Bible Belt: A Study in Religion, Politics, and Ideology. *American Politics Quarterly* 10:255-272.

Patterson, John W. 1983. Thermodynamics and Evolution. In Laurie R. Godfrey (Ed.), *Scientists Confront Creationism*. New York: W. W. Norton.

Pawlikowski, John T., O.S.M. 1986. Modern Catholic Teaching on the Economy: An Analysis and Evaluation. In Bruce Grelle and David A. Krueger (Eds.), *Christianity and Capitalism*. Chicago: Center for the Scientific Study of Religion, 3-240.

Penning, J. M. 1986. Changing Partisanship and Issue Stands Among Catholics. *Sociological Analysis* 47:29-49.

Perkins, Jerry. 1983a. The Effects of Evangelicalism on Southern Black and White Political Attitudes and Voting Behavior. In Tod A. Baker, Robert P. Steed, and Laurice W. Moreland (Eds.), *Religion and Politics in the South*. New York: Praeger, 57-83.

_____. 1983b. Popular Evaluations of the Moral Majority. Paper delivered to the Western Social Science Association Convention, Albuquerque.

Petrocik, J. R. 1981. *Party Coalitions: Realignments and the Decline of the New Deal Party System*. Chicago: University of Chicago Press.

_____. 1987. Realignment: New Party Coalitions and the Nationalization of the South. *The Journal of Politics* 49:347-373.

Petrocik, J. R. and F. T. Steeper. 1987. The Political Landscape in 1988. *Public Opinion* 10:41-44.

Phillips, Keven P. 1986. The Era of Republican Ascendancy May Already Have Ended. *The Washington Post National Weekly Edition* 28:23-24.

Pollock, John C. et al. 1981. *The Connecticut Mutual Life Report on American Values in the '80s: The Impact of Belief*. Hartford: Connecticut Mutual Life Insurance Company.

Poloma, Margaret. 1982. *The Charismatic Movement: Is There a New Pentecost?* Boston: Twayne Publishers.

Polsby, Nelson and Aaron Wildavsky. 1984. *Presidential Elections*, 6th ed. New York: Scribner's.

Powell, G. Bingham. 1982. *Contemporary Democracies: Participation, Stability and Violence*. Cambridge, Mass.: Harvard University Press.

Ray, J. J. 1976. Do Authoritarians Hold Authoritarian Attitudes? *Human Relations* 29:307-325.

_____. 1979. Does Authoritarianism of Personality Go With Conservatism? *Australian Psychologist* 31:9-14.

_____. 1984. Alternatives to the F Scale in the Measurement of Authoritarianism: A Catalog. *Journal of Social Psychology* 122:105-119.

Reichley, A. James. 1985a. *Religion in American Public Life*. Washington, D.C.: The Brookings Institution.

———. 1985b. Religion and Realignment. *The Brookings Review* 31:29–35.

Rhodes, A. Lewis. 1960. Authoritarianism and Fundamentalism of Rural and Urban High School Students. *Journals of Educational Psychology* 34:97–105.

Riker, William H. 1962. *The Theory of Political Coalitions*. New Haven, Conn.: Yale University Press.

Ripley, Randall. 1985. *Congress: Process and Policy*. New York: W. W. Norton.

Rokeach, Milton. 1969–70. The Paul H. Douglass Lecture for 1969: Part 1, Value Systems In Religion. *Review of Religious Research* 11:3–23; Part II, Religious Values and Social Compassion, 24–39; Religious Values and Social Compassion: A Critical Review, 136–162.

Roof, Wade Clark. 1978. *Community and Commitment: Religious Plausibility in a Liberal Protestant Church*. New York: Elsevier.

Roof, Wade Clark and William McKinney. 1987. *American Mainline Religion*. New Brunswick, N.J.: Rutgers University.

Rothenberg, Stuart and Frank Newport. 1984. *The Evangelical Voter*. Washington, D.C.: The Free Congress Foundation.

Rothman, Stanley and S. Robert Lichter. 1982. *Roots of Radicalism: Jews, Christians and the New Left*. New York: Oxford University Press.

Rose, Richard and Derek Urwin. 1969. Social Cohesion, Political Parties, and Strains in Regimes. *Comparative Political Studies* 2:7–67.

Ross, Gary M. 1984. Churches Gone Political: The Recent Controversy over Vatican Recognition. Paper presented to the Conference on Faith and History.

Sabato, Larry. 1988. *The Party's Just Begun: Shaping Political Parties for America's Future*. Glenview, Ill.: Scott, Foresman.

Salisbury, Robert H., John P. Heinz, Edward O. Laumann, and Robert L. Nelson. 1986. Who Works With Whom? Patterns of Interest Group Alliance and Opposition. Paper presented to the American Political Science Association, Washington, D.C.

Schaeffer, Francis A. 1968. *The God Who Is There*. Downers Grove, Ill.: Intervarsity Press.

———. 1972. *He is There and He is Not Silent*. Wheaton, Ill.: Tyndale House.

Scholzman, Kay L. and John T. Tierney. 1985. *Organized Interests and American Democracy*. New York: Harper.

Scott, Eugenie C. 1987. Antievolutionism, Scientific Creationism and Physical Anthropology. *Yearbook of Physical Anthropology* 30: 21–39.

Seaman, Jerrol M., Jerry B. Michel, and Ronald C. Dillehay. 1971. Membership in Orthodox Christian Groups, Adjustment and Dogmatism. *Sociological Quarterly* 12:252–259.

Setterfield, Barry, 1983. The Velocity of Light and the Age of the Universe (Technical Monograph). Creation Science Association (Australia).

Shackford, John W. 1917. *The Program of the Christian Religion*. Nashville: Lamar and Barton.

Shafer, Byron E. 1985. The New Cultural Politics. *PS* 28:221–231.

Shapiro, Robert Y. and Harpreet Mahajan. 1984. Gender Differences in Policy Preferences: A Summary of Trends from the 1960s to the 1980s. *Public Opinion Quarterly* 48:42–61.

Shupe, Anson and William Stacey. 1983. The Moral Majority Constituency. In R. Liebman and R. Wuthnow (Eds.) *The New Christian Right*. New York: Aldine.

Sigelman, Lee, Clyde Wilcox, and Emmett Buell. 1987. An Unchanged Minority: Popular Support for the Moral Majority in 1980 and 1984. *Social Science Quarterly* 68:876–884.

Simpson, John. 1983. Support for the Moral Majority and its Sociomoral Platform. In D. Bromley and A. Shupe (Eds.), *New Christian Politics*. Macon, Ga.: Mercer University Press.

Smelsner, Neil. 1963. *Theory of Collective Behavior*. New York: Free Press.

Smidt, Corwin, 1983. Born-Again Politics: The Political Behavior of Evangelical Christians in the South and Non-South. In Tod A. Baker, Robert P. Steed and Laurence W. Moreland (Eds.) *Religion and Politics in the South*. New York: Praeger, 27–56.

_____ . 1985. Evangelicals and the 1984 Election: Continuity or Change? Paper presented at the annual meeting of the Society for The Scientific Study of Religion, Savannah, Ga.

_____ . 1986. Self-Identification as a Measurement Approach in the Study of Religion and Politics. Paper presented at the annual meeting of the American Political Science Association, Washington, D.C.

_____ . 1987. Evangelicals and the 1984 Election: Continuity or Change? *American Politics Quarterly* 15:419–444.

_____ . 1988a. Evangelicals in Presidential Elections: A Look at the 1980s. *Election Politics* 5:2–11.

_____ . 1988b. Evangelicals within Contemporary American Politics: Differentiating between Fundamentalist and Non-fundamentalist Evanglicals, *The Western Political Quarterly* 41:601–620.

_____ . 1988c. The Mobilization of Evangelical Voters in 1980; An Initial Test of Several Hypotheses. Forthcoming, *Southeastern Political Quarterly*.

_____ . 1989. Praise the Lord Politics: A Comparative Analysis of the Social Characteristics and Political Views of American Evangelical and Charismatic Christians. *Sociological Analysis*. Forthcoming.

_____ . (Forthcoming). *Contemporary Evangelical Political Involvement*. Washington, D.C.: University Press of America.

Smidt, Corwin and Lyman Kellstedt. 1987. Evangelicalism and Survey Research: Interpretative Problems and Substantive Findings. In Richard J. Neuhaus (Ed.), *The Bible, Politics, and Democracy*. Grand Rapids, Mich.: William B. Eerdmans, 81–102, 131–167.

Smidt, Corwin and James Penning. 1982. Religious Commitment, Political Conservatism, and Political and Social Tolerance in the United States: A Longitudinal Analysis. *Sociological Analysis* 43:231–246.

Smith, Gary Scott. 1985. *The Seeds of Secularization*. Grand Rapids, Mich.: William B. Eerdmans.

Smith, Tom W. (Ed.). 1984. The Polls: Gender and Attitudes Toward Violence. *Public Opinion Quarterly* 48:384–396.

Sniderman, Paul M. With Michael Gray Hagen. 1985. *Race and Inequality: A Study in American Values*. Chatham, N.J.: Chatham House.

Snyder, Edward F. 1971. The Churches' Role in Washington. *The Christian Century* 88:69–70.

Solbach, Vern. 1987. Interview with Mary T. Hanna, Walla Walla, Washington, January 13.

Spanier, John W. 1968. *American Foreign Policy Since World War II*, 4th rev. ed. New York: Praeger, 1968.

Stanley, H. W., W. T. Bianco, and R. G. Niemi. 1986. Partisanship and Group Support Over Time: A Multivariate Analysis. *American Political Science Review* 80:969–976.

Stark, Rodney and Charles Y. Glock. 1968. *American Piety: The Nature of Religious Commitment*. Berkeley: University of California Press.

Steeper, F. T. and J. R. Petrocik. Forthcoming. New Coalitions in 1988. *Public Opinion*.

Stephenson, William. 1953. *The Study of Behavior: Q-Technique and its Application*. Chicago: University of Chicago Press.

Stockman, David. 1986. *The Triumph of Politics*. New York: Avon.

Stockton, Ronald. 1984. The Falwell Core: A Public Opinion Analysis. Presented at the annual meeting of the Society for the Scientific Study of Religion, Chicago.

———. 1987. Christian Zionism: Prophecy and Public Opinion. *The Middle East Journal* 41:234–253.

Storms, Roger C. 1972. *Partisan Prophets: A History of the Prohibition Party* Denver: National Prohibition Foundation.

Stouffer, Samuel. 1955. *Communism, Conformity and Civil Liberties*. New York: Doubleday.

Straus, Hal. 1988. Robertson Wins Backing of S.C. Clergy. *Atlanta Journal*, March 1, 1988.

Strege, Merle D. 1986. Jerry Falwell and The Simple Faith on Which This Country Was Built. In Stephen D. Johnson and Joseph B. Tamney (Eds.), *The Political Role of Religion in the United States*. Boulder, Colo.: Westview Press, 103–124.

Streiker, Lowell D. and Gerald S. Strober. 1972. *Religion and the New Majority*. New York: Harper.

Sullivan, John, James Piereson, and George Marcus. 1982. *Political Tolerance and American Democracy* Chicago: University of Chicago Press.

Sullivan, John, Michael Shamir, Patrick Walsh, and Nigel Roberts. 1984. *Political Tolerance in Context: Support for Unpopular Minorities in Israel, New Zealand, and the United States*. Boulder, Colo.: Westview Press.

Suro, Roberto. 1988. Papal Encyclical Says Superpowers Hurt Third World. *New York Times*, February 20. 1,5.

Tabb, William K. (Ed.). 1986. *Churches in Struggle*. New York: Monthly Review Press.

Tamney, Joseph B. and Stephen D. Johnson. 1983. The Moral Majority in Middletown. *Journal for the Scientific Study of Religion* 22:145–157.

———. 1987. Church-State Relations in the Eighties. *Sociological Analysis* 48:1–16..

———. Forthcoming. Explaining Support for the Moral Majority. *Sociological Forum*.

Tamney, Joseph B., and Ronald Burton, and Stephen Johnson. Forthcoming. Christ-
    ianity, Social Class, and the Catholic Bishops' Economic Policy. *Sociological
    Analysis.*
Tesh, Sylvia. 1984. In Support of "Single-Issue" Politics. *Political Science Quarter-
    ly* 99:27–44.
Thompson, James J. 1982. *Tried As By Fire: Southern Baptists and the Religious
    Controversies of the 1920s.* Macon, Ga.: Mercer University Press.
Turner, Helen Lee and James L. Guth. 1988. The Politics of Armageddon. Paper
    presented at the annual meeting of the Midwest Political Science Association,
    Chicago.
U.S. Congress. 1986. House-Senate Joint Economic Committee. *Poverty Ethics
    and Economics.* C-Span telecast.
Vergote, A. 1969. Concept of God and Parental Image. *Journal for the Scientific
    Study of Religion* 8:78–79.
_____. 1970. The Vertical and Horizontal Dimensions in Symbolic Language
    about God. *Lumen Vitae* 25:9–32.
_____. 1972. Parental Images and Representations of God. *Social Compass* 19:
    431–444.
Wald, Kenneth D. 1987. *Religion and Politics in the United States.* New York: St.
    Martin's Press.
Wald, Kenneth D. and Michael B. Lupfer. 1983. Religion and Political Attitudes in the
    Urban South. In Tod A. Baker, Robert P. Steed, and Laurence W. Moreland
    (Eds.), *Religion and Politics in the South.* New York: Praeger, 84–102.
Wald, Kenneth D., Dennis E. Owen, and Samuel S. Hill, Jr. 1988. Churches as
    Political Communities. *American Political Science Review* 82:531–548.
_____. Forthcoming. Evangelical Politics and Status Issues. *Journal for the Scien-
    tific Study of Religion.*
Walzer, Michael. 1965. *The Revolution of the Saints.* Cambridge, Mass.: Harvard
    University Press.
Warner, R. Stephen. 1979. Theoretical Barriers to the Understanding of Evangelical
    Christianity. *Sociological Analysis* 40 (1):1–9.
Wattenberg, M. P. 1986. *The Decline of American Political Parties 1952–1984.*
    Cambridge, Mass.: Harvard University Press.
Weakland, Rembert. 1986. "New Draft Tackles Lifestyles, World Debate." *Na-
    tional Catholic Reporter* 22: June 6, 1–20.
Weber, Max. 1952. *The Protestant Ethic and the Spirit of Capitalism.* New York:
    Scribner's.
Weber, Paul J. 1981. Religious Interest Groups in American Politics. Paper pre-
    sented to the American Political Science Association, New York.
_____. 1982a. Examining the Religious Lobbies. *This World*, No. 1.
_____. 1982b. The Power and Performance of Religious Interest Groups. Paper
    presented to the Society for the Scientific Study of Religion, Providence.
_____. 1986. Religious Interest Groups: An Update. Paper presented to the Socie-
    ty for the Scientific Study of Religion, Washington, D.C.
Weber, Timothy P. 1987. *Living in the Shadow of the Second Coming: American
    Premillennialism, 1875–1982.* Chicago: University of Chicago Press.

Welch, Michael R. and David C. Leege. 1989. Religious Predictors of Catholic Parishioners' Sociopolitical Attitudes: Devotional Style, Closeness to God, Imagery, and Agentic/Communal Religious Identity. *Journal for the Scientific Study of Religion*. Forthcoming.

West, Cornel. 1986. Neo-Aristotelianism, Liberalism, and Socialism: A Christian Perspective. In Bruce Grelle and David A. Krueger (Eds.), *Christianity and Capitalism*. Chicago: Center for the Scientific Study of Religion, 70–90.

Whitcomb, John C. Jr., 1973. Origin of the Planets. In Kelly L. Segraves (Ed.), *And God Created* (2). San Diego: Creation-Science Research Center.

Wikse, John R. 1977. *About Possession: The Self as Private Property*, University Park, Pa.: Penn State University Press.

Wilcox, Clyde. 1984. The New Christian Right and the Mobilization of the Fundamentalists. Presented at the annual meeting of the Midwest Political Science Association, Chicago.

——— . 1986a. Evangelicals and Fundamentalists in the New Christian Right: Religious Differences in the Ohio Moral Majority. *Journal for the Scientific Study of Religion* 25:355–363.

——— . 1986b. Fundamentalists and Politics: An Analysis of The Impact of Differing Operational Definitions. *Journal of Politics* 48:1041–1051.

——— . 1987a. Popular Approval of the Old Christian Right: Explaining Support for the Christian Anti-Communism Crusade. *Journal of Social History*, September 1987.

——— . 1987b. Popular Support for the Moral Majority in 1980: A Second Look. *Social Science Quarterly* 68:157–167.

——— . 1987c. Religious Orientations and Political Attitudes: Variations within the New Christian Right. *American Politics Quarterly* 15:274–296.

——— . 1989. The Fundamentalist Voter: Politicized Religious Identity and Political Attitudes and Behavior. *Review of Religious Research*. Forthcoming.

Wilcox, Clyde, Lee Sigelman, and Elizabeth Cook. 1989. Some Like it Hot: Individual Differences in Responses to Group Feeling Thermometers. *Public Opinion Quarterly*. Forthcoming.

Wilson, James Q. 1962. *The Amateur Democrat*. Chicago: University of Chicago Press.

——— . 1973. *Political Organizations*. New York: Basic Books.

Wirls, Daniel. 1986. Reinterpreting the Gender Gap. *Public Opinion Quarterly* 50:316–330.

Wolfinger, Ray and Michael G. Hagen. 1985. Republican Prospects: Southern Comfort. *Public Opinion* 8–13.

Wolfinger, Raymond, Barbara Wolfinger, Kenneth Prewitt, and Sheilah Rosenhack. 1964. America's Radical Right: Politics and Ideology. In David Apter (Ed.), *Ideology and Discontent*. New York: Free Press.

Woll, Peter. 1985. *Congress*. Boston: Little, Brown.

Woodward, Kenneth L. with Donna Foote. "The Bishops Call A 'Halt.'" *Newsweek* 10 (May 16, 1983): 26.

Wright, James Edward. 1974. *The Politics of Populism*. New Haven, Conn.: Yale University Press.

Wuthnow, Robert. 1983. The Political Rebirth of American Evangelicals. In R. Liebman and R. Wuthnow (Eds.), *The New Christian Right*. New York: Aldine.

Yankelovich, Daniel. 1981. Stepchildren of the Moral Majority. *Psychology Today* vol. 15 5–6.

Yinger, Milton. 1969. A Structural Examination of Religion. *Journal for the Scientific Study of Religion* 8:88–99.

Yinger, Milton and Stephen Cutler. 1984. The Moral Majority Viewed Sociologically. In D. Bromely and A. Shupe (Eds.), *New Christian Politics*. Macon, Ga.: Mercer University Press.

Zwier, Robert. 1982. *Born-Again Politics: The New Christian Right in America*. Downers Grove, Ill.: Intervarsity Press.

_____ . 1987. Coalition Strategies of Religious Interest Groups. Paper, American Political Science Association.

Name Index

Subject Index

absolutism, moral, 93–95
agentic dimension, of religious belief, 49, 52–54, 56. *See also* individualism
American Civil Liberties Union, 177, 245, 260
American Council of Christian Churches, 244–245
American Legion, 236
American Medical Association, 236
American National Election Studies, 26, 111, 116–117, 124–125, 128. *See also* Center for Political Studies
Americans United, 177
amillenialism, 187–207
Anglicans, 45. *See also* Episcopalians
Anti-Defamation League, 269
Armageddon, 187–196
Assemblies of God, 6, 266
Association for Public Justice, 183
authoritarianism, 93–107
authority-mindedness: as distinguished from authoritiarianism, 94–97; measurement, 100

Baptist Joint Committee, 177, 180
Baptist Ministers, Southern, 187–207
Baptists, *xiv*, 4, 6, 27, 46, 93, 148, 181, 184, 262, 265, 270

Benedictines, 214
Bible: fundamentalist view of, 95–96; inerrancy, 9, 11–14, 32–36, 71, 76–77, 79, 81, 158, 193; literalism, 9, 11–14, 32–36, 76–77, 79, 84, 88, 225–227; measures, 3–19, 32–36
Bible belt, 260–261
born-again, as component of evangelicalism, 3, 5–6, 9–12, 14, 19, 26–32, 37–38, 142–146, 227
Bread for the World, 183

Calvinism, 67–68, 70
capitalism, 67–82, 212
Catholic Bishops, American: on economics, 67, 69–71, 209–221; on nuclear war, 209, 215; and political activity, *xiii–xiv*, 171, 174, 182, 209–221, 264
Catholics, Roman, 5–6, 179; and creationism, 83–92; and elections, 139–156; as evangelicals, 6–8, 14, 142–143; as fundamentalists, 71–72, 77–81; and party identification, 110–113
CBS/New York Times Poll, 113, 135, 223
Center for Political Studies, 4, 6, 19, 21, 26, 28, 41–42, 124, 141–143,

301

About the Editor and Contributors

Ted G. Jelen is Professor of Political Science at Illinois Benedictine College. His main research interests are in the political mobilization of religious belief, the politics of abortion, and public attitudes toward feminist issues. His work has appeared in a number of scholarly journals and books.

Ronald Burton is Associate Professor of Sociology at Ball State University. He is the author of numerous articles in *The Review of Religious Research* and *Sociological Analysis*, and has presented his research at many scholarly conferences.

James D. Fairbanks is Assistant Vice President for Academic Affairs and Professor of Political Science at the University of Houston–Downtown. His interest in the impact of religion on politics began with doctoral dissertation work on the determinants of morality policies, and continues to be reflected by his published research in such journals as the *Policy Studies Journal*, *Midwest Quarterly*, *Presidential Studies Quarterly*, and *Western Political Quarterly*.

John C. Green is the Acting Director of the Ray C. Bliss Institute of Applied Politics at the University of Akron. He has published numerous articles on campaign finance and religion and politics, and has studied the Robertson campaign.

James L. Guth is Professor of Political Science at Furman University. His work on religion and politics has appeared in many scholarly journals and books. His current research includes studies of the political activism of conservative Protestant clergy and of Republican and Democratic campaign donors.

Mary T. Hanna is faculty chair and Miles C. Moore Professor of Political Science at Whitman College. Her books include *Summer in the City*, on the community action program in New York City (published under her maiden name, Mary Cole), and *Catholicism and American Politics*. She has just completed a manuscript on Catholic and fundamentalist political activity in the 1980s entitled *Politicizing the Gospel*.

Allen D. Hertzke teaches Political Science at the University of Oklahoma and is also Assistant Director of the Carl Albert Congressional Research and Studies Center. He is author of *Representing God in Washington*.

Samuel S. Hill, Jr., has been Professor of Religion at the University of Florida since 1972, before which he held a similar position at the University of North Carolina, Chapel Hill. His primary research interest is in religion in the U.S. South, a field in which he has published extensively.

Stephen D. Johnson is Professor of Sociology at Ball State University. His specialties are in the areas of religion and politics, social psychology, race relations, and statistics. He has published many articles on interpersonal attraction, racial prejudice, and religion and politics, and is the co-editor of *The Political Role of Religion in the U.S.*

Lyman A. Kellstedt is Professor of Political Science at Wheaton College. His research interests in recent years have been concentrated in the field of religion and politics with a special focus on evangelicals and political behavior. His work has appeared in various conference papers and professional publications.

Henry C. Kenski is an Associate Professor holding joint appointments in the Departments of Communication and Political Science at the University of Arizona. He has published numerous journal articles and book chapters on U.S. politics, and has a major research interest in religion and politics.

David C. Leege is Professor of Government, Director of the Hesburgh Program in Public Service, and Director of the Program on Religion, Church, and Society at the University of Notre Dame. Author (with Wayne Francis) of *Political Research: Design, Measurement, and Analysis*, Leege has written several articles on religion and politics, voting behavior, and methodology, and is the principal author and co-editor of the Notre Dame Study of Catholic Parish Life *Report* series.

William Lockwood is a computer analyst in the Department of Political Science and a doctoral candidate at the University of Arizona. He is the co-author of three recent papers on religion and politics.

Alfred R. Martin is Associate Professor of Biology at Illinois Benedictine College. He has studied the scientific merit of claims made by creation "scientists" for a number of years, and is Illinois Liaison for the Committee of Correspondence, an organization that opposes the efforts of creation "scientists" to force creationism into public schools.

Dennis E. Owen is Assistant Professor of Religion at the University of Florida. He specializes in the area of religion in contemporary U.S. culture and is co-author, with Samuel Hill, of *The New Religious-Political Right in America*.

Jerry Perkins is Director of the Center for Public Service and Professor of Political Science at Texas Tech. His work appears in such leading scholarly journals as *The American Political Science Review*, *The Journal of Politics*, *Polity*, *Public Opinion Quarterly*, *Women and Politics*, *Publius*, and *Political Behavior*.

Corwin Smidt is Professor of Political Science at Calvin College in Grand Rapids, Michigan. He has published articles in the areas of political socialization, voting behavior, and religion and politics. His present research efforts have centered primarily upon the completion of a book analyzing the contemporary evangelical involvement in U.S. politics. His most recent work on evangelical political behavior has appeared in *American Politics Quarterly*, *Western Political Quarterly*, and *Election Politics*.

Joseph B. Tamney is Professor of Sociology at Ball State University. His recent publications include *Religious Switching: Religious Mobility in Singapore* (with Riaz Hassan), *The Political Role of Religion in the U.S.* (co-edited with Stephen D. Johnson), and articles on religion and politics in *Sociological Analysis*, *Review of Religious Research*, and *Journal for the Scientific Study of Religion*.

Helen Lee Turner teaches in the Religion Department at Furman University. She studies a variety of U.S. religious groups, although her special focus is on Southern Baptists. She has also done work in Jewish-Christian relations and on the place of children and children's religious literature in Western religious traditions.

Kenneth D. Wald teaches political science at the University of Florida. His work on religion and politics has appeared in two books (*Religion and Politics in the United States* and *Crosses on the Ballot*), several chapters and journal articles, and various conference papers.

Clyde Wilcox is Assistant Professor of Government at Georgetown University. He has written a number of articles on the influence of evangelical religion on politics, and on campaign finance.

Robert Zwier is Associate Professor of Political Science at Northwestern College in Orange City, Iowa. Professor Zwier is the author of *Born Again Politics*, as well as articles in *Legislative Studies Quarterly* and *Christian Scholar's Review*.